SAN JUAN, VIEQUES & CULEBRA

GW00992091

FIRST EDITION

SAN JUAN, VIEQUES & CULEBRA: PUERTO RICO

Zain
Deane

The Countryman Press
Woodstock, Vermont

ISBN 978-1-58157-043-4

Cover photo © QT Luong/terragalleria.com
Interior photos by the author unless otherwise specified
Book design Bodenweber Design
Page composition by Melinda Belter
Maps by Mapping Specialists, Ltd., Madison, WI, © The Countryman Press

Published by The Countryman Press, P.O. Box 748, Woodstock, Vermont 05091

Distributed by W. W. Norton & Company, Inc., 500 Fifth Ave., New York, NY 10110

Printed in the United States of America

10 9 8 7 6 5 4 3 2 1

Great Destinations Puts the "Guide" in "Guidebook"

Recommended by *National Geographic Traveler* and *Travel & Leisure* magazines.

[A] CRISP AND CRITICAL APPROACH, FOR TRAVELERS WHO WANT TO LIVE LIKE LOCALS. — *USA Today*

Great Destinations™ guidebooks are known for their comprehensive, critical coverage of regions of extraordinary cultural interest and natural beauty. The authors in this series are professional travel writers who have lived for many years in the regions they describe. Each title in this series is continuously updated with each printing to insure accurate and timely information. All the books contain more than one hundred photographs and maps.

Current titles available:

The Adirondack Book
Atlanta
Austin, San Antonio & the Texas Hill Country
The Berkshire Book
Big Sur, Monterey Bay & Gold Coast Wine Country
Cape Canaveral, Cocoa Beach & Florida's Space Coast
The Charleston, Savannah & Coastal Islands Book
The Chesapeake Bay Book
The Coast of Maine Book
Colorado's Classic Mountain Towns: Great Destinations
The Finger Lakes Book
Galveston, South Padre Island & the Texas Gulf Coast
The Hamptons Book
Honolulu & Oahu: Great Destinations Hawaii
The Hudson Valley Book
Las Vegas
Los Cabos & Baja California Sur: Great Destinations Mexico
The Nantucket Book
The Napa & Sonoma Book
Palm Beach, Miami & the Florida Keys
Phoenix, Scottsdale, Sedona & Central Arizona
Playa del Carmen, Tulum & the Riviera Maya: Great Destinations Mexico
Salt Lake City, Park City, Provo & Utah's High Country Resorts
San Diego & Tijuana
San Juan, Vieques & Culebra: Great Destinations Puerto Rico
The Santa Fe & Taos Book
The Sarasota, Sanibel Island & Naples Book
The Seattle & Vancouver Book: Includes the Olympic Peninsula, Victoria & More
The Shenandoah Valley Book
Touring East Coast Wine Country

If you are traveling to, moving to, residing in, or just interested in any (or all!) of these enchanting regions, a Great Destinations guidebook is a superior companion. Honest and painstakingly critical, full of information only a local can provide, Great Destinations guidebooks give you all the practical knowledge you need to enjoy the best of each region. Why not own them all?

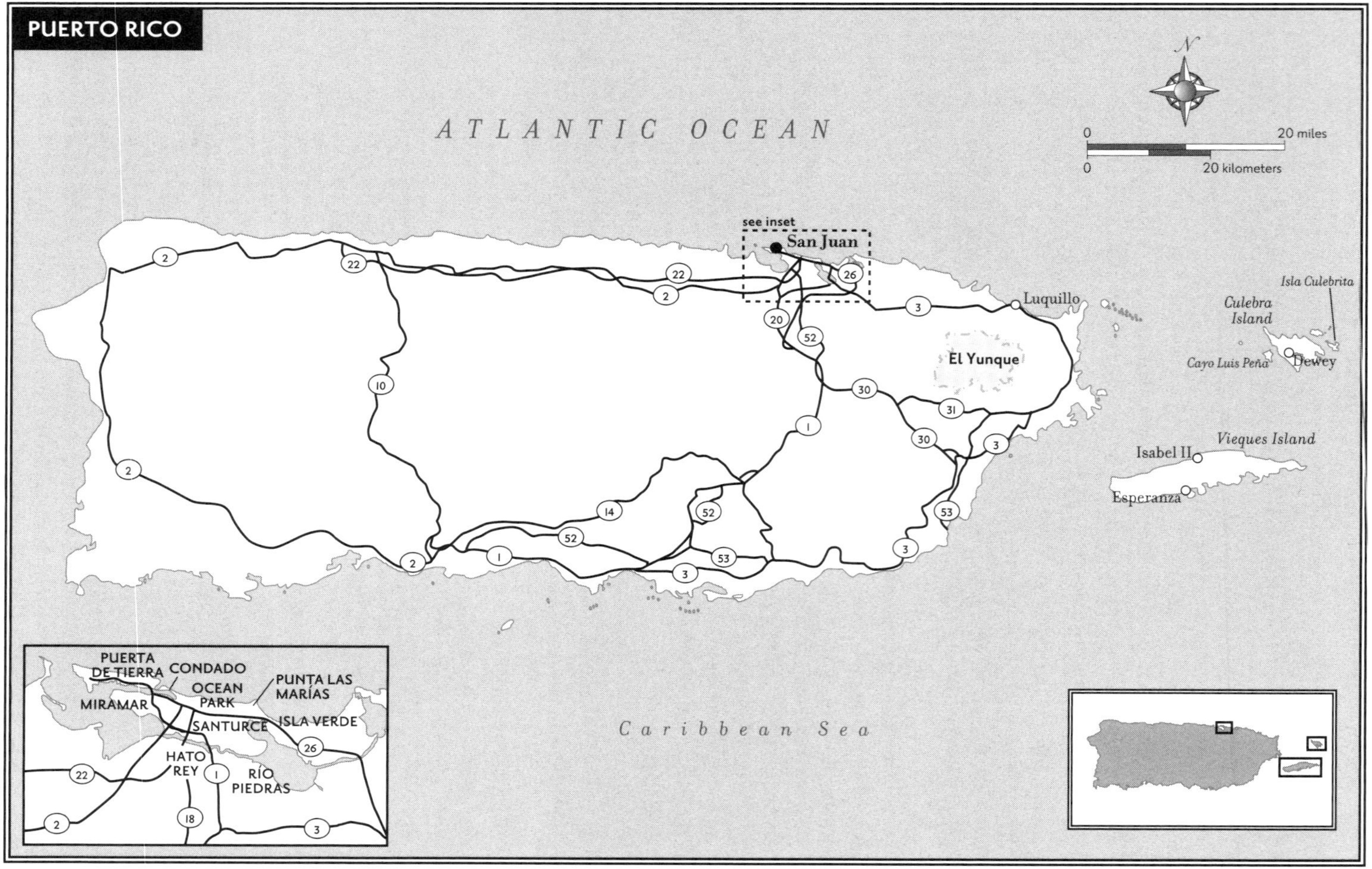

PUERTO RICO

ATLANTIC OCEAN

Caribbean Sea

El Yunque

San Juan

see inset

Luquillo

Isla Culebra
Culebra Island
Cayo Luis Peña
Dewey

Vieques Island
Isabel II
Esperanza

20 miles
20 kilometers

PUERTA DE TIERRA
CONDADO
OCEAN PARK
PUNTA LAS MARÍAS
ISLA VERDE
MIRAMAR
SANTURCE
HATO REY
RÍO PIEDRAS

CONTENTS

San Juan and the Surrounding Area

The Islands

9

C<small>ULEBRA</small>

Breathtaking Beaches, Part 2

248

C<small>ULEBRITA AND</small> C<small>AYO</small> L<small>UIS</small> P<small>EÑA</small>   258

A F<small>EW</small> I<small>DEAS</small>

10

P<small>UERTO</small> R<small>ICO ON A</small> . . .

275

Acknowledgments

Writing a guidebook about a much-loved tourist destination is no simple task. As much as my affection for Puerto Rico fueled my research, this book would not have been possible without the concerted efforts of several key contributors. At the forefront of this list are Kim Grant, who selected my book proposal and recommended it to The Countryman Press, and Kermit Hummel, who commissioned the work.

Carlos Muñoz Acevedo was at once my fact-checker, critic, and fountain of knowledge about his homeland. Nicolas Muñoz Muñoz helped me to better understand, and write about, the political climate and dynamics of today's Puerto Rico. Ariadne Comulada gave me her time, her resources, and her contacts to get me in and out of some of San Juan's best restaurants and places to visit. Cuca and Bibi Del Rincón were ambassadors of art and hospitality. José Alegría graciously allowed me to bother him several times. Marilyn and John and the Doghouse gang made Vieques feel like home. And Jim Galasso introduced me to a Culebra I never knew existed. The Puerto Rico Tourism Company sent me a wealth of information, and the National Register of Historic Places provided invaluable background material for my historical research.

It would take an entire chapter to mention and thank the people who threw open their doors to me as I compiled the research for this book. So many of the owners and managers of the hotels, restaurants, shops, and attractions I visited reinforce Puerto Rico's image of warmth, friendliness, and charm. I'm deeply indebted to all of them.

My fiancée has borne my wanderlust with patience and undying support. My sister encouraged me through every step. And last, I must acknowledge my parents, for without their support I wouldn't be writing any of this. Thanks, guys.

INTRODUCTION

When I first agreed to go to San Juan for Thanksgiving, I expected nothing more than a quiet, lazy few days spent on an idyllic beach while listening to a tropical melody and sipping something out of a coconut husk. It turns out that I was sorely mistaken, and it was this error in judgment that led me to fall in love with the place. Don't get me wrong: If it's a beach you seek, Puerto Rico has some of the best beaches in the world . . . but they're only the tip of the tropical iceberg. In many ways, this island is more than it seems.

Puerto Rico is at once a verdant, lush landscape and a concrete jungle; a sun-splashed paradise and an indoor shopping mecca; a modern society and a place of deep history and tradition. Its people are intensely proud of their heritage but divided in their opinions about their homeland's political status. Puerto Rico is a cultural, commercial, geographic, and historic meeting point between old and new, *el Gringo* and *el Latino*. Yet it is the dichotomy of Puerto Rico that makes it a unique destination. Its diversity extends to the type of vacation it offers to the millions of tourists who flock here. Where else can you lie on a beach in the morning, hike through a rain forest during the day, spend the evening within the ancient walls of a colonial city, and play roulette until the sun returns? Puerto Rico is a paradise for a family, a romantic getaway for a couple, and a fascinating destination for an explorer. The island serves up an incredible variety of activities, catering to the active, athletic type; the history buff; the elite socialite; and the indolent sunbather. If you enjoy the nightlife, San Juan will oblige. If you adore the outdoors, you'll have access to a full banquet of natural wonders. And if you love to eat, the Puerto Ricans will love you back. There is music in the air at all times, and at night, the island's most unusual voice, that of the coquí tree frog, will accompany you.

San Juan, Vieques, and Culebra are the most popular tourist destinations in Puerto Rico. The latter two are islands of breathtaking beauty, boasting sands so white they glitter. The waters surrounding them are so pristine that when you look out your airplane window, you'll see several shades of turquoise between the shore and the deep blue of the ocean. What separates these island beaches from those on the main island is a sense of remoteness. Beyond the vacation homes, guesthouses, and boutique hotels, Vieques and Culebra bestow a delicious sense of isolation and tranquility on visitors.

San Juan is your entry to Puerto Rico, and you may never want to go any farther. The oldest European city under the American flag, San Juan has a heritage that dates to the 1500s. Also Puerto Rico's commercial, political, historic, and cultural hub. San Juan is most famous for its old city center; with its narrow streets, Colonial architecture, and two mighty forts, Old San Juan is a charming reminder of a bygone era. Beyond Old San Juan's ramparts, modern San Juan sprawls outward, offering luxury resorts, beaches, shopping malls, and all the amenities (and problems) of a large metropolis.

Think of this book as a tour from an unabashedly biased guide, from someone who has lived in Puerto Rico's hotels as a visitor, as well as in its suburbs as a member of a Puerto Rican family. Rather than provide a detailed catalog of restaurants, hotels, and places to visit, for this guide I have compiled a list of places that I would recommend to friends. I have also tried to duplicate what Puerto Rico seems to manage so easily: to offer something for everyone, regardless of age, interest, or income.

I underestimated Puerto Rico when I planned that first Thanksgiving trip and also ignored my sister's passionate vow that she would move here permanently if the opportunity presented itself. But I quickly realized that that trip would be the first of many visits to this land of plenty. I wrote this guide to help you avoid the mistake I made, and I hope that it gives you the same sense of wonder that I feel whenever I return to my favorite island in the sun.

—Zain Deane

How to Use This Book

Although San Juan, Culebra, and Vieques are relatively small, they have so much to offer that the development of this book required much planning and thought. I hope it will not only familiarize you with the region's many delights but also give you something to think about and relish that goes beyond the obvious attractions. This is a place of fascinating culture, turbulent history, and tremendous artistic expression, and I wouldn't do Puerto Rico or its people justice if I didn't explore these aspects of its society in detail. They help make Puerto Rico truly La Isla Del Encanto (The Enchanted Isle).

I compiled the information about the area's restaurants, hotels, sites, and incredible range of activities from my journeys to Puerto Rico. My travels and experiences there run the gamut: from the dirt cheap to the extravagantly expensive, from a typical family gathering in a quiet suburb to an enchanted destination wedding at a landmark hotel. I have met and befriended so many people whose warmth, kindness, and hospitality overwhelmed me that I have come to believe that it's the people of Puerto Rico who are its greatest asset. During my visits, I developed certain biases. For example, I prefer the boutique hotels over the more familiar chains, if only because they reflect so much care and individual expression. Similarly, as much as I enjoy Puerto Rican food, I have a particular affinity for those places that blend international flavors with those of the Caribbean, offering one's palate unique pleasures.

Where possible, I have avoided experiences easily found in the United States (for example, this book doesn't mention the Hard Rock Café in San Juan); although there is nothing wrong with these places, I prefer to talk about and share with you the things that make Puerto Rico unique. Although my preferences have naturally influenced this book, I've tried to cast a wide net; from the variety offered, you can select the lodging, dining, and entertainment options that best suit your fancy, as well as your budget.

Prices

Prices fluctuate often. Instead of listing exact rates, I've used the following chart to help you decide where to go, what to eat, and what to see and do. It's important to note that, in a land with hardly any variance in temperatures, Puerto Rico nevertheless is very much a seasonal destination, and this is reflected in its prices. From May to November, a four-star hotel might be available at a two-star price. This is not always the case, but it happens. The major trade-off, of course, is the chance of a hurricane or tropical storm interfering with your beach outing. Again, this is not always the case, but it happens.

The discrepancies in rates are large enough in some cases that you'll see hotel descriptions in the book with the designation $–$$$$. The spike in rates for some services (like car rentals) is relatively minor and doesn't warrant my noting a price range. You will also notice that the price range for attractions is relatively large. This is because activities in Puerto Rico range from free museums to adventure excursions that cost several hundred dollars per adult.

Please note that these prices do not include taxes or gratuities. A 15 percent tip is standard. Make sure to check your bill at restaurants, as some include the tip.

Price Guide

Code	Lodging (double occupancy)	Restaurants (per entrée)	Attractions (per adult)
$	Up to $125	Up to $10	Up to $10
$$	$126–$225	$11–$25	$11–$50
$$$	$226–$325	$26–$35	$51–$100
$$$$	More than $325	More than $35	More than $100

1

FROM COLONY TO COMMONWEALTH

A Brief History

Knowing Puerto Rico's past is integral to understanding the cultural, political, and social dynamic of the island today. Like the history of the rest of the New World, Puerto Rico's past can be segmented into three pivotal eras: the pre-Columbian period, colonial times, and the modern age. Similarly, Puerto Rico reflects the story of three peoples: the various indigenous tribes who claimed it at one time or another, the Spanish invaders (accompanied by their African slaves), and the Americans. The island's culture retains strong ties to each of these roots; everything—from the food, to the festivals, to the identity of today's *boricua* (a common term referring to descendants of the island's indigenous peoples)— pays homage to its past.

Puerto Rico's history has been shaped by the military concerns of the Spanish, the commercial interests of the colonial powers, and a period of relative anonymity following the Spanish-American War. Its beauty, popularity, and unique culture have never been more appreciated or celebrated as they are today. Because of its status as a commonwealth, Puerto Rico today is not completely clear about its place in the world; but it has come a long way since the days of Juan Ponce de León.

THE FOUNDING OF A MILITARY OUTPOST

Columbus landed on the island of Boriquén during his second tour of "the Indies," as he famously and erroneously believed, in 1493. The great explorer claimed the land in the name of Spain, christened it San Juan Bautista (Saint John the Baptist), and promptly left two days later to colonize Santo Domingo and acquire more territory for his queen and country. Of course, Columbus didn't walk into a desolate, unpopulated place. At the time, Boriquén (Land of the Brave Lord), belonged to an Arawak Indian tribe who called themselves the Taíno.

The Taíno were the latest in a series of indigenous peoples to occupy the land. Their reign in Puerto Rico spanned several hundred years, and they were an advanced society. The Taíno boasted a developed agriculture, which enabled them, unlike other nomadic cultures, to settle permanently in the land they called Borikén. (The Spanish would later interpret this as Boriquén, which has since become synonymous with native Puerto Rico.)

A garita (sentry box)

The tribe flourished as a society, producing artifacts that have survived and are replicated to this day, holding elaborate ceremonies, and even sporting events at *bateyes* (ball courts), which can still be seen on the island.

But if the Taíno were awestruck by the sudden arrival of Columbus and his fellow sailors, he gave them plenty of time to get over it. For more than a decade after his hurried baptism, Columbus and the Spanish left the people of Boriquén to themselves; after all, there was plenty of flag planting and colonizing to be done in the New World. There were Spanish governors installed on the island, but, as they didn't do anything of note, their presence was negligible. The island's relative anonymity ended in 1508, when Juan Ponce de León arrived with a force of 50 men to colonize it. On August 8 of that year, the founder of modern Puerto Rico established the town of Caparra, on the northern coast of the island. A year later, he moved his men to an islet with a better harbor, and named the new town Puerto Rico (Rich Port). By the 1520s, this had become the name of the island, while the port town was renamed San Juan.

Ponce de León served as governor during the colony's first formative years. A mere four years into his reign, however, he decided to chase after a mystical "fountain of youth" —a quest that would lead him to the discovery of Florida and, eventually, and most ironically, to his death. Still, during his tenure, Ponce de León established the foundations of modern-day Puerto Rico. Sadly, he also set in motion the now-similar pattern of subjugation practiced by colonizing powers throughout much of North and South America. In Puerto Rico, their enslavement all but decimated the Taíno as an independent ethnic group.

The Taíno did not go down without a fight; in 1511, they revolted against the Spanish. (What really got them going was when they drowned a Spanish soldier, who naturally died, thereby debunking the theory that these men were gods.) The Spanish easily crushed the rebellion, however, and some of the Taíno gradually died out while others merged with the Spanish and African population of Puerto Rico until they became intertwined with the island's society, culture, and heritage. As the Taíno population decreased, African slaves replaced them. First brought to the island in 1513, this new community would eventually put its stamp on Puerto Rican culture and society.

The Spanish were not the only ruling authority to lay claim to the island. The Roman Catholic Church, not to be left out of the westward rush, established a diocese in Puerto Rico; it was one of three in the New World, and it was given to the Canon of Salamanca, Alonso Manso. In 1512, Manso became the first bishop to arrive in America. The role of the

Church would have a profound influence on the island, which remains fervently Catholic to this day. In addition to building two of the oldest churches in the Americas—the Catedral de San Juan and the Iglesia de San José—the Church established the first school of advanced studies on the island. In time, Puerto Rico became the headquarters of the Roman Catholic Church, as well as the epicenter of the Spanish Inquisition, in the New World.

While Ponce de León pursued immortality, his family remained in Puerto Rico and flourished. In 1521, the tiny European settlement had grown to about 300 people, and the Ponce de León family built the Casa Blanca (White House), which remains one of Old San Juan's most important historic buildings. Still, for the remainder of the 1500s, the settlement grew at a sluggish pace, numbering only about 2,500 people by 1590. This was mostly due to the normal-for-the-time hardships of Indian attacks and disease, but it was also the result of Puerto Rico's relatively poor opportunities for wealth. With rich deposits of silver and gold being discovered throughout the Americas, Puerto Rico became an unattractive destination for European settlers in search of fortune.

Iglesia de San José

Ironically, however, this newfound wealth was also pivotal to Puerto Rico's development and its importance in the eyes of the mother country. With ship after ship, literally worth their weight in gold, crossing the oceans, the Spanish realized they had to protect their investment. The city of San Juan, overlooking the bay and located immediately along the shipping route, became a focal point for the empire. If the island were to fall into enemy hands, the treasure of the New World would be in jeopardy. And so began Puerto Rico's rise as a military stronghold.

Puerto Rico versus the Pirates of the Caribbean

Ponce de León's Casa Blanca was the first building on the island to serve a defensive military purpose, but Spain quickly perceived the need for additional fortifications. Puerto Rico's first true fort, called simply La Fortaleza (The Fortress), was built in 1537. Its construction was spurred on by a vicious attack in 1528 by the French, who destroyed many of the island's original colonies in their desire to wrest control of Puerto Rico from the Spanish. Seven years later, the Spanish, realizing that the protruding eastern headland of the island was much better suited to house a fortification, began construction of the imposing Castillo San Felipe del Morro. El Morro was enhanced and fortified frequently, until it became a self-contained bastion of military muscle overlooking San Juan Bay.

The island's defenses were tested hotly and frequently. Throughout the 1500s, pirates assailed the outpost, trying to break the citadels of San Juan to gain easy access to the treasure convoys the city protected. Among the notable corsairs who attacked the Puerto Rican forces were Sir Francis Drake, in 1595, and George Clifford, the Earl of Cumberland, in 1598. Throughout the repeated battering, El Morro fell only once, to Clifford's troops when the earl took the back door approach, destroyed a small battery on the eastern edge of the islet called El Boquerón, and captured the fortress by land. The British held the island for several months, before an outbreak of dysentery proved more fatal to Cumberland's forces than did the Spanish troops. Obligingly, Cumberland looted and burned the old city on his way out.

The British success revealed a glaring weakness in the Spanish defense; although their fortifications were powerful enough to repel virtually any attack by sea, they were naked to a land assault. The threat of further invasions by the British and the Dutch led to the construction, in 1634, of Castillo de San Cristóbal and the city walls. The new citadel was El Morro's neighbor and partner in the city's defense, protecting El Morro as well as any approach on land from the east, in case Cumberland's plan was repeated. The El Boquerón battery, which overlooked the bridge connecting the old city from the rest of the island, was also rebuilt; smaller than the other fortifications, it was renamed Fortín de San Gerónimo.

San Juan's defenses went beyond fortresses. The high, formidable walls (which varied in thickness as they snaked around the city but reached, at points, 20 feet) formed a layer of armor for the city of San Juan. Their remnants still stand, punctuated by elegantly crafted *garitas* (sentry boxes), and by the San Juan Gate. (Of the five gates into the old city, this is the only one left; the others were torn down as the city expanded over time.) Despite these efforts, Puerto Rico remained a prime strategic target of the British, Dutch, and French. The island faced wave after wave of attacks well into the 18th century, and, after over a century of relative peace, was thrust into the Spanish-American War in 1898.

One of the most famous of these invasions in Puerto Rican history was the 1797 British attack by Sir Ralph Abercromby and Admiral Henry Harvey. With the British forces outnumbering the defenders almost three to one, Harvey blockaded San Juan harbor while Abercromby landed 3 miles east of San Juan and made for the Martín Peña and San Antonio bridges into the old city. Here, he met stiff resistance from the Spanish who, under the leadership of Governor Ramón de Castro, prevented the invaders from reaching Old San Juan. The battle has spawned one of the most poetic legends of Puerto Rico: In their darkest hour, the remaining citizens of the old city gathered for a religious procession that was mistaken by British scouts as reinforcements. Facing what they thought was an onslaught of fresh troops, the British withdrew, and Old San Juan remained free.

The role of Puerto Rico during this period of unprecedented wealth for Spain became critical to the colony's survival and growth. As a natural resource, the island provided almost nothing to the Crown when compared to its other colonies. But as one of the principal guardians of the sea lanes and protectors of Spanish ships, Puerto Rico carved a small but vital role for itself. As a result, the mother country's investment in the island was mainly limited to establishing its armed strength. The oldest and most magnificent structures in Puerto Rico today are its fortresses, government buildings, and churches—the main elements of a military settlement.

Indeed, Spain's consideration of Puerto Rico mirrored Columbus's treatment of it. By and large, the mother country, like its adopted explorer, passed over the island on its way to richer pastures. As such, aside from the necessary fortifications, the development of the island stagnated under the aegis of the Crown's rule. Further crippling Puerto Rico's growth was Spain's constricting policies, which prevented trade among the colonies by mandating that all commerce be solely with the mother country.

It's no surprise, then, that 200 years after Columbus first met the Taíno, Puerto Rico's population still numbered less than 10,000. By 1700, a meager 7,500 people lived in eight towns on the island. With little development, smuggling became a way of life in Puerto Rico, with the United States serving as a principal partner for contraband goods. But Puerto Rico's days of languishing under the inattention of the Spanish soon came to an end. The island's agricultural resources would finally be exploited. More important, the New World was changing rapidly. A new dynamic was evolving between the colonized and the sovereign powers in Europe. Even Puerto Rico's small voice would be heard as the winds of change and the rising ideology of freedom and autonomy swept through the Americas and altered the history of the world.

GROWTH IN THE 1800S AND THE RISE OF THE JÍBAROS

By 1800, Puerto Rico was home to 150,000 residents. Considering that only 50 years ago, fewer than 50,000 people lived on the island, this was truly a population explosion. Why the sudden growth spurt? One of the biggest factors was the expansion of the island's agriculture. Although tobacco and sugar were grown and exported, the real boom came in the late 1700s with the introduction of coffee, which soon became the island's principal export. With the boom in coffee production came the settling of the rugged interior of the island and the advent of the *Jíbaros.*

These were the country folk, laborers from the highlands who came to be a celebrated part of the island's folklore. The Jíbaros worked in *haciendas* (plantations), serving the *hacendados* (landowners). It was a typical relationship of the time: landowner and laborer. The Jíbaros were not slaves, but they were poor, uneducated, and illiterate. They did, however, find expression in music; and the songs of the Jíbaros are one of their most lasting legacies in Puerto Rico.

Coffee was not the only reason that Spain suddenly started paying attention to Puerto Rico. The 1700s were a volatile and unfriendly time for the imperial powers in Europe. Social and political unrest, demands for civil rights, and a growing bitterness with the mother country rippled through much of the New World. When the European nations tried to clamp down on their overseas subjects, the results were disastrous for Europe. The American Revolution in 1776 jump-started a global movement of oppressed against oppressor, and the Spanish empire was one of the chief targets.

When Spain began losing its precious possessions, it hurried to secure its remaining footholds in the region, which during the 19th century had dwindled until they included only Puerto Rico and Cuba. The political climate was hardly peaceful in either colony; as a result, the Crown invested in the development of the island and its settlers. In 1812, the Spanish granted conditional citizenship to Puerto Ricans. Three years later, the Royal Decree of Grace lifted the trade embargo the Spanish had imposed among the colonies, giving Puerto Rico commercial opportunities with other nations. (Of course, these opportunities existed before in the form of smuggling, but their legalization contributed significantly to Puerto Rico's financial growth.) In addition, foreigners were allowed to enter the

Castillo de San Cristóbal, and El Morro in the distance

island for the first time, and even received free land in exchange for their sworn fealty to Spain and the Roman Catholic Church. These freedoms were shortly revoked, but they did contribute to the growth and diversity of the island's population.

The colony expanded in size and importance, and its population reached nearly 1 million by the turn of the 20th century. During this time, the landscape of San Juan as we see it today was shaped. In 1835, the slave trade came to a merciful end in the Spanish colonies, although slavery was still practiced on the island. In 1897, the eastern and southern walls of the city were torn down to allow for the city's expansion. Architecture, art, education, and trade all flourished during this period, but so too did political awareness and a new consciousness—the desire for autonomy.

Fortunately for the Spanish, the thirst for independence was not as strong in Puerto Rico as it was in other colonies. While all agreed that the colony should be awarded certain political and civil rights, the people were divided as to what lay in their best interests. Some called for total separation from the Crown, while others preferred self-rule without autonomy. It would not be the last time the Puerto Ricans found themselves in this predicament.

These divisions came to a head on September 23, 1868, when a physician named Ramón E. Betances planned a revolt in Lares, a small town in the north of the country. Several hundred disgruntled men and women took to the streets against the Crown. The uprising, which became known as El Grito de Lares (The Cry of Lares), was notable not for its ferocity or longevity; the rebels were defeated the very next day. Rather, it was, and remains, the only native challenge ever launched by the Puerto Rican people against the Spanish. Considering that this occupation spanned 400 hundred years, the revolt is a remarkable footnote in the island's history.

El Grito de Lares reflected the growing mood of the people, a general unrest that would lead to important reforms on the island, including the abolishment of slavery in 1872. In 1870, Puerto Rico saw the establishment of its first political parties: the Traditionalists, who called themselves the Liberal Conservative Party, and the Autonomists, who formed the Liberal Reformist Party.

The man behind the Autonomy movement was Luis Muñoz Rivera, "the George Washington of Puerto Rico." Rivera led a delegation from his party to Spain in 1896. His persistence finally paid off in 1897 and Puerto Rico received its first taste of freedom. The Spanish government ratified the Carta Autonómica (Autonomic Charter), which gave Puerto Ricans political and administrative authority. February 9, 1898, marked the first day of the new, independent government of Puerto Rico, with Muñoz Rivera as its unquestioned leader. And then the Americans invaded.

THE SPANISH-AMERICAN WAR: NEW FLAG, SAME RESULT

The battle for Puerto Rico lasted approximately four months. The catalyst for the last war against Spanish interests as a colonial power was the enigmatic explosion of the USS *Maine* in Havana Harbor. Shortly after Teddy Roosevelt and his Rough Riders charged up San Juan Hill in Cuba, the fighting came to the city of San Juan. The first volleys were fired on May 10, 1898, Spanish forces at San Cristóbal engaged the USS *Yale*. Two days later, 12 American ships bombarded San Juan. On June 25, the USS *Yosemite* barricaded San Juan harbor; and on July 25, the USS *Gloucester* landed at Guánica, on the southern coast of the island.

Facing an overwhelming 16,000 troops, the Spanish defenses offered nominal resistance. The strongest opposition to the U.S. forces would have been in San Juan, but that contest never took place. On August 13, Spain and the United States signed a peace treaty. (The formal transfer of power would not occur until December 10, 1898, when Spain signed the Treaty of Paris, relinquishing its claim on Cuba and ceding Guam and Puerto Rico to the Americans.) On October 18, General John R. Brooke became Puerto Rico's first American military governor. Two years later, the military government would be replaced by a civil administration.

The introduction of U.S. government was the start of Puerto Rico's evolution into the modern commonwealth that it is today. After suffering under the yoke of Spanish colonial rule, the island's residents welcomed these new conquerors, thinking that their lot would improve under this democratic, liberal regime. And indeed, the rights that the Americans had so recently wrested from the British—freedom of assembly, speech, press, and religion—were accorded to the United States's newest acquisition. New roads and bridges were constructed, and a centralized public health service was introduced. In addition, new political groups came to the forefront, including the Republican Party and the American Federal Party: Both factions advocated full annexation to the United States.

But in other ways, switching flags left the same imprint of a dual personality on the island, and a sociopolitical rift among its citizens. Following his brief glimpse of autonomous government, Luis Muñoz Rivera would continue to campaign for self-rule. He went to Washington, DC, where he served as the island's resident commissioner. Despite his efforts, Muñoz Rivera and his supporters found that the Americans offered less autonomy than the charter they had secured from the Spanish. After existing primarily as a colony, the United States was unused to having one, and Puerto Rico was not the only challenge the fledgling nation faced in the early 1900s.

Puerto Rico would prove valuable to the United States for two main reasons, sugar and location. As a military outpost, it gave the United States a foothold far beyond its territorial borders; unfortunately, the U.S. military presence in Puerto Rico has had an ugly history that has lasted into the new millennium. But the fomenting nationalism that had built to a crescendo before the Spanish-American War continued into the 20th century, as local workers galvanized to combat the exploitation of land and people to serve the mercantile interests of U.S. corporations.

Muñoz Rivera died in 1916 without seeing his vision for Puerto Rico realized. His final attempt was made before Congress in 1915, which led to the Jones Act of 1917. This law made Puerto Rico a United States territory that was "organized but unincorporated." Under the act, all Puerto Ricans were granted U.S. citizenship, along with conscription to the U.S. Army. Following the American model, the bill introduced three branches of government: executive, legislative, and judicial. It also gave Puerto Rico a Bill of Rights and made English the official language of the local courts.

In the 20th century, Muñoz Rivera's son, Luis Muñoz Marín, would continue where his father left off. One of the most beloved figures in Puerto Rico's history, Muñoz Marín transformed the island's economy, political structure, and society. Like his father's before him, Muñoz Marín's efforts earned him a catchy moniker: "the Father of Modern Puerto Rico."

THE DEVELOPMENT OF MODERN PUERTO RICO

Luis Muñoz Marín, Puerto Rico's prodigal son, had his work cut out for him. At the turn of the century, the United States had acquired a predominantly rural, agricultural colony with minimal infrastructure, education, and civic institutions or services. It was a poor place with few prospects, and in the next few decades, Puerto Rico fell under the yoke of a new tyrant: "King Sugar."

The 1920s saw a major spike in the price of sugar, now Puerto Rico's principal export. The resulting wealth paid for needed enhancements to the island's infrastructure, including new schools and roads, and housing to accommodate a rising wealthy social class. However, the powerful sugar interests undermined the democratic process on the island; votes were bought and secured by and for the magnates of the sugar industry, ensuring an uneasy status quo for Puerto Ricans.

The Roaring Twenties took on another meaning in Puerto Rico; it was a time of draconian policies, political awakening, and civil unrest. The American government took steps to bring the island further into the fold of the Union by trying to prohibit Spanish from being spoken on the island, and declared it illegal to fly the Puerto Rican flag. Political unrest spilled over into several skirmishes.

In 1922, following the Jones Act, the Puerto Rican Nationalist Party was founded. In the 1930s, the party clashed with authorities, attacking Puerto Rico's governor, chief of police, and one of its judges. In 1936, San Juan's police chief was killed. A year later, the police

Old San Juan and Puerta de Tierra

shot at a party parade, killing 20 people and wounding 100 in what became known as the Ponce Massacre.

The sugar boom also suffered in the 1930s as Puerto Rico, along with the United States, languished under the Great Depression. Puerto Rico's economic woes were exacerbated by Hurricane San Ciprián, which fell upon the island in 1932, killing more than 200 people, causing over $30 million in damage (an astronomic sum at that time), and effectively shutting down the sugar industry. Another blow to the island's economy came from an unexpected source. In 1938, the United States enacted a minimum-wage law of 25 cents per hour. This legislation decimated Puerto Rico's textile production, as two-thirds of the industry's workers earned lower salaries.

Into this tumultuous climate walked Luis Muñoz Marín, after spending his childhood and early adulthood in the United States. Realizing that Puerto Rico needed significant reforms at all major levels of society, Muñoz Marín launched a grassroots campaign promoting social change through the democratic process. He won over the Jíbaros, who then elected his Popular Party to the legislature in 1940. Six years later, President Truman appointed Jesus Toribio Piñero governor of Puerto Rico; he was the first island-born official to serve in this capacity. In 1947, the United States expanded Puerto Rico's self-government powers to allow local elections, and one year later, Muñoz Marín became the first governor of Puerto Rico to be elected by Puerto Ricans.

The new governor went to work immediately. He limited the land available to the powerful sugar interests and invited U.S. companies to the island, offering tax concessions to investors building manufacturing plants. Muñoz Marín also lowered wage scales to curb unemployment. These measures, coupled with the natural attraction for American companies of avoiding both federal taxes and import duties, helped Puerto Rico transition rapidly from an agricultural economy to an industrial one.

While Muñoz Marín is duly acknowledged as the man behind Puerto Rico's transformation, the engineer of its economic revival was Teodoro Moscoso. It was Moscoso who devised the plan to get the island out from under the yoke of King Sugar, the first critical step in the island's commercial evolution. The program he initiated in 1948 to improve living conditions and wean Puerto Rico from its agrarian dependency came to be known as Operación Manos a la Obra (Operation Bootstrap; not a literal translation).

On the political front, the culmination of Muñoz Marín's efforts came in 1950, when President Truman signed Public Act 600, allowing Puerto Rico to draft its own constitution. Its ratification two years later marked the beginning of a new political relationship with the United States: the evolution of the island from a "protectorate" to a "commonwealth," or "free associated state," which granted local autonomy to the island and allowed public displaying of the Puerto Rican flag. It was a big step, and it seemed to satisfy Muñoz Marín, since he did not pursue independence. Yet this was not the end of the age-long debate. Instead, the question of autonomy versus colony became one of independence versus statehood versus commonwealth.

The 1950s saw the rise of textile manufacturing, sewing enterprises, and other light industries. Another factor in the island's growing economy at this time was the introduction of a new, hitherto untapped source of revenue—tourism. It was during this period that hotels and high-rise condominiums sprang up by the fabulous beaches along Isla Verde and Condado, giving Puerto Rico a beachfront skyline reminiscent of Fort Lauderdale, Miami, and Cancún. Ironically, in the midst of this transformation, nearly 70,000 residents chose to leave their island for the United States. Most settled in New York City, where they formed a Puerto Rican community with strong ties to its native heritage.

In the 1960s and '70s, textiles and manufacturing gave way to petrochemicals, oil refining, and pharmaceuticals—the businesses of a new, industrial middle class. The Fomento, which was the Spanish name for Puerto Rico's Economic Development Administration, helped companies establish thousands of factories on the island. Despite the influx of bigger business, unemployment continued (and continues) to be a problem, far exceeding the U.S. national average.

After serving four consecutive terms as governor, The Father of Modern Puerto Rico chose not to run for a fifth term. The mantle of leadership was assumed by Roberto Sánchez Vilella in 1964 but also gave rise to a new crop of prominent nationalist figures. Among these was Luis A. Ferré, a successful industrialist-turned-politician. An elected representative of the Puerto Rican House of Representatives, Ferré championed statehood and union with the United States. He saw a golden chance to sway the population in 1967, a pivotal year for Puerto Rico because it marked the first time a referendum was held to determine the island's political status. Puerto Ricans voted to stick with the commonwealth, and Ferré responded by establishing the New Progressive Party (NPP).

Running as his party's candidate, Ferré became governor of Puerto Rico in 1968. Although his tenure lasted only one term, he opened the door for a growing minority of *estadistas* (statehooders). One of the most respected leaders of Puerto Rico, Ferré also founded Museo de Arte de Ponce (Ponce Museum of Art) and *El Nuevo Día* (The New Day), the island's most widely read newspaper.

The 1970s brought U.S.–Puerto Rican relations and the clash over Puerto Rico's political status into sharp, violent relief. A few catalysts fomented this unrest. In 1970, the U.S. Navy took control of almost all of Culebra Island. In 1976, Carlos Romero Barceló, the mayor of San Juan and a staunch advocate for statehood, became governor of Puerto Rico. He defeated a dynamic figure, Rafael Hernández Colón, who in 1972 had become, at age 36, the youngest governor of the island. Colón fought against President Ford's efforts to make Puerto Rico the 51st state, but he also implemented stiff taxes and governed the island during an economic recession. Colón and Barceló dominated Puerto Rican politics for the next 20 years.

Barceló worked hard to relieve Puerto Rico's economic malaise, and in this, he was aided greatly by the implementation of section 936 of the U.S. IRS tax code in 1976. This legislation exempted American companies with operations on the island from paying taxes, marking the dawn of significant investment and fiscal growth on the island. The 1970s also saw the rise of a controversial group known as Los Macheteros, made up of activists who were diametrically opposed to Barceló's beliefs and party. Los Macheteros (The Machete Wielders) took their name from a local band of Puerto Ricans who resisted the American army during the 1898 war; they were also known as the Ejército Popular Boricua (Boricua Popular Army), and they wasted no time carrying out the first of a series of attacks designed to undermine American influence over the island and the local parties that supported the statehood movement. Among other activities, the group was responsible for blowing up 11 jet fighters of the Puerto Rican National Guard, murdering three naval soldiers, and, their most brazen assault (as it took place Stateside), robbing a Wells Fargo depot of $7 million in Connecticut, in 1983. They were, and still are, considered a terrorist organization in the United States and by the majority of Puerto Ricans.

In the 1980s, Puerto Rico's economy began to decline. Rafael Hernández Colón returned to the spotlight in 1984, defeating Barceló by the slimmest of margins. He served for two terms, plagued by the sagging economy, before rumors of rampant scandal and corruption in his Popular Democratic Party forced him to step down.

In 1992, the world marked the 500th anniversary of Columbus's discovery, but few did it more enthusiastically than Puerto Rico. In the same year, Pedro Rosselló took over as governor. A controversial figure, he was known for his tough-on-crime policies and large-scale government projects, including the Tren Urbano (Urban Train).

The 1967 decision to remain a commonwealth was brought to the vote again in 1993 and 1998. In both cases, the people chose not to change their status. While results were mixed, several patterns in the voting are indicative of local sentiment. A small minority want independence; a growing number of people have warmed to the idea of statehood; but the prevailing view, for the moment, seems to be to let sleeping dogs lie. The results proved curiously inconclusive in 1998, as 50 percent of the vote was for "None of the Above."

Rosselló was the governor in office when a botched naval exercise on Vieques in 1999 led to the death of a civilian, sparking protests and drawing an international spotlight on U.S. military operations on the island. Together with President Clinton, he began the process that would result in the navy's leaving Vieques in 2003.

Puerto Rico Convention Center © 2005 Puerto Rico Convention Center

2

Puerto Rico Today

Who Are We, Where Are We, Why Do We Feel This Way?

Puerto Rico today is unlike any place in the United States or the Caribbean. The smallest and easternmost island of the Greater Antilles, it boasts the largest metropolis of its island neighbors. As such, the relaxed "joie de vivre" of the tropics is matched by a bustling economy. With nearly 4 million residents, it is among the most densely populated places in the world (its population density per square mile is greater than that of any U.S. state), and at the same time is home to isolated stretches of land that sparkle in their unspoiled beauty. Puerto Rico enjoys most of the freedoms and advantages of the United States, which has facilitated its urban development; but those it doesn't have are a source of constant debate. The continued elusiveness of autonomy has formed a more politically charged society than that of, say, the Bahamas.

Puerto Rico's people are as unique as their homeland. Their diverse backgrounds are vividly expressed in their culture. Beyond the aforementioned Spanish and African additions to the indigenous populations, Puerto Rico's melting pot has newer ingredients. U.S. citizens from the mainland have been flocking here since 1898. In the 1960s, refugees fleeing Cuba made for the island. More recently, thousands of impoverished Dominicans have reached Puerto Rico's shores on *yolas* (small wooden boats), risking their lives to enjoy a better future. Other minorities who have lived here since the 19th century include Lebanese, Italian, French, German, and Chinese immigrants, as well as people from all over the Caribbean.

CULTURE & BELIEFS

Puerto Rican culture is a vibrant, joyous union of religion, art, heritage, and nationality. There is a strong emphasis on arts and crafts, with celebrated traditions that go back centuries. Locally made products—as diverse as papier-mâché folkloric demon masks (*vejigantes*), hand-carved Catholic saints (*santos*), and Native Indian lacework (*mundillos*)—represent the different elements of Puerto Rico's past. Art and literature tell the story of the humble Jíbaros, the ancient Taíno, and the Spanish colonizers, as well as the American and Nuyorican identities. Even local fashion is emerging on the global stage.

Vejigantes *(demon masks)* at El Galpón in Old San Juan

Music & Dance

Music is the lifeblood of Puerto Rico's culture. Recently, the fusion of Puerto Rican and American sound in *raggaetón*—accompanied by its own style of dance—has achieved world-wide fame. But *raggaetón* and its *perreo* dance are only the newest form of musical expression to come out of the island. There are many more:

Salsa is the most famous, a six-step routine twisted and turned into some of the most inventive and sensual dance movements on earth. Salsa, which most agree originated in the Puerto Rican community in New York City and later evolved on the island and in Latin America, put Puerto Rico on the musical map. Watching seasoned *salseros* whip and glide around each other to a trumpet-heavy Latin beat is a marvel, and that addictive beat will make even the most left-footed among us want to take the floor.

Bomba y plena are often grouped together, but they are actually two different types of music, with different histories. Bomba is an African music form featuring a percussion ensemble of drums, sticks beaten together, and maracas. The drum complements the movement of the dancer in a duel of beat versus body. Plena incorporates Spanish and Taíno influences, using native instruments like the *güiro*, a dried-out gourd husk marked with a series of notches that, when rubbed with a stick, produces a raspy sound; the *cuatro*, a 10-stringed guitar; and the *pandero*, or tambourine. Together, *bomba y plena* is a much-loved staple of Puerto Rican music, and a highlight of any parade.

The **décima** (tenth) is an early blending of Spanish culture and Jíbaro folk music. A poem of 10 lines (five couplets) each comprising eight syllables, the *décima* is typically accompanied by the **seis** (sixth), a melody featuring the *cuatro*, guitar, and *güiro*. These songs, often ballads of love or woe, are closely associated with the mountainfolk of Puerto

Rico. There are many types of *seis* today, varying in speed and dance style. *Seis* are named either for their author, the city in which they originated, or the choreography that accompanies them. They are simple, nostalgic, and sometimes haunting melodies. It is believed that the name *seis* comes from the custom of six couples, the men aligned facing the women, dancing to the music.

The *décima* is also found in **aguinaldos**, which are Puerto Rican versions of Christmas carols. *Aguinaldos* are sometimes sung by *parrandas*—groups of revelers much like carolers, but far less solemn, who to this day go from house to house in their neighborhoods, receiving free food and drink for their efforts.

While the *décima* and *seis* recall the agrarian roots of Puerto Rican society, the **danza** is perhaps the island's most refined musical offering. This is Puerto Rico's adaptation of European classical music. *Danzas* are harmonic and most closely resemble the waltz. They can be either romantic or festive. A good example of the former is *La Borinqueña*, Puerto Rico's national anthem.

If the various types of native music and dance aren't enough indication, let me make it clear: Puerto Ricans love to party. San Juan explodes on weekend nights, with after-hour bars, lounges, and clubs welcoming the dawn before they close their doors. In rural communities, there's always someone willing to beat a drum and others ready to sing. A dizzying number and variety of parades, festivals, and other public celebrations occur all over the island. With all that rum and all those tropical cocktails, it's no exaggeration to say they love their drink as well. Mix the two, and the festivity routinely continues into the wee hours.

Flamenco performance at Divino Bocadito restaurant in Old San Juan

Are You Not Entertained?

Given its emphasis on the arts, it's not surprising that some of the most famous Latin stars in the entertainment business have some Puerto Rican blood in their veins. You may have heard of a few of them:

- Urban art legend **Jean-Michel Basquiat**
- Salsa king **Tito Puente**
- Über-guitarist **José Feliciano**
- Star CHiP **Erik Estrada**
- Crooner **Marc Anthony**
- Baseball Hall-of-Famer **Roberto Clemente**
- Classical cellist **Pablo Casals**
- Boxer **Felix Trinidad**
- Actors **Benicio Del Toro** and **Joaquin Phoenix**
- Hip-shaker **Ricky Martin**
- World-famous-backside owner **Jennifer Lopez**

Local musicians at Juanita Bananas Courtesy of Harbour View Villas & Suites/Juanita Bananas

Santos *at Siena Art Gallery in Old San Juan*

Religion & Folklore

Catholicism is the dominant religion on the island, reaching about 85 percent of the population. Introduced by the Spanish five centuries ago, it has played a key role in the evolution and identity of Puerto Rico. But even Catholicism isn't untouchable, and you'll find, sprinkled here and there and everywhere, indigenous and Caribbean influences added to Catholic tenets. Like so many other aspects of Puerto Rican life, religion has been adapted, over time, to meet the needs of a complex culture.

You don't have to look far to see the influence of Catholicism here. The most centrally located and noticeable building in most cities is the town church, the centerpiece of the main plaza. Geographically, the town revolves around its nexus. Following Spanish tradition, there is a patron saint for each town in Puerto Rico, who serves as its spiritual protector and guardian. Once a year, these towns honor their patron saint with a festival. Add it up, and you're talking about 78 festivals per year to celebrate Catholic saints. These events are not small, pious occasions; on the contrary, they are often the biggest bash of the year for the town, lasting between 3 and 10 days. All and sundry participate in the festivities, which, depending on the town's budget, include processions, parades, fireworks, live music, and food.

Each saint is also honored through *santos*. These hand-carved miniatures are created by artisans known as *santeros,* who are respected in Puerto Rico as a living link to the island's present and past. The *santero* tradition goes back to the 16th century, when churches were few and far between in the more rural parts of the island, and people made

Godzilla's Caribbean Counterpart

Okay, so maybe it won't trample innocent hordes as it rampages across San Juan, but Puerto Rico does have its own monster. Up until very recently, the island was besieged by the sinister **Chupacabra**. First sighted on the island in the 1990s, this fearsome beast has since moved on to other destinations in the Caribbean, but not before drawing international notoriety, and comedy, to the island. The Chupacabra, which literally means "Goat Sucker," is so called because of its ability, and affinity, to drain goats of all their blood. Goats aren't its only diet, however. The Chupacabra's prey includes dogs, chickens, and sheep. There have been no reported human fatalities . . . yet.

So what does it look like? Hard to tell, as descriptions vary wildly. It's green, or maybe gray. Some believe it has a snakelike tongue. Others claim it is has batlike wings. Still others say it has sharp quills running down its back. It's believed to be a biped (meaning it walks upright like human beings do . . . although it supposedly hops around a lot too) and ranges from 3 to 6 feet in height. No tracks have been found, but it certainly leaves a distinct calling card: the bloodless carcasses of its victims, with puncture wounds on their necks. It's also prolific: There have been over 2,000 reported cases of Chupacabra attacks in Puerto Rico alone.

Where does it come from? Again, theories abound. The creature is unknown to modern-day science. Some people say it's a type of dinosaur. Others are convinced it's an alien. Most think of it as an undiscovered species. Whatever it may be, this mythical local celebrity has drawn heavy hitters like *Inside Edition* and *National Geographic* to Puerto Rico to investigate it.

do with homemade altars. To this day, you'll find *santos* in many local homes, and these wood, clay, stone, or even gold carvings are a popular souvenir that typifies Puerto Rico. In addition to this homage to individual saints, the two biggest cultural and festive events on the island are Catholic holidays: Christmas, which lasts from early December until mid-January, and the San Sebastián Street Festival in Old San Juan.

While Catholics may be the clear majority on the island, all major faiths are represented, and some precede the Spanish Church. The Protestant community is rapidly growing, to the point that many believe Catholicism—despite the statistics—is no longer predominant. Evangelical churches have flourished and have found a popular following. Santeria has a strong foothold as well, although it does not have the public presence of Catholicism. Sadly, Santeria has been vilified in Hollywood and in the Western media, so much so that these days we associate it only with chicken blood and black magic.

Introduced in the Caribbean centuries ago by slaves from the Yoruba tribe, Santeria is a highly spiritual blending of African and Catholic beliefs. In fact, many practitioners of Santeria are devout Catholics who worship Jesus and the Virgin Mary along with the Yoruba deities and spirits; this isn't officially sanctioned by the Church, but it is an accepted reality in Puerto Rico. (Incidentally, Santeria priests, also called *santeros*, are not to be confused with the sculptors of the *santos*.)

Espiritismo is another alternative belief system that is practiced concurrently with other religions. Believed to date to the Africans and Taíno, it is a little more nebulous than an organized faith. Some people follow it as a religion, others believe it is more philosophical, and a large number of Puerto Ricans turn to Espiritismo for its healing attributes. Espiritismo centers on the acceptance of a spirit world that interacts with the material world. This spirit world is comprised of "ignorant" spirits, who seek to harm humans, and good spirits who can protect us. Communication between people and spirits is the most essential practice of this belief, and spiritist centers exist where people afflicted by a spiritual malaise can attempt to establish a dialogue with the spirit whom they believe is responsible for their condition. As with Santeria, these centers are often decorated with *santos* and portraits of Jesus and the Virgin Mary.

A more cultural superstition is the *mal de ojo* (evil eye), which is found throughout Latin America. People who believe in *mal de ojo* speak of a negative force that is generated by the mere act of one person's looking at another (and especially looking at babies or children) in the wrong way: that is, with avarice, jealousy, and other unkind motives. To combat this bad luck, some Puerto Ricans arm their kids with *azabache* bracelets, which are made of gold and adorned with a black or red coral charm.

POLITICS & ECONOMICS

The Government

As a commonwealth, the responsibility of governing Puerto Rico falls, ultimately, on the U.S. Congress. A resident commissioner is elected every four years to represent the commonwealth in Congress. Most federal laws apply as if Puerto Rico were a state; however, the island exercises self-government in all domestic affairs, with the governor acting as the chief executive officer of the island. Like the U.S. president, the governor is elected every four years but, unlike the president, can serve any number of consecutive terms.

Puerto Rico's government closely mirrors the American model. Along with its own constitution, there is a senate representing 8 districts, and a house of representatives with 40 districts. Two senators and one representative are elected every four years. In addition, voters elect 11 senators and 11 representatives "at large," who represent the commonwealth as a whole rather than a particular district.

The Supreme Court is the highest court on the island; its seven justices are appointed by the governor. The governor also appoints the 33 judges who preside over the Circuit Court of Appeals, but the U.S. president selects the 7 judges for the U.S. District Court for Puerto Rico. Beyond the executive branches, local governance falls to the 78 municipalities that constitute the commonwealth. Residents of each municipality elect a mayor and an assembly. There are three main political parties: the Popular Democratic Party of Puerto Rico, whose platform supports the island's commonwealth status; the New Progressive Party of Puerto Rico, which continues Ferré's legacy and desire for statehood; and the Puerto Rican Independence Party.

The Economy

The efforts of Puerto Rico's leaders in the last 50 years have altered the economic landscape of the island. Agriculture has given way to industrial and service sectors. Pharmaceuticals are a vital business here, as are food products, electrical equipment, machinery, medical and scientific equipment, and clothing. Rubber, glass, leather, and printed products are also made here. There are about 2,000 factories on the island, which together contribute more to Puerto Rico's gross domestic product than does any other industry.

Tourism is a multibillion-dollar business that provides over 80,000 direct and indirect jobs on the island. It is one of the economic sectors that has shown consistent growth over the past few years, even as many local business leaders believe Puerto Rico has yet to tap its full potential as a tourist destination. For this reason, Puerto Rico continues to invest both in promoting itself and in improving its facilities and infrastructure to better accommodate visitors.

Agricultural output includes coffee, a great variety of fruits (of which bananas are the most commercially important), tobacco, and sugar. Rum is Puerto Rico's largest export, and it goes principally to the United States. The local government has made a concerted effort to boost its livestock. Not surprisingly, fishing is an important industry as well, with an annual fish catch valued at approximately $20 million. Caribbean lobster, which is abundant here, is its most precious commodity.

Other industries that fuel Puerto Rico's economy include mining, electric power, transportation, and communication. While most of its trade is with the United States, Puerto Rico also has "foreign trade zones" set up in its three largest cities, offering foreign companies a place to process, warehouse, and reship goods without paying customs duties.

All that said, the economy is an issue of some concern in Puerto Rico today. It is largely dependent, in one form or another, on the United States, and this relationship has undergone a significant transition in the last 20 years. The tax incentives that mainland U.S. companies enjoyed were curtailed in 1993, when new legislation linked the tax credit to wages paid by those companies rather than to profits. Naturally, these changes in the tax code affected private sector interests on the island. More to the point, Puerto Rico's economy is fueled in great part by federal aid—never a position of strength for a largely autonomous society. The local government remains the main employer on the island, and growing debt and the rising cost of services have resulted in a new tax structure introduced in 2006. Add to this the lack of abundant natural resources on which to base a heavy industry, and it's understandable that the viability of Puerto Rico's long-term economic outlook is fiercely debated.

Boricua and *Criollo*

Whatever their political affiliations, Puerto Ricans are staunch nationalists, in a cultural sense. They are extremely proud of their *boricua* (native) heritage, and they celebrate this more than their American or Spanish roots. Another term used to describe local culture—especially music, cooking, and the arts—is *criollo* (creole). *Comida criolla* is a term you'll see and hear a lot in restaurants to describe local specialties.

Through time, Puerto Ricans have absorbed in various ways the cultural influence of the outsiders who at one point or another called this island home, and have made it their own. This is true of Puerto Rico's relationship with the United States. Elements of American society as diverse as the Constitution and rap music have been adopted and adapted to the Puerto Rican way of life.

THE DEBATE OVER STATEHOOD

You could argue that Hawaii and Alaska never had it so good. What if you were asked if you would like to stop paying federal income taxes but continue to enjoy all the benefits of citizenship, save one: the right to vote in federal elections? Considering the high percentage of citizens who *don't* vote as it is, you can imagine how tempting this proposition might be for many Americans. In Puerto Rico, however, the unique quasi-statehood it enjoys under the United States is still considered a work in progress.

Puerto Ricans are an intensely political lot. Talk to most locals and they will be happy to debate the merits and weaknesses of their current and potential status in the world, and do so with knowledge and passion. You'll find three main camps:

1. **Leave well enough alone:** Although many residents want a definitive answer to the question of statehood, the strongest faction seems to favor preserving the hybrid status quo of the island. And who can blame its champions? With its own local government, Puerto Rico is largely left to its own devices from a political perspective. Puerto Rico receives billions of dollars each year from the federal government, and these funds impact almost every aspect of life on the island. Even though Puerto Rico receives less from the United States than does any state, its status as a commonwealth affords certain liberties, such as no federal income taxes. Why rock the boat?

   Rather than fully commit to either alternatives, supporters of the commonwealth suggest tweaking the current state of affairs to provide a greater degree of autonomy to the island, while keeping Puerto Rico firmly and permanently tied to the United States. Some of these proposed changes have included instituting dual U.S. and Puerto Rican citizenship, giving Puerto Rico sole decision-making authority over international trade, and allowing the island's government to forge independent ties to foreign nations.

2. **Enough already, let's become a state:** For a politically enlightened society, the lack of a vote obviously chafes the public conscience. With no senators or representatives in Congress, the island's residents are acutely aware that decisions are made in the Capitol without their input yet directly impact Puerto Rico. And the resident commissioner whom Puerto Ricans elect every four years to represent them in Congress has no vote in any final legislation passed by the House of Representatives, so he or she is seen as relatively powerless.

   One can imagine how Puerto Rico could carry significant leverage and power in Washington, DC, if it were a state. It would almost certainly receive an economic boost from the federal government, and would be a stop on the campaign trail. Given its population, I believe that Puerto Rico would be an active and vociferous player in the electoral process. Looking beyond the political issues, proponents of statehood argue that the island's status is a direct cause of its economic woes: Puerto Rico's average personal per capita income is below that of Mississippi, the poorest state in the nation. And many believe the United States is growing weary of giving Puerto Rico a "free ride." On the other hand, as a state, Puerto Rico would be eligible to receive more than double the amount of federal funds it currently gets from the U.S. government.

3. **State of independence:** Sitting at the other extreme, naturally, are those who want to create an altogether independent island-state, an autonomous member of the Caribbean. Over time, support for a fully autonomous Puerto Rico has dwindled, as even loyalists agree that full separation from the United States would come at a stiff price. The economy would suffer tremendously from the sudden absence of federal support. In addition, it would be easy to predict the effect of independence on American capital investment, once Puerto Rico had no more political ties to the

United States than, say, Jamaica. Without federally backed initiatives or guarantees, the appeal of investing in the island would naturally diminish.

So why go through with it? Well, the strongest reason is the surge of nationalism that would galvanize the spirit and identity of the local people, a culmination of centuries of being under the yoke of another power. (After all, the Founding Fathers faced harsher economic realities when they declared independence from the British.) Independence would also give Puerto Rico sole authority to create its own economic, immigration, monetary, and foreign policies. As a Republic, Puerto Rico would have a vote in the United Nations, and could enter into trade agreements and treaties with other nations.

WHAT IS AMERICAN, AND WHAT IS NOT

I was amazed to find that guidebooks on Puerto Rico are shelved in the "Foreign Travel" section at my local Barnes & Noble bookstore. Another eye-opener, several travel-related Web sites refer to Puerto Rico as a country, and some domestic airlines call it an international destination. Although Puerto Rico is not a state, it certainly isn't foreign territory. But leading Americans to believe they are traveling to international soil adds to Puerto Rico's ubiquitous duality.

Even I am sometimes confused. The winner of the 2006 Miss Universe pageant was Miss Puerto Rico, *not* Miss USA. In the Olympic Games, the Puerto Rican flag marches with that of other nations, and yet the U.S. armed forces include Puerto Rican soldiers. Puerto Ricans are U.S. citizens, accounting for approximately 1.3 percent of the total population. As with the 50 states, the government annually allocates federal funds to Puerto Rico. Its residents don't file federal income tax returns (unless they work for the federal government), however. This is an unusual political, economic, and social relationship.

If you visit the island, you'll certainly feel like you're not in Kansas anymore. Still, there are reminders that Puerto Rico is U.S. soil. At the most basic level, you'll never need to exchange any dollars (although the locals sometimes call dollars *pesos*). You'll see the American flag, the U.S. Postal Service, and those familiar green highway signs (which are written in Spanish). Most businesses have English names, and a lot of information is posted in both languages—such as museum and cultural signage, restaurant menus, and

Nuyorican Souls

A large number of Puerto Ricans living in the United States call New York City their home. Here, a vibrant, vocal, and close-knit society has emerged, a community that has come to be known as Nuyorican. Nuyorican style, attitude, and culture draw on their Latin roots but retain their urban NYC edge.

Nuyoricans are also an artistic and intellectual group that has helped spread Puerto Rican culture in the United States since the 1960s and '70s. Its more celebrated members include author Jesús Colón, who is considered the father of the Nuyorican movement, and the incomparable Tito Puente. With their unique literary and musical expressions of Latin and American identities, Nuyoricans aptly represent what is American about Puerto Rico, and what is not.

hotel instructions. You won't need adaptors or voltage converters, and a call to anywhere on the home front is just an area code away. Your cell phone should work. There are malls and movie theaters, Macy's and other department stores, fast-food chains like McDonald's and Burger King, and other examples of Americana.

But that's where the similarities end. In most ways, Puerto Rico looks and feels like another country, but one that has made a special effort to welcome Americans. The people who cater to tourists—the waiters, shopkeepers, guides, and the like—speak fluent English, albeit with a strong Spanish accent. (The police aren't nearly as proficient, however.) But if you walk among a crowd of "Sanjuaneros," you probably won't hear English spoken too often. And this is not a class issue, incidentally. Blue- and white-collar people alike will prefer their native tongue to English, and they will appreciate your efforts to communicate in Spanish. The farther away you move from the major tourist destinations, the more essential your grasp of the language.

Everything from the tropical foliage to the bright, brilliant architecture screams of a different place. In addition, Puerto Rico makes you intensely aware of its history in a way that precious few places in the United States are able to. Its Spanish and Catholic roots are strong. The towns and rural areas on the island are similar to what you'd find in South and Central America. If you rent a car and drive out to a remote beach or to the rain forest, you will likely leave almost every vestige of American life behind.

And this is why Puerto Rico is such an exciting destination. It is American, and yet most distinctly un-American. It is the Caribbean, and at the same time so much more than the Caribbean. People who are familiar with South and Central America will comment on how American the island is, while those who have never ventured farther south than Florida will tell you how different it is from "back home." In Puerto Rico, you can feel like you're in a new world while knowing you haven't fully left America behind. It is a part of the United States in which you can explore a history that precedes the very existence of the 13 colonies. Where else can you do that?

Go Ahead and Say, "Hola!"

With all of the uncertainty surrounding U.S.–Puerto Rico relations, you might wonder how Americans are received on the island. The honest truth is I get mixed reviews. Many people have commented on how friendly the island is, how you'd be hard-pressed to find a better welcome as an American traveling "overseas." Even though you may not *feel* it, the people greeting you as you leave the airport are U.S. citizens. Plus, the vast majority of the tourists who make up an overwhelming percentage of the island's GDP are visitors from the States. In 2005, over 1.2 million Americans registered themselves at a hotel on the island. The next largest group of tourists was from the Caribbean, which checked in at just over 53,000 visitors.

A large number of Americans live on the island, concentrated in the main cities and on Vieques and Culebra. And Puerto Rico is a popular business destination for American corporations, due both to its excellent conference and meeting facilities as well as its extensive menu of "team-building" exercises and corporate retreats. So familiar faces abound pretty much year-round.

That's not to say that the locals will be laying flowers at your feet as you step off the plane or ship. Not everyone loves the United States and its hold on the island. Quite a few people express contradictory feelings of being left behind by the United States while at the same time being too connected to America. Whether their justifications are right or wrong, many locals feel they're getting a raw deal, especially concerning the United States involvement on matters like federal funding and investment in the island. Another sore spot: well-documented problems that the people of Vieques and Culebra have had with the U.S. Navy.

Having said that, I can comment with certainty only on my experience after several trips to Puerto Rico. As a tourist and as a writer compiling research for this book, I met hundreds of people from every walk of life: schoolchildren, struggling waiters, bohemian artists, community leaders, and affluent businessmen. The welcome I received from every one of them was nothing less than amazing. More than once I was told, "Esta es tu casa" (This is your house). The people of Puerto Rico are generally humble, easygoing, and affable. They certainly went out of their way to help me, whether it was in their interests or simply because it's in their nature to make visitors feel at home. So I have no problem encouraging you to go ahead and say, "Hola!"

A HIGHLY ABRIDGED DICTIONARY OF PUERTO RICAN SLANG, TÚ SABES

So you took six years of Spanish in high school and college, read Gabriel Garcia Marquez's *100 Years of Solitude* in the original Spanish, and generally have a mastery of the language. You should have no problem in Puerto Rico. Right? Well . . . get ready to scratch your head and look confused. Spanish, like English, has dialects, accents, and colloquialisms that vary from country to country, and region to region. Latin and South America all have manipulated the mother tongue and come up with their own collection of slang, phrases, and names.

Puerto Rican Spanish is a unique animal. The language of the *boricua* is almost a snapshot of their culture and history. There's a certain casual "What? Me worry?" dropping and substituting of extraneous letters, especially *r* and *l,* that has resulted in interesting pronunciations: A good example is *Puerto Rico,* which is typically pronounced *"Puelto Rico."* (Note that *Rico* retains the *r* sound; the switch to *l* occurs when a consonant follows the *r.*) The same substitution occurs with *s* and *j,* but not as ubiquitously. And the influx of American culture has added a lot of English to the mix—so much so that sometimes, the English word will be better understood than the Spanish one. If you don't believe me, listen to a *raggaetón* rap and see how many words you can decipher.

What follows is a compilation of "Puerto Ricanisms" that you may find useful in any prolonged conversation with a local. This is by no means a complete list; there are enough colloquialisms to fill a dictionary. Not all of these terms are exclusive to Puerto Rico, but it's highly doubtful that you'll find them in your Spanish-language textbooks.

Words & Slang

Acaramelado . . . . Lovey-dovey.
Agallao . . . . Pissed off.
Arrancao . . . . Broke (monetarily).
Balneario . . . . A public beach.
Bayú . . . . A get-together.

Bichote . . . . A drug dealer, or an important boss-type figure.

Birra . . . . Beer (although the more universal *cerveza* will do just fine).

Brutal . . . . Awesome.

Cafre . . . . An all-purpose insult, used to describe someone uneducated, crude, or unrefined.

Chavo/Chavito . . . . . . Loose change or pocket money.

Chévere . . . . Cool (you hear this in other parts of South America as well).

Chillo/Chilla . . . . A lover on the side. (*Chillo* also means "red snapper," so if you hear it at a restaurant, you're probably not intruding on a personal conversation.)

Chiringa . . . . A kite.

Cuero . . . . Prostitute. (As you can imagine, there are several words for this.)

Desmadre . . . . A disaster.

Diez Cuatro . . . . Literally, "10-4," with the same meaning.

Dron . . . . A trash can.

Echón/Echona . . . . . . A show-off.

Esnú . . . . A modification of *desnudo*, which means "naked."

Espejuelos . . . . Eyeglasses.

Flechao . . . . Smitten (literally, "arrowed").

Fleje . . . . A synonym for *cuero*, also the term for a very ugly (and typically very thin) person.

Gallera . . . . A cock-fighting ring.

Greñú . . . . Hirsute.

Guagua . . . . Can be either a bus, small truck, or van.

Heavy . . . . Cool.

Jonrón . . . . The "spanglified" pronunciation of *home run*, with the same literal and figurative meanings.

Leche . . . . Luck (also used in its original definition, "milk"); you may hear the phrase *tener más leche que un palo de pana*, which means "someone's very lucky."

Ligar . . . . To stare at (in a very suggestive way).

Mahón . . . . Jeans.

Malecón . . . . A boardwalk.

Mime . . . . A small, very annoying insect like a mosquito or gnat.

Mitin . . . . Another English word gone local: a meeting (usually political or business).

Negro . . . . Literally "black" but has nothing to do with race; it's a term of endearment, similar to *dear* and *sweetie*.

Oficial . . . . No doubt about it; for sure.

Pana . . . . .A friend or buddy (also the word for breadfruit).

Parisear . . . . .To go partying.

Peso . . . . .A unit of currency in some South American nations, it's what the locals call dollars; they also say *dollars*, but nobody uses the Spanish equivalent, *dolares*.

Piragua . . . . .A snow cone. (In Puerto Rico, you'll get a wide variety of tropical flavors—try out a few; as one intrepid vendor claims, you haven't been to Puerto Rico until you've tasted a *piragua*.)

Quitado . . . . An easy thing; piece of cake.

Rechonchón . . . . An elderly party animal.

Relajo/Relajar . . . . . . A joke/to joke.

Revolú . . . . A mess or fiasco.

Sendo . . . . A common reference meaning "plenty of something" or "something big."

Siquitraque . . . . A firecracker.

Tapón . . . . A traffic jam.

Titi . . . . An affectionate term for *aunt*.

Todavía . . . . This is a tricky one; unlike its meaning, "still" in the rest of the Spanish-speaking world, *todavía* in Puerto Rico means "not yet."

Trililí . . . . A cheap, poorly made product.

Vacilón . . . . A party, but also a general mess or chaotic scene.

Wiken . . . . A mangled pronunciation of *weekend*—you won't hear *fin de semana*.

Zángano . . . . Also spelled *sángano;* means "jerk" or "idiot."

Common Phrases

Aquí hay gato encerrado . . . . Something's not right here.

Caerle como bomba . . . . Usually used in a social sense to mean it's not going too well, flaming out.

Darse un palo . . . . To have a drink.

Esos son otros veinte pesos . . . . Literally, "that's another twenty dollars"; means "that's a whole different issue."

Estar al palo . . . . To be fashionable and hip.

Estar del caray/Estar del mero . . . . . . To be out of line, to go overboard.

Estar pelao . . . . To be broke.

Feliz como lombriz . . . . The Puerto Rican version of "happy as a clam"; literally, "happy as an earthworm."

Juan del pueblo . . . . The Puerto Rican version of Joe Blow; literally "John from town."

Le importa un pirulí . . . . Couldn't care less.

Le puso en un tres y dos . . . . To put someone in a confusing position; literally, "put in a three and a two."

Llamar para atrás . . . . A to-the-letter literal translation of "to call back."

Me cago en nada . . . . A general expletive.

Mucha mecha, poca dinamita . . . . . . All talk; all bark and no bite.

Ni pa . . . . No way.

No es para tanto . . . . It's not all that (used to describe a gross exaggeration).

No me fuñas . . . . Leave me alone; don't bother me.

No pegar ni una . . . . To be totally and completely wrong or way off the mark.

O te peinas o te haces rolos . . . . Make up your mind.

Perder la chaveta . . . . To lose your temper.

Por allí para abajo . . . . Straight ahead. (Good to know if you're asking for directions, because this literally means "over there and down.")

Por si las moscas . . . . Just in case.

¿Qué es lo tuyo? .... What's your deal? (In written Spanish, all questions are framed by two question marks: an upside down mark before the sentence, and a regular one at the end.)

Rabo del ojo .... The corner of the eye; means giving someone a sideways look.

Se botó .... Refers to a person who goes all out or goes above and beyond what is expected.

Se deja comer .... Used to refer to food that is decent, but not great; like saying "it'll do."

Ser como jamón del sandwich ...... Get caught in the middle.

Ser patriota .... Looks like it means "being patriotic," right? Actually, it's a crude reference to a woman with large breasts.

Si no es Juan es Pedro .... Literally, "if it's not John, it's Peter," meaning "if it isn't one thing, it's another."

Tantas curvas y yo sin freno .... The spoken equivalent of a wolf whistle; literally, "all those curves and me with no breaks."

¿Te pica el coco? .... Are you nuts?

Tirar bomba .... To stand someone up.

Tomar el pelo .... Literally, "to take someone's hair," it's the Puerto Rican interpretation of "pulling your leg."

Tú sabes .... You know (usually attached to the end of a sentence); you'll hear this about a million times if you talk at length with a local.

Ultimo grito de la moda .... The latest fad.

Vestida de novia .... Literally a bride's dress, this is also used to describe a beer bottle frosted with ice.

Ya tú sabes .... Along with *tú sabes,* this is a popular phrase that means "you know how it goes."

Puerto Rican society is a great crossroads of culture and people; this union of different customs and ideologies can be seamless or conflicting, joyful, or bitter. But, as each occupant of this land has left its indelible mark on the island, so has the island blended the traditions, beliefs, governments, arts, and essence of all its inhabitants through time to create something uniquely Puerto Rican. Welcome to the land of the *boricua.*

3

PLANNING YOUR TRIP

The Checklist

The main island of Puerto Rico measures about 110 miles east to west and 35 miles north to south, about the size of Connecticut. In some ways, it's like a condensed continent; the topography includes everything from rugged mountains to rolling plains to sun-drenched beaches. It's probably the most accessible island in the Caribbean, a major air-travel hub and a main destination for many cruises. Before you pack your bags, here is some information that will help you plan your trip and make the most of it.

In Case You Need It
✓ Any emergency   911
✓ Department of Health   787-766-1616
✓ Medical emergency   787-754-2550
✓ Dental emergency   787-795-0320
✓ Fire department   787-725-3444
✓ Police   787-343-2020
✓ Tourist Zone Police
In Condado   787-726-7020
In Isla Verde   787-728-4770
✓ Weather   787-253-4586

CLIMATE

Good news: You can put your coat back in the closet. It's summer year-round on the island, with temperatures ranging from 71 to 89°F, so you're almost guaranteed to get some sun. While its weather is usually postcard-perfect, Puerto Rico does get quite a bit of rainfall, mostly in the mountainous interior. The driest months are January through April, but it rains in spurts throughout the year. (By the way, the forecast in San Juan is not always the same as in Culebra and Vieques, so be sure to check the forecasts separately when planning your trip.)

Like the rest of this region, Puerto Rico has a hurricane season, which officially lasts from June 1 to November 30. Several hurricanes have passed over the island or grazed its coast in past decades, but Puerto Rico has not suffered a Category 4 or 5 storm since the 1930s. Hurricane Georges in 1998 was the last to have a major impact on the island, and it was the only one to hit the island directly in the past 60 years.

All that said, a storm doesn't need the notorious "hurricane" label to ruin your day. Tropical Storm Jeanne in 2004, for example, caused significant havoc in Puerto Rico. If you're thinking of traveling to Puerto Rico during this season, it's a good idea to check any of the following resources for up-to-the-minute forecasts:

The **National Weather Service's Climate Prediction Center** provides online statistics and predictions at www.cpc.ncep.noaa.gov.

The **Weather Channel** (www.weather.com) offers daily, weekly, and monthly data on every city it covers. For a charge of 95 cents, you can call 1-800-WEATHER to hear about up-to-date conditions.

When to Go

Because of its temperate climate and dedication to the tourism industry, any time is a good time to head to Puerto Rico. Still, the tourist season follows the weather. The peak travel period is winter, when sun-deprived throngs from the U.S. East Coast descend on the island by boat- and planeloads. As a result, travelers visiting the island from December to April can expect to pay the highest prices for hotels. Make your plans well in advance, especially if they include spending Christmas in Puerto Rico. During the low season, between May and November, travelers can find great deals on most island hotels.

TRANSPORTATION: GETTING TO THE ISLAND

Coming into Puerto Rico is like traveling anywhere within the United States. American citizens don't need a passport or any documentation other than a valid form of photo ID, such as a driver's license. This is especially convenient when you consider that, beginning in July 2007, all U.S. citizens will need their passports to travel to any destination in the

Cruise ships docking at the piers in Old San Juan

Caribbean except Puerto Rico and the U.S. Virgin Islands. There's no need to go through customs or worry about vaccinations. Canadian citizens must carry proof of citizenship, and international travelers must show a passport. The island is on Atlantic time, which is one hour ahead of Eastern time, but there are no daylight savings adjustments.

As for your method of transportation, you have your choice of traveling by air or by sea. For a small island, Puerto Rico has busy skies and crowded ports. There are 30 airports (13 of these have unpaved runways, catering more to private charters and island-hopping) and over 20 airlines servicing the main cities and islands. Luis Muñoz Marín International Airport is the main gateway to Puerto Rico for domestic and international airlines (although you can fly directly to other parts of the island from many U.S. cities). It is also the regional hub for American Airlines which, along with its sister airline, American Eagle, has over 100 flights a day from the island to the U.S. mainland and most Caribbean destinations.

Sample Air Travel Times to San Juan

From Miami	2.5 hours
From New York City	4 hours
From Chicago	5 hours
From Los Angeles	7.5 hours

Of course, you can elect to travel by boat rather than plane. The Caribbean is the most popular cruise ship destination, and San Juan is the second-largest cruise port in the Western Hemisphere. It makes for an interesting contrast, peaking through a 400-year-old sentry box and seeing, in the distance, an ultramodern cruise ship sailing into the old city. If you walk along the piers of Old San Juan, you can't miss them: massive, floating cities that dot San Juan Bay, waiting to dock. And they can't miss you: Chances are that your Caribbean cruise will include this island. The piers in Old San Juan welcome over a million visitors from cruise ships every year, giving passengers easy access to the old city. The following cruise lines all count Puerto Rico among their Caribbean ports of call:

Carnival Cruises	1-888-CARNIVAL
Celebrity Cruises	1-800-722-5941
Costa Cruises	1-800-377-9383
Cunard Line	1-800-7CUNARD
Diamond Cruise	1-800-333-3333
Holland America Line	1-877-SAIL HAL
Majesty Cruise Line	1-800-532-7788
Norwegian Cruise Line	1-866-625-1160
Princess Cruises	1-800-PRINCESS
Regent Seven Seas	1-877-505-5370
Royal Caribbean	1-800-398-9819
Seabourn Cruise Line	1-800-929-9391
Silver Sea Cruise Line	1-800-722-9955
Windstar Cruises	1-800-258-SAIL

To promote tourism from the cruise ship industry, the Puerto Rico Tourism Office has instituted the San Juan Fun Card for passengers disembarking in the city. Participating establishments—including hotels, restaurants, and bars—offer discounts to cardholders.

TRANSPORTATION: GETTING AROUND THE ISLAND

Luis Muñoz Marín International Airport is in Carolina, about 3 miles from San Juan. Many hotels offer shuttle service to and from the airport, and taxis to the main tourist neighborhoods of Isla Verde, Condado, and Old San Juan have flat rates between $10 and $20. You'll pay metered rates for other destinations on the island. The airport also offers bus service to the old city and its outlying neighborhoods. Most major car-rental agencies have a desk here or within shuttle distance, but you'll pay a 10 percent airport tax to rent directly from the airport.

You can travel within Puerto Rico by taxi, bus, train, ferry, rental car, *público* (a privately owned van service), tour bus, charter boat, or, to really ritz it up, small plane. This section focuses on the main island. *Transportation to and around Vieques and Culebra are covered in their respective sections.*

By Taxi

The best way to get around metropolitan San Juan is by taxi. Taxis are easily recognizable; they're all-white cars and vans with logos featuring the iconic Puerto Rican sentry box. You can call a taxi on the phone, arrange a pickup from your hotel, or hail one (in Old San Juan, there are several stands where you can grab a taxi). For those of you who have experienced unsavory or dingy-looking cabs in parts of Latin and South America, don't worry, these are safe, clean, and reputable.

Several independent taxi companies operate in Puerto Rico. Here are a few in the San Juan area:

Astro Taxi   787-727-8888
AA American Taxi, Inc.   787-982-3466
Metro-Taxi Cab, Inc.   787-725-2870
Cooperativa de Servicio Capetillo Taxi   787-758-7000
Cooperativa Rochdale Radio Taxi   787-721-1900

Puerto Rico's public transportation options aren't New York City's, but they're practical and cheaper than a taxi.

By Bus

The main island has a public bus system (you'll hear the buses referred to as *guaguas*), with two routes serving the principal tourist areas: Bus A5 travels between Old San Juan and Isla Verde, and Bus B21 can take you from Old San Juan to Condado and on to the Plaza Las Americas mall. Bus stops are indicated by yellow signs marked *Parada* (Stop). The one-way fare is 50¢, and service runs daily. For routes and more information on bus service, call 787-767-7979. The new Metrobus runs from San Juan to Río Piedras; call 787-763-4141. Finally, a free trolley runs within the old city (see chapter 4, "Old San Juan").

By the Tren Urbano (Urban Train)

A relatively new development is the Tren Urbano, an 11-mile rapid-transit rail line that runs from Bayamón to Santurce, connecting the business district to San Juan and sur-rounding communities. While this is basically a commuter rail designed to alleviate local traffic (there is no service from Old San Juan), you can use it to visit some areas outside Old San Juan; and the designers have gone out of their way to make the stations architec-turally and artistically appealing (check out the wall sculpture made from 60,000 spools of thread at the Centro Médico station, or the 25,000-foot cast iron orange tree at the Martínez Nadal station). The fare is $1.50 and includes transfers to buses (students, the disabled, and passengers over 60 pay 75¢; passengers over 75 and children under 6 travel for free). Trains run from 5:30 AM to 11:30 PM seven days a week. For more information, call 1-866-900-1284.

By Rental Car

Most of the major national car-rental companies, along with several local agencies, oper-ate in San Juan. The cost of renting a car isn't exorbitant, and this is a great way to explore the island. The highway system is well planned, and if you have the time, excursions away from San Juan offer an experience far removed from the world of resorts and guided tours. You'll pay a bit more than the average price in the States, but you may get better deals from local companies. You may also have to pay liability insurance. Credit cards that offer auto coverage in the continental United States don't always extend that coverage to Puerto Rico, and your own car insurance company may not include coverage for the island.

Before you get behind the wheel, it would be helpful to familiarize yourself with the fol-lowing interesting facts about driving in Puerto Rico:

Should You Bother?—Some people love to head straight from baggage claim to the car-rental agency to kick off their vacations, and this is wise in many popular destinations in the United States. But does it work for Puerto Rico? That depends on what you want to do. If your time will be predominantly spent in Old San Juan, with the occasional excursion to Condado or Isla Verde, forget the rental car—everything is accessible by foot or a short cab ride, and parking can be problematic. But if you plan on flitting around Greater San Juan and want full mobility, having a car is a good idea.

At least know how to ask, "Donde está San Juan?"—For those of you who have to look that one up, it means, "Where is San Juan?" If you're heading out to the hinterlands, it would be in your best interests to have a basic understanding of Spanish. English is widely spoken and understood in the tourist zones, but once you hit the road, only Spanish is spoken. If you don't speak Spanish, pay special attention to your map. (Make sure you get one from the rental company.) Puerto Rico's roads have numbers as well as names, so getting around isn't complicated. The only problem is asking for directions; most Puerto Ricans know the roads by name rather than number, while highway signs often list just the route number.

Miles and Kilometers—For some bizarre reason, Puerto Ricans use both; distances are in kilometers, but speed limits are posted in miles. Have fun calculating how long it will take you to travel 50 kilometers at 60 miles per hour. (For the record, there are 1.6 kilometers to 1 mile.) Gas is sold in liters, not gallons.

Road Rules—They do things a little differently around here. Puerto Rican motorists have been trained at the same school as NASCAR racers and New York City cabdrivers. People don't always heed stop signs, so be careful when you're at an intersection. (This is especially true at night, when motorists frequently run red lights.) It is legal to make a right turn at a red light after coming to a stop. Many drivers think it's also legal to make a left turn at a red light. Also, motorists pass on the right here, rather than on the left. Actually, they'll pass you any way they can. This is an accepted way of life on the island. Nobody seems to get overly offended by the aggressive driving, and you'll rarely hear a horn blaring in anger. But it takes some getting used to.

Avoid Rush Hour—This is true of most large cities, and San Juan is no exception. From 7 AM to 10 AM and from 4 PM to 7 PM, chances are you'll regret driving around the city, and you'll hate your destination before you get there. Also, if there's a concert or any other main event in Old San Juan, God help you. Traffic is not confined to just the city; it can delay your trip out to Fajardo or other coastal cities much longer than you might have anticipated. A helpful tip: If you're taking the expressway from San Juan to another part of the island, you'll hit tollbooths, and you'll be grateful if you have *cambio exacto* (exact change).

Parking—Parking is a major problem, not just in the old city, but in most tourist areas. San Juan just wasn't designed to accommodate the huge number of cars that congest its roads. As such, the number of spots where you can park is very limited. The police understand this and are therefore somewhat lenient when issuing parking tickets. In Old San Juan, some roads are so narrow that parallel parking becomes an unhappy adventure. The other reality you'll face is paying for parking just about everywhere you go. Most hotels will charge you for parking, even if you're their guest. Many restaurants also charge, whether in the form of a valet fee or tips. (The most hysterical example of this that I saw was a small café that had two parking spots right in front of it, with a $2 valet parking sign displayed in one of them.) Every casino hotel has parking fees.

Those flashing lights—Whether you're a pedestrian or a motorist, you'll frequently see San Juan police cars driving along with their lights flashing but no sirens blaring. After about the fifth time I had pulled over, only to see that the cop wasn't getting out and was actually waiting for me to resume my journey, I learned that the police always drive around like this. The lights are meant to help drivers identify police cars at night.

The following is a partial list of the national and local car-rental companies operating on the island. Many agencies provide additional services, such as free pickup from the airport, a cruise ship, and/or hotels, and car rentals.

AAA Car Rental
787-726-7350; 787-726-7355
www.aaacarrentalpr.com

Located in Isla Verde, this agency offers free pickup and return service, and unlimited mileage.

Avis
1-800-331-1212
www.avis.com

Avis has several locations, including the airport, hotels in San Juan, the Plaza Las Americas mall, and cities across the island.

Budget Rent-A-Car
1-800-527-0700
www.budget.com

Budget has offices in the airport, Howard Johnson Hotel, and Normandie Hotel.

Charlie Car Rental
1-800-289-1227; 787-728-2418
www.charliecarrentalpr.com

Offices are in the airport, Isla Verde, and Condado. Charlie offers free shuttle service from the airport and hotels, as well as free drop-off service to cruise ships from its Condado office (787-721-6525).

Dollar Rent-A-Car
787-725-5500 (at Luis Muñoz Marín International Airport)
www.dollar.com

Offices are in the airport, at the Holiday Inn in Isla Verde, in Ponce, and in Carolina. With the exception of the Holiday Inn, all offices are in or near the airport.

Hertz Rent-A-Car
1-800-654-3030
www.hertz.com

Hertz is all over the island, with offices in over 15 locations, including the Sheraton in Old San Juan, the Caribe Hilton in Puerta de Tierra, and the San Juan Marriott Hotel & Casino in Condado, and in nearby neighborhoods Hato Rey and Río Piedras.

Lanes Car & Truck Rental
787-268-6161; 787-268-6162
www.lanescarrental.com

Located in San Juan, Lanes offers free drop-off and pickup service to the airport, hotels, offices, and residences. Also, visitors renting for a week get the seventh day free.

Pier Car Rental
787-962-6555

Located in the Sheraton lobby, Pier is the first car-rental company in Old San Juan. Its location is ideal for anyone thinking about renting a car for the day, and they offer free pickup within 10 miles.

Quality Car Rental
1-866-497-3155; 787-791-3800
qcarrent@coqui.net

Quality is an affiliate of Advantage Rent-A-Car. Located in Isla Verde, it provides a free shuttle from the airport. They also give customers the option of renting with cash or credit card.

Specialty Car Rental, Inc.
787-340-4040
www.exoticcarrentalpr.com

Located in Isla Verde, this is the place to go if you want something beyond the standard sedan. Anything from a Mini to a Hummer to a Lotus Elise is available.

Thrifty Car Rental
1-800-FOR-CARS; 787-253-2525
www.thrifty.com

Located at Luis Muñoz Marín International Airport, Thrifty provides pickup and drop-off service at most major hotels in the Condado and Isla Verde area. It also has offices in other parts of the island and is one of the few that provide drop-off service in Fajardo, which is convenient if you plan to go to Vieques or Culebra.

By Two-Wheeler
For a more flexible and affordable rental, you might want to try a moped, scooter, or bike. Mopeds and scooters can be a lot of fun, especially on the winding, hilly roads of the old city and on brief trips to the beach. Just remember that traffic can get a little crazy, so ride with care. You can rent a moped or scooter through many of the island's hotels, or go straight to the source:

Hot Dog Cycling
787-791-0776
www.hotdogcycling.com
Plazoleta shopping center in Isla Verde

Hot Dog is all about bikes: selling, renting, and servicing. Their rental bikes have grip shifts, bar ends, low gearing, and fat tires. You can also rent helmets, rack straps, leg straps, locks, air pumps, and other accessories.

JM Rentals, Inc.
787-727-6611
www.scooterspr.com

JM rents in the San Juan area as well as in Culebra. They offer pickup anywhere within the area they service, including Luis Muñoz Marín International Airport, hotels, and ferry terminals.

Pier Car Rental
787-962-6555

Pier rents scooters in addition to cars, with free pickup within 10 miles.

San Juan Motorcycle Rental
787-630-2300

Located in Old San Juan, immediately off Pier 4. You can rent scooters here at hourly, three-hour, or daily rates.

Specialty Car Rental, Inc.
787-340-4040
www.scooterrentalpr.com

Specialty Car rents bikes and scooters, along with a variety of exotic and sports cars. They'll deliver to your hotel.

By Ferry
If you're going to Culebra or Vieques, the ferry is the most economic option. To use this service, however, you must first make your way to Fajardo. A taxi ride to Fajardo will cost between $50 and $60. There's also seasonal (December through April) high-speed ferry service from Old San Juan directly to the islands. For more details on transportation to the islands, check the "How to Get There and When to Go There" sections in the Culebra and Vieques chapters.

Within the old city, you can take a ferry from Old San Juan to Hato Rey or Cataño from the **AquaExpreso** in Pier 2, near the cruise ship docks. The fare to Cataño (from here you can take a quick cab ride to the Bacardi rum distillery) is 50¢ each way; to Hato Rey, it's 75¢ each way. One advantage of the Hato Rey stop is that it links the old city with the Tren Urbano (787-729-8714), which has a station right next to the dock.

By *Público*
If you want a uniquely Puerto Rican travel experience, get on a *público*. These independently owned and operated passenger vans make daily trips to many towns and hard-to-reach rural areas. *Públicos* can be identified by their yellow license plates ending in *P* or *PD*. They are cheap but make frequent stops, and some routes don't operate on a set schedule.

These are clearly options for students, visitors who have spare time, and the "lets-wing-it" crowd who crave the adventure of getting there as much as the destination itself. Just make sure you don't mind road trips and aren't sticking to a schedule: If your destination is the western edge of the island, you could be in a van for several hours, as the *público* makes several stops along the way. On Vieques and Culebra, however, which are small and free of congestion, *públicos* are a great travel option if you're not renting a car. In San Juan, you can call any of the following *público* companies, which offer routes to various parts of the island:

Blue Line
787-765-7733

Goes to Aguadilla, Moca, Isabela, and other destinations on the northwest coast.

Chóferes Unidos de Ponce
787-764-0540

Goes to Ponce and other destinations.

Línea Boricua
787-765-1908

Goes to Lares, Ponce, Utuado, San Sebastián, and other destinations.

Línea Caborrojena
787-723-9155

Goes to Cabo Rojo, San Germán, and other destinations on the southwest coast.

Línea Sultana
787-765-9377

Goes to Mayagüez and other destinations on the west coast.

Terminal de Transportación Pública
787-250-0717

Goes to Fajardo and other destinations on the east coast.

Camuy and Arecibo

Two of the most visited sites in Puerto Rico are the **Río Camuy Cave Park** and the **Arecibo Observatory.** Both are a few hours west of San Juan. The Camuy subterranean cave system, the third largest in the world, is the result of over a million years of nature's inexorable landscaping. You don't have to be in prime shape to negotiate the easy trails, which take you through fern-filled ravines, to the gaping mouths of caves over 600 feet deep, and to an underground river. Science buffs may prefer the Arecibo Observatory, and many of you have seen it before: Remember that scene in *Goldeneye* when James Bond fights the bad guy while hanging onto the end of a telescope? That was the radio telescope at Arecibo, the largest single-dish radio telescope in the world.

Tours

Of course, you can let someone else do all the work. For every major destination in Puerto Rico, there will be at least one tour company willing to take you there. The tours offered can be as basic as guided jaunts around the old city to multiple-day, activity-intense treks into the interior. Most hotels can arrange them, and many tour companies will arrange transfers and pickups from the airport. Several operators allow you to tailor the tour to your preference.

Tour operators in San Juan are more than abundant, and through them you'll have unprecedented access to all of Puerto Rico. Most of these companies provide a variety of trips, and a few specialize in aquatic, nature, or adventure excursions. These latter tours are covered in greater detail under "Puerto Rico on a . . . Dare" (see chapter 10). The companies listed below form a partial selection and include the ones I have either come to know or have consistently received rave reviews for, from tourists and locals alike.

AAA Island Tours

787-793-3688
www.aaaislandtours.com

Offers an extensive array of tours and packages, including the Arecibo Observatory, the Bacardi rum factory, the bioluminescent bay, Río Camuy Cave Park, Cabezas de San Juan (site of an ecological reserve and ancient lighthouse), El Yunque, Guánica Dry Forest, Humacao (a wildlife refuge), Luquillo Beach, Ponce, and Old and New San Juan, and various shopping tours. AAA also provides biking, diving, fishing, hiking, kayaking, sailing, and snorkeling trips; tailors tours for photographers, bird-watchers, and golfers, and has nighttime tour packages.

Acampa

787-706-0695
www.acampapr.com

Acampa offers a range of nature tours and excursions that take you to places most other operators don't reach. Among the destinations they help you discover are Enrique Monagas Recreational Park, Caja de Muerto Island, Mona Island ("the Galapagos of the Caribbean"), San Cristóbal Canyon, Tanamá River, El Yunque and Toro Negro rain forests, and a full-day tour to an old plantation in Ciales.

American Tours of Puerto Rico

1-800-250-8971
www.americantoursofpr.com

Bus and van tours of the Arecibo Observatory and Camuy caves, Ponce, Luquillo Beach, El Yunque, Old San Juan (with or without the Bacardi rum factory), as well as private and VIP tours.

Aquatica

787-531-3593
http://aquaticapuertorico.com

Aquatica offers a 1.5-hour guided Jet Ski tour that takes you around Old San Juan and lets you see La Fortaleza, the city walls, and the two main forts from a nautical point of view. This tour offers a very different experience from the land tours, for two reasons: First, you're skimming across San Juan Bay on a Jet Ski; and second, the land tour gives you the perspective of the Spanish troops who occupied the city; Aquatica shows you what the pirates and invading forces saw when they approached the city's formidable defenses. The tour includes pickup and drop-off at your hotel.

Audioguía
787-507-2905
www.audioguiapr.com

This do-it-yourself company furnishes tourists with handheld audio equipment and a map, and sets them loose to discover Old San Juan at their leisure. A cool new addition to their service is the ability to download the audio tour on an MP3 player.

Countryside Tours
787-723-9691
www.freewebs.com/countrysidetourspr

Countryside runs tours of the Arecibo Observatory, the bioluminescent bay, the Camuy caves, and El Yunque. A garden tour includes the botanical garden, and gardens in Old and New San Juan.

Legends of Puerto Rico
787-605-9060
www.legendsofpr.com

An interesting menu of customized tours covering Old San Juan (by day and by night), El Yunque and Guajataca forests, and a coffee plantation. The various tours of Old San Juan, which combine culture, history, sightseeing, and, depending on the tour, food and drink, are very popular. As an add-on to some tours, you can book a rum-tasting event that lets you sample different varieties of the liquor, learn about the history and making of rum, and combine the experience with dishes from one of San Juan's fine restaurants.

Number I Wheelchair Transportation & Tours
787-883-0131

The only company to provide tours, drivers, and vans dedicated to special-needs visitors. Tours of Old and New San Juan, and the Bacardi rum distillery, are offered. The trips include transfers from a hotel or cruise ship. All tours must be booked in advance.

Legends of Puerto Rico offers "Night Tales in San Juan," a tour and with rum tastings.

Yokahú Kayak Trips, Inc.
787-604-7375
http://yokahukayaks.com

Yokahú offers ecotours, specializing in kayak trips out into Fajardo's bioluminescent bay (your best option if you're not going to Vieques).

By Small Plane

Flying around the island might seem like an expensive proposition, but it's really not a bad way to get from place to place; and Puerto Rico is remarkably well equipped to handle all the air travel. Small airports are located in every major city, and on Vieques and Culebra. Two airports serve San Juan, and a good number of local flights depart from the city's smaller Isla Grande Airport. Many local and international airlines that service major points on the island, as well as the local airlines, can also take you to several destinations in the Caribbean. Here are just a few of those companies:

Air America, Inc.
787-268-6951
www.airamericacaribbean.com

Air Flamenco
787-724-6464
www.airflamenco.net

American Eagle
1-800-433-7300
www.aa.com

Cape Air
1-800-352-0714; 787-253-1121
www.flycapeair.com

Charter Flights Caribbean, Inc.
787-791-1240; 787-398-3181
www.charterflightscaribbean.com

Isla Nena Air Services
1-877-812-5144
www.islanena.8m.com

Vieques Air Link
1-888-901-9247; 787-741-3266
www.vieques-island.com/val

LODGING: WESTERN COMFORT & LATIN CHARM

True to its commitment to you, the tourist, Puerto Rico offers a dizzying number and variety of lodging options, and your experience here can be tailored as much by your choice of hotel as your choice of activities and recreation. The good news is this, whatever the budget, there are warm and friendly places to stay when you're visiting Puerto Rico.

Consider the following sections as an overview of what you can expect to find on the island. Most of the hotels mentioned are covered in detail in their respective chapters. One thing to note when you book your hotel is the tax structure. You'll pay an 11 percent tax on rooms in hotels with casinos, a 9 percent tax in hotels without casinos, and a 7 percent tax in small inns.

Go West(ern)

Some travelers want to be assured of the familiar feel, service, and standard of the hotels they've stayed in countless times before. Most major hotel chains are represented on the island, surrounded by or close to all the fun. Puerto Rico as a "home away from home" is reinforced by the presence of all-American institutions like **Howard Johnson** and **Hampton Inns.** Seldom available when you travel abroad, they're all here.

At the same time, many of these Western standbys have succumbed—in a good way—to the lure of the Caribbean. The curved facade of the **Sheraton Old San Juan**, for example, is a beautiful nod to Colonial architecture. The faux lagoon at the **Embassy Suites** features palm trees and a waterfall. The **Caribe Hilton** threw in a tropical garden and bird sanctuary along with its business center, spa, and other more typical amenities. These hotels provide the same comforts and quality that you'll find stateside, only with a tropical twist.

Reception area of the Gallery Inn in Old San Juan

Sleek, Chic & Boutique

I have to admit I'm a big fan of Puerto Rico's boutique hotels. There's something to be said for owners and developers who go out of their way, and spend a significant amount of money, to stamp their own personality on a place. In Puerto Rico, quite a few of them have gone about it with a zeal and passion that will leave a huge smile on your face. Meeting the people who run these hotels (In many cases, the owners are on-site) is just as delightful.

Of course, you pay for all that personality. Boutique hotels typically aren't cheap, but a few in Puerto Rico are very reasonable, and even the more expensive ones are usually worth the higher price. The majestic **Normandie Hotel,** which resembles an ocean liner, arose from a love story to match James Cameron's *Titanic*. The **Gallery Inn** is as much an art gallery and history museum as it is a hotel, and it's the only one I know of whose social director is a parrot. *Condé Nast Traveler* called the **Water Club** one of the world's coolest hotels. In Vieques, **Hix Island House** takes the boutique concept, quite literally, into the Stone Age.

B&B . . . & B

Bed & Breakfast Inns can be a delightful alternative to a hotel. These places usually have a story to tell, and the owners are usually around to tell it. They are like the first cousins of the boutique hotel, and put you in mind of cheerful hospitality and understated pride. In Puerto Rico, B&Bs could add an extra *B* to their name, as they tend to be close to the beach.

At the trio of **El Canario Inn**, **El Canario by the Lagoon**, and **El Canario by the Sea**—all in Condado—you can have your sun and eat your breakfast too. **Casa del Caribe,** a block from Condado Beach, typifies the laid-back Caribbean B&B concept. In addition to a full American breakfast, you can order a picnic lunch prepared in a handy backpack at **Hacienda Tamarindo** in Vieques. With marble floors in every room and an Italian motif, the **Coral Princess Inn** is a nice retreat in Santurce.

Bargain Bets

Even in the heart of the tourist district, you'll find a cheap place to stay. More important, most of the budget hotels I visited were clean and comfortable. The ones I've listed below have advertised year-round rates under $100. (Depending on when you go, you can even get a room for less than $50.) They're not the only ones, but these hotels make that bang for your buck resonate just a little bit more.

In Isla Verde, the bright blue **Borinquen Beach Inn** is well run, affordable, and close to the beach. At the **Coqui Inn,** an amalgamation of two former budget hotels—Casa Mathiesen and Green Isle Inn—you'll get poolside complimentary coffee, tea, and pastry service every morning. It's not easy to find truly "budget" accommodations in Old San Juan, which in general caters to a well-heeled crowd, but **La Caleta Realty** offers very affordable lodgings.

Once you get out to the more remote islands, prices drop even further. On Culebra, **Posada La Hamaca** will throw in free beach towels, coolers, and ice for your trip to the beach. Owners Penny and Ruthyc Miller make the **Sea Gate Guest House** not only an affordable but also a friendly and rustic option on Vieques. The rooms at **Amapola Inn**, on the island's southern shore, are cute and comfortable.

Lust for Luxury

Some travelers just want to get pampered silly, and worry as little as possible—about

Presidential Suite at Chateau Cervantes in Old San Juan

anything—while they're on vacation. These people pay top dollar for top-class service in top-of-the-world accommodations, and they'll find both in Puerto Rico. You can spend over a thousand dollars per room, per night, in Puerto Rico. And for that kind of money, you'll stay where the stars do when they visit the island.

Located in Río Grande, The **Paradissus**, the island's first all-inclusive, all-suite resort, is a bit removed from all the action, but it will offer you every amenity. The ultrachic **Chateau Cervantes** will present you with your very own butler if you and your wallet so desire. **Hotel El Convento** doesn't have the grandeur of the bigger resort hotels, but it makes up for it with a perfect balance of luxury, rustic charm, and outstanding service. The **Ritz-Carlton** is stately elegance. The **Martineau Bay Resort & Spa** is a manicured anomaly amid the wild vegetation of Vieques.

Eco-rific

On the other end of the spectrum from the "spoil-me" tourists are the naturalists; the ones who don't mind roughing it as long as they can wake up holding a shot of wheatgrass juice. Fortunately, the eco-resorts here do their best to ensure your comfort as well as your proximity to nature. Most of these nature-focused establishments cluster around El Yunque National Forest, requiring a rental car or transportation from the airport. You will leave the casinos and the beaches behind, and replace the chatter of cars and people with the singing of frogs and parrots. And that's probably exactly what you're looking for.

I'm quite sure that anyone who has stayed at **Villa Sevilla** wouldn't call the experience "roughing it," but its location just a few miles from the peak of El Yunque puts it in the heart of the rain forest. The **Río Grande Plantation Eco-Resort** is built on a 200-year-old sugarcane plantation. **Casa Grande Mountain Retreat**, a former coffee plantation, has its rooms dotting the mountainside, and boasts a freshwater swimming pool. **Casa Cubuy Ecolodge** offers a natural Jacuzzi.

Beachfront Property

This is where you'll find the vast majority of hotel options in Puerto Rico. Taking advantage of its most prized natural resource, the island has developed stretches of its finest beachfront and stocked it with hotels for every budget and taste. For every hotel that is as close to the water as you can get, there are several a few blocks from the beach. As you can imagine, price often dictates proximity; but you won't have to pay a lot to be a stone's throw from the Atlantic Ocean.

The **Caribe Hilton** is the only hotel to boast its own private beach. Others have simply muscled their way onto a section of beach for their guests. In peak season, this access can be a very good thing. If you want to be close to the beach as well as Old San Juan, head to the **Normandie Hotel,** which is adjacent to El Escambrón, the only public beach near the old city.

There is a string of fancy beach-bordering hotels along Condado and Isla Verde, including the **InterContinental San Juan Resort & Casino, El San Juan Hotel & Casino, Ritz-Carlton,** and **Condado Plaza**. **Hostería del Mar** and **Numero Uno Guest House** are economical options located on the edge of Ocean Park, whose beach is well loved by the locals for its sands as well as its laid back tranquility. Luquillo Beach, perhaps the most popular beach, especially for Sanjuaneros, is a hike from the city; but it's accessible from the **Westin Río Mar Beach Golf Resort & Spa**, which has its own lush sands to lure you away from San Juan.

Private Property

There is a thriving market of privately owned furnished apartments and villas for rent in Puerto Rico, and they can be rented nightly, weekly, or monthly. This affordable alternative is also often an attractive option for families who want to avoid spending too much money in restaurants, and for families who have pets. The listings are more prevalent in Vieques and Culebra, but there are many property owners in San Juan who will open their doors to you.

Ocean Park is a residential neighborhood as much as it is a tourist destination, so you'll find vacation rentals here. In addition to its hotel rooms, **El Prado Inn** has a well-appointed, two-story villa and a basic one-bedroom apartment for rent. The owners of the **Bóveda** souvenir shop have apartments in the heart of Old San Juan. The **ESJ Towers** is a rare condo-hotel and vacation ownership property in a prime location in Isla Verde. Many property owners in Vieques will rent out rooms, suites, or entire floors to tourists. In Culebra, you can live like a king for a week or more in a $1 million cottage.

Room for Roulette

It's an indescribable feeling, if you like to gamble: to leave your room, press the *C* button on the elevator, and emerge in the eye of a storm of bells, whistles, sirens, hoots, tinkles, cheers, and applause. It's the siren song of the hotel casino, and it's the only reason many of us ever go to Las Vegas. Puerto Rico's hotels haven't quite reached those inspired facades or wondrous heights, but the casinos are a big part of the fun here. The gaming culture follows the European mold: elegant, old-fashioned halls and settings that remind you of Bond movies, complete with old classics like baccarat, roulette, blackjack, and craps. Ironically, Texas Hold 'Em, the most addictive card game on the planet, hasn't taken hold in Puerto Rico, and many casinos don't offer it.

In an effort to ensure the quality and security of the gaming business, the government regulates casinos and permits them only in hotels. Not all are open 24 hours a day, but you can at least lose your money until 4 in the morning. And everyone from slot specialists to high rollers will find a home, and a game, to suit their style. Here's an informal guide to help you target the one that's right for you.

With 17,500 square feet of gaming space, the largest casino on the island is the **Ritz-Carlton**, and it is one of the most elegant. The only casino hotel in Old San Juan is the Sheraton. The largest hotel casino, in terms of number of rooms, is easily the massive **Wyndham El Conquistador Resort & Country Club.** The most games can be found at the **Condado Plaza** and **San Juan Marriott Resort & Stellaris Casino.** The Condado Plaza also has the largest number of slot machines in San Juan. The **InterContinental San Juan Resort & Casino** in Isla Verde and **Radisson Ambassador Plaza Hotel & Casino** in Condado are good destinations for poker fans.

Paradores

Paradores (country inns) are Puerto Rico's best effort to get you out of Metropolitan San Juan (as well as well-known Vieques & Culebra) and into its relatively untapped western, southern, and interior regions. Part marketing gimmick, part bargain, *Paradores* dot the island, most of them hugging the coast. Check the Puerto Rico Tourism Company's Web site (www.gotopuertorico.com) for special deals on these inns.

The 23 inns classified as *Paradores* are something of a mixed bag. They tend to be strategically located near a beach or popular tourist attraction, but a few revel in their isolation. Because each is privately owned, the inns vary greatly according to location, theme, and accommodations. They range in style from a restored coffee plantation in the mountains to a beachfront resort. The term *country inn* usually denotes a rustic charm, but not all Paradores fit the image. More than a few *Paradores* resemble typical, modern hotels found in Condado or Isla Verde. Among those that do recall a bygone era are **La Hacienda Juanita**, in Maricao, and **Hacienda Gripiñas**, in Joyuya.

SHOPPING FOR ARTS & CRAFTS & DEMON MASKS

Like its hotels and restaurants, Puerto Rico's shops cater to diverse tastes and budgets. People love to shop here, and there is an abundance of good-quality merchandise on the island. At many stores, even the smallest arts and crafts are well made. Americans will quickly recognize retail outlets of some of their favorite chains on the island, and seasoned vacationers will notice a few international brands as well.

Souvenirs of Boricua

If you find it hard to leave the island without a souvenir, you're not alone. The arts and crafts industry here is excellent. What's more, it is distinct. Souvenirs in the Caribbean can be predictable, after all—the bottles of multicolored sand, those polished pink sea shells that you stick next to your ear and then strain to hear the ocean, and innumerable T-shirts

Máscaras de Puerto Rico

with witty slogans—we've all seen them. But the souvenirs you'll find here are several notches above these trinkets because Puerto Rico has deep and proud artistic roots. Arts and crafts in Puerto Rico draw from two main cultural wells: religion and the mixed heritage of the island's population.

Spend more than a few hours here and you can't miss one of Puerto Rico's most popular and unique artifacts: the *caretas.* These papier-mâché demon masks, traditionally worn at carnivals by revelers known as *vejigantes,* are an explosion of color, design, creativity, and teeth. (Many locals call the masks *vejigantes* as well.) Horns and fangs sprout from everywhere on the fantastic faces of the masks, which make striking wall decorations. They range in price, size, and complexity, from $10, palm-sized miniatures to massive, complex constructions that run into the thousands of dollars.

The *caretas* have a cousin of sorts—if the masks are too thorny for your tastes, you can purchase a painted, polished, and decorated husk of gourd or coconut from many of the stores that specialize in the masks. The style and origins of the masks draw on Puerto Rico's Spanish, native Taíno, and African heritage. Strange though they may seem at first, the *caretas* will draw your eye, and you might end up gingerly carrying one home . . . as I did. You can buy them at several locations throughout Puerto Rico and in Old San Juan, in particular. A popular source is the **Puerto Rican Art and Crafts** store on Fortaleza Street, in Old San Juan.

If demon masks are Puerto Rico's most dramatic craftswork, *santos* are perhaps its most ubiquitous. These carved icons can be found all over the island. Their history dates to Puerto Rico's earliest Catholic roots. Even the artisans who carve these figurines are given a name: *santeros.* The *santos* can be made from clay, gold, stone, or, in their most widely available form, cedar wood. They typically vary in size from 8 to 20 inches, making them conveniently portable souvenirs.

Santos are deeply linked to Puerto Rican society, both past and present; it's not only tourists who buy these figurines. Most easily recognized are the images of Los Tres Reyes Magos (The Three Kings) and the Virgin Mary. If you're in the old city, you'll find them in various shops on Cristo and Fortaleza streets. **Siena Art Gallery** on San Francisco Street has a small but fine collection of higher-end pieces.

Ceramic wall hangings are also common artifacts that recall the tropical architecture of the island. These painted replicas of the more well-known and beautiful buildings in Puerto Rico are cute reminders of the island's beauty. They are also widely available, especially at **Mi Pequeño San Juan** on Cristo Street.

Mundillos (tatted fabrics) are the product of Puerto Rican bobbin lacework, which had all but vanished until a recent resurrection and promotion through the Puerto Rican Institute of Culture. The work is particular to Puerto Rico and Spain, where it originated. Its patterns are often elaborate and intricate, not unlike those of some Native American crafts found on the U.S. mainland. A good place to look for them is **Mundillo Lace,** in front of Pier 4 in Old San Juan.

A Passion for Fashion

Fashion, and high fashion in particular, is a big deal in Puerto Rico. It ranges from basic beachwear to sophisticated couture, but there's a common theme: Puerto Ricans like to look good and dress smart (if you have any doubts about this, step out at night). On Vieques and Culebra, almost everyone is in full beachwear, of course, but fashion is important on these islands, too.

There's a strong push to launch Puerto Rican fashion on an international stage. Local designers have flourished, with a few big names in the vanguard of the fashion scene. There is no consistent theme to Puerto Rican fashion but, generally speaking, sexy is in. Puerto Ricans' Latin roots are very much on display in their fashion sense, but anyone expecting the Caribbean's tropical themes to duplicate themselves on fabric are mistaken;

you won't find too many garish palm-tree patterns and lime green arrangements. Fashion is serious, and serious business. Well-known local designers stage the biannual Fashion Week in San Juan, where they showcase the latest in Puerto Rico style and flair. These are major productions, covered by the international media and attracting hundreds of people.

Some of Puerto Rico's best-known designers include the following:

David Antonio

Talk about one-of-a-kind: Antonio makes only one garment in each size. He's also known for his men's line.

Luis Antonio

JLo is one of many celebrities on his client list. Antonio's ready-to-wear collection is available in New York City, Miami, Tokyo, Munich, and, of course, San Juan.

Gustavo Arango

Dressed Miss Universe 2001. 'Nuff said.

Lisa Cappalli

Designer for many models, singers, and TV personalities. Cappalli's designs run the gamut of women's wear. Her distinct style is easily recognized, and her items are known especially for their meticulous, detailed work.

Ruben Dario

Another regular on the beauty-queen circuit, Dario personally fits each of his customers at his atelier. His ready-to-wear collection is available in San Juan.

Nono Maldonado

Known as much for dressing beauty queens as for his sophisticated casual and formal menswear and women's clothing.

Stella Nolasco

One of Puerto Rico's youngest leading designers, Nolasco specializes in modern casual clothing for young women.

Harry Robles

An internationally known women's-wear designer who will attend to you personally in his boutique, Harry welcomes customers by appointment only. There are few set pieces available in his shop; even the gowns you'll see in catalogs will be tailor-made for you.

A typical fashion for men is the *guayabera* shirt, which is a cross between a jacket and a shirt. *Guayaberas* are traditional clothing for men throughout the Caribbean and are acquiring a foothold in the U.S. market. They are light, comfortable, and come in casual and evening-wear designs. You can find these, in varying degrees of quality, in many souvenir and clothing shops. A reliable selection is available at **Clubman**, which has a store in Old San Juan.

If the local flavor's not your thing, don't worry. Most of the world's most well-known brands have established a presence on the island. Puerto Rico is home to the Caribbean's largest shopping center: **Plaza Las Americas** is a sprawling, three-story mecca decorated with fountains and sculptures, and stocked with over 300 stores. Smaller malls are located throughout the island, including very exclusive mini–shopping centers housing **Louis Vuitton**, **Cartier**, and similar top-shelf retailers.

Of particular appeal is the cluster of high-end outlet stores from such brands as **Polo Ralph Lauren**, **Dooney & Bourke**, and **Coach** in the old city. A bit removed from San Juan, shoppers can go nuts at the **Belz Factory Outlet World**, which features over 400,000 square feet of discount retail merchandise, or at **Prime Outlets**, which lies between San Juan and Arecibo.

Two Drinks & a Smoke

Puerto Rico has a quite a few consumable exports, but it is best known for one of them. I'm referring, of course, to rum. Rum is pervasive in Puerto Rico. From the plethora of rum-based drinks found in bars, to the cultural and historical significance of the drink, to the business of rum (over 70 percent of the rum sold in the United States comes from the island), for many people rum is a huge part of the Puerto Rican experience.

The locals are proud of their rum, even if they sometimes get sick of the ever-present piña colada. Puerto Rico is the only rum-producing country to adhere to a minimum aging law for the drink. The Bacardi distillery, across the bay from Old San Juan, is a popular tourist attraction. There are many varieties of rum available on the island, sorted into three main categories: light, dark, and *añejo* (aged). Have fun picking the right one to take home with you.

It may not be as strong as the rum, but Puerto Rico's coffee is also quite good. Given the fame of Venezuelan coffee, Jamaican blends, and the legendary status of Juan Valdez, it's

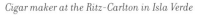

Cigar maker at the Ritz-Carlton in Isla Verde

odd that Puerto Rico has not done more to market this product in recent years. At one time Puerto Rico was among the largest coffee producers in the world, and coffee is still a principal export. But the household status enjoyed by beans from Kona, Colombia, and Brazil, among other nations, has thus far eluded the Puerto Rican coffee bean.

The best coffee plantations are in the verdant mountains in the southwest. The combination of tropical rainfall, the locally grown Arabica bean, and the volcanic soil are responsible for the rich flavor of the coffee. The city of Yauco, nestled among the mountains, is known as El Pueblo del Café (The City of Coffee) for its rich product, and the **Café Yauco Selecto** brand is among the best-known premium blends around. Another brand, **Alto Grande**, is considered of super premium quality, which is the worldwide gold standard of coffee—it is only one of three coffees to carry this label.

Finally, Puerto Rico has a small share in the hand-rolled cigar industry. Like the coffee and sugar industries, cigar production and export used to be big business in Puerto Rico, but the industry dwindled in the 20th century. It does, however, have the somewhat questionable honor of being home to the biggest cigar ever produced (pending Guinness World Records authorization): Patricio Peña's 62-foot-long stogie, made in January 2005 and stuffed with over 20 pounds of tobacco.

Puerto Rican cigars, along with more popular brands like **Cohiba** and **Partagas**, are available in many gift shops on the island. Recent attempts to revive the industry have been led by **Don Collins**, a local brand whose manufacturer claims to be the world's oldest cigar-making company.

The Fine Arts

"There has been a major boom in art in Puerto Rico over the last five to ten years," says José Alegría, director of Obra Art Gallery in Old San Juan, pointing out the tens of millions of dollars spent producing inspired temples to artistic expression. A few examples: the $58 million restoration of the Museo de Arte de Puerto Rico (Puerto Rico Museum of Art) in nearby Santurce, and the $40 million spent on the Museo de Arte Contemporáneo (Museum of Contemporary Art). Along with the outstanding Museo de Arte de Ponce (Ponce Museum of Art), these centers have renewed international attention in Puerto Rican art. According to Alegría, this emphasis has fueled the demand of local artists, many of whom are currently in vogue on the international stage. Several of the old masters have already carved out their place in the art world.

Beyond the three large and well-known museums, there are distinct monuments to art in Puerto Rico that underscore its prominence on the island. You have only to walk into one of the serene and beautiful galleries in Old San Juan to see a variety of sculpture, photography, paintings, and ceramics.

The man considered to be the founder of the artistic movement in Puerto Rico is **José Campeche**, and Puerto Rico could not ask for a more appropriate champion of the arts. Of mixed descent, Campeche was born in 1751, the son of a freed slave. He never left the island, but his works, which focused on religious themes and historical portraits, earned him a place of reverence in the pantheon of Puerto Rican artists. He is considered to be one of the most important artists (if not *the* most important artist) of the 18th century to come out of the Americas.

Of equal fame in Puerto Rico and abroad is **Francisco Manuel Oller Cestero,** who arrived on the fledgling arts scene in the late 1800s and became known as the only Hispanic artist to contribute to the impressionist movement. He is also well loved in

Puerto Rico for his subject matter: He painted vivid portrayals of the romantic and rugged life of Puerto Rico's working classes, from landscapes to depictions of slaves, Jíbaros, and peasant life. His most famous work, *El Velorio,* currently hangs in the Museum of History, Anthropology, and Art in Río Piedras, and is a beautiful if eerie representation of an old Puerto Rican custom: the "celebration" of a child's death.

Two of Puerto Rico's modern artists are very well known to the art community and the general public in the United States. **Jean-Michel Basquiat**, whose mother was Puerto Rican, took urban art to new heights. A contemporary of Warhol and Haring, Basquiat has developed a cult following since his death. Because of his impact on the arts and his short-lived,

Museo de San Juan in Old San Juan

tumultuous career, he was aptly named "the art world's closest equivalent to James Dean" by the *New York Times.* On the island, his work has recently been exhibited in the Obra Gallery as well as the Museo de Arte de Puerto Rico.

Puerto Rico's other contemporary art rebel has been leaving enigmatic, prophetic messages all over New York City. His chalk depictions have been copied by closet revolutionaries and grassroots ideologists throughout the tristate area. Few have captured New Yorkers' imagination through street art to the degree that **James De La Vega** has. (Ironically, one of the only other legitimate claimants to profound street artistry was Basquiat.) De La Vega's work has ranged from politically and socially charged messages to humanistic expressions.

These four artists are just the tip of a rich history of art on the island. But whereas Basquiat and De La Vega made their homes and their careers in New York City, the homegrown talent has only recently begun to garner international acclaim. In fact, local leaders in the artistic community believe Puerto Rico is entering a commercial and international golden age of sorts, as newer artists explore hitherto uncharted territory and branch out beyond the traditional form.

The meshing of art, culture, and entertainment is perhaps best captured in the new tradition of the **Noche de Galerías** in Old San Juan, when the city's galleries stay open late so that locals and tourists can drop in, view some of the island's best work, enjoy a glass of wine, and breathe in the magic of the ancient city at night.

The Sparkly Stuff

Puerto Rico is a fantastic destination for jewelry shopping, if only because you'll be hardpressed to find such a staggering concentration of vendors in so small an area anywhere else (see also "Where to Shop," below). You'll find a range of quality, design, and store specials here, and window-shopping is easy because many retailers are also neighbors. **Tiffany, Luca Carati, David Yurman**, and **Harry Winston** are among the brand names available in San Juan's jewelry shops.

The number of "discount" jewelry stores has contributed to Puerto Rico's reputation as a bargain hunter's dream, but that's not necessarily the case. You will get good-quality merchandise, but I haven't seen too many spectacular deals. There are niche stores—for example, **Emerald Isles** in Old San Juan stocks Colombian emeralds; **Argenta**, is the exclusive supplier for Elle Jewelry in the Caribbean; and **Atena Gold** specializes in hand-made Greek designs—and there are purveyors of jewelry from all over the world.

Where to Shop

Plaza Las Americas, the Caribbean's mega-mall, is in the Hato Rey district of San Juan and is worth a visit for those who love large shopping centers. If you crave the local fashion scene, Puerto Rico's most posh designers have planted stores in Old San Juan, Condado, and nearby Santurce. Condado's Ashford Avenue is the island's Fifth Avenue, a broad, busy road where you can browse high-end boutiques. A very ooh-la-la address here is **1054 Ashford Avenue**, an ultra–strip mall where you can drop in for a bejeweled watch at **Cartier**, a facial at the **Zen Spa**, and a snazzy pair of shoes at **Ferragamo**.

Outlet stores are grouped together on Cristo Street in Old San Juan, but the sprawling **Belz Factory Outlet World** is just outside the city, in Canóvanas. Souvenirs and local artifacts are sold all over the island but are especially omnipresent in Old San Juan. If you're hunting for jewelry, Fortaleza Street will make your head spin. They line the street here, which makes it easy to comparison shop. Cristo Street and the malls also have a decent selection of jewelry shops. As a general rule, I steer clear of shops in hotels, fearing overpriced goods and limited selection. But some hotels on the island have a decent selection, or a signature boutique, that's worth checking out.

Shopping is the last thing on people's mind when they head out to Vieques and Culebra. And, beyond a smattering of gift shops and local artisans, these islands don't offer much. What they do provide, however, is transportation to nearby St. Thomas, a duty-free shopping mecca in the Caribbean. So if the isolation is getting to you, and you absolutely must breathe the air of polished leather and discount prices, boats and planes await your command.

DINING WITH KING PLANTAIN

"Buen provecho!"

You'll hear this often when you dine in Puerto Rico, and it means "enjoy your meal." On this island, it's hard not to. It's a familiar tune by now, but Puerto Rican cuisine is a hybrid, and an interesting one at that. Every race to call Puerto Rico home has contributed something tangible to its food. Their indelible marks have shaped a cuisine that is at once exotic and basic, hearty and varied, simple and rich.

The Taíno influence is obviously the oldest, and it is principally found in the staples of the Puerto Rican diet: seafood, tropical fruit, cassava, *achiote* (annatto seed), and corn. The Spanish came along and changed everything. The biggest dietary revolution they spawned was the introduction of meat (beef, pork, and chicken), garlic, rice, and olive oil to the island's cuisine. Many dishes served in Puerto Rican restaurants today, such as *bacalao* (salted cod) and *arroz con pollo* (chicken with rice), are direct imports from Spain. The Spanish love of pork has translated seamlessly to the island; pork is not just "the other white meat" here. Indeed, Spanish food in Puerto Rico is more true to the mother country than in any other Latin American nation. The Spanish also brought the Africans, who contributed their own ideas and recipes, as well as okra, taro, and plantains. Both cultures introduced sugarcane to the palates of the local population, and it has played a pivotal role in the food and drink of the island.

Historical insights can be drawn from Puerto Rican cuisine today, and the plantain is a good example. It makes sense that this fruit is now an integral ingredient in local food; after all, African slaves typically cooked in the kitchens of the Spanish aristocrats who lived in Puerto Rico. Similarly, it is said that Puerto Ricans don't waste edible parts of the foods they eat, and this holds true in some of their most typical dishes. *Gandinga* and *mondongo* are two classics that use the less choice meats of the animal: Pigs' feet and ears make up part of the meal. This economy of food again points to social custom; the African slaves used the leftovers when preparing their food. Their recipes have lasted over time to become mainstays today.

Mix all of these together, and you have the beginnings of **criollo** (creole) cooking. The tastes and flavors of criollo cuisine rely on a few secrets. The first is *sofrito,* a seasoned sauce made with tomatoes, garlic, peppers, coriander, and onions, and whatever personal touch the cook throws in. *Sofrito* is a base for many of the island's main dishes, stews, and soups. The second is *achiote,* which is used to color food as well as give it an earthy, rich flavoring. Third, we have *adobo,* a common seasoning for meat that includes peppercorns, oregano, garlic, salt, olive oil, and lime juice. And the last is not really a secret, but a natural advantage: Practically everything one eats in Puerto Rico is freshly prepared. The islanders consume what they grow, and there is little need to import the ingredients, at least for local specialties.

Two other critical elements contribute to homegrown cooking and are found in most island kitchens: the *caldero* (cauldron), without which a good *arroz con pollo* is inconceivable, and the mortar and pestle. You'll find mortar-and-pestle combinations of all sizes in gift shops and local stores on the island, because grinding up oregano, coriander, and other herbs is essential to local cuisine. Puerto Ricans love to season their food with herbs and spices, without making it spicy.

The Puerto Rican diet is heavy on beans, rice, and meats. But, as far as raw materials go, if there is one mainstay of Puerto Rican cuisine, it's the plantain. A plantain is a type of banana that is generally eaten when cooked. It's a larger, coarser, less-sweet cousin of the fruit we know on the mainland. And Puerto Ricans, forgive the pun, go bananas over it. It is the most ubiquitous side dish on the island, in part because the plantain has an unexpected range when cooked. Plantains can be baked into hard patties called *tostones,* boiled into a mash, or fried and served golden-brown, crispy on the outside and sweet and flavorful on the inside. The latter are called *amarillos* (*amarillo* literally means "yellow"). *Mofongo,* the signature dish of Puerto Rico, begins with a mashed mound of plantains, into which is added a combination of seafood, meat, or vegetables. Go to any criollo restaurant, from the casual to the most refined, and you'll see *mofongo* on the menu.

Flan

Another local favorite is *asopao*, a kind of stew that is considered the most traditional Puerto Rican dish. Usually made with chicken or seafood, *asopao* is like curry, in that there are many varieties and "Mom's special recipe" versions of the dish. Other choice selections include a variety of *sopóns* (soups). The most common soups are chicken-with-rice (*sopón de pollo con arroz*), fish (*sopón de pescado*), and chickpea-with-pig's-feet (*sopón de garbanzos con patas de cerdo*). Most tourists will be more familiar with the well-known black bean soup (*frijoles negros*), and those who have traveled in Spain might recognize one of its imports, *caldo Gallego* (Galician broth), which is made with pork, ham, beans, and vegetables.

There are two great loves in the Puerto Rican diet: meat and fried foods. Between popping an astounding variety of fried fritters (*frituras*), gnawing on roast pig (the famous *lechón asado*), and wolfing down large quantities of *arroz con pollo*, you can gain a lot of weight if you're not careful. Then again, if you visit Puerto Rico and plan to stick to a diet, you'll miss out on one of the island's best attributes.

If you *must* diet, your choices are limited. Puerto Ricans aren't big on salads, although the growing number of tasty tropical salads on restaurant menus has been encouraging. Vegetables feature prominently in the cuisine, but raw vegetables are typically hard to come by at restaurants. Soups and stews are hearty and filling, and Puerto Rico's seafood and shellfish are excellent.

With the abundance of tropical fruits, you'd expect a variety of exotically flavored desserts, and you'll find specialties made with banana, pumpkin, guava, and pineapple. For the most part, however, Puerto Ricans prefer to stick to the basics. Coconut dominates the dessert scene. You can get crunchy coconut squares, coconut bread pudding, and many other dishes laced with this stalwart of the Caribbean. One local choice is *tembleque*, made with coconut, vanilla, and cornstarch. The most popular dessert on the island is flan, a caramel custard introduced by the Spanish. Flan can be prepared and flavored with a variety of local ingredients, including rum, breadfruit, cheese, pineapple, and pumpkin. Rum cake is also widely enjoyed, and also tailored to the chef's imagination.

The aforementioned *tembleque* is a purely 'Rican invention, as are *cazuela*, which is made with sweet potato, pumpkin, and coconut, and *majarete*, a basic porridge of coconut milk, cinnamon, and rice. *Arroz con dulce*, a Puerto Rican take on rice pudding, is enhanced with ginger and spices. The local interpretation of sweet potato pie is *nísperos de batata*, which is sweet potato balls fried with coconut, cloves, and cinnamon. Like other Latinos, the islanders also enjoy guava with cheese. The coolest name on the dessert menu is *amor de polvo* (love powder), a crispy concoction of grated coconut and a lot of sugar.

More recently, Puerto Rican cooking has been influenced by immigrants and cultures from lands as far away as Japan, Thailand, and India. Sushi is becoming popular on the island, and I sampled "Pan-Asian-Latin" fusion food for the first time in Old San Juan. You'll find restaurants from all over the world, sometimes from unexpected places. Many of the chefs combine what they know with ingredients that Puerto Rico grows, offering unusual, but very tasty, tropical twists on their native cuisine.

So, what to drink with your food? If you're 18, you can legally drink anything you want. And the number of choices is staggering. Cocktails, liquor, coffee, and fruit mixes abound.

Rum is by far the most consumed drink on the island, but that's a huge oversimplification. There are roughly 200 varieties of rum in Puerto Rico, including dark, light, gold, and flavored varieties. It is poured, squeezed, or blended into a range of tropical drinks.

A Brief Dictionary of Puerto Rican Culinary Terms (for speakers and nonspeakers of Spanish alike)

Acerola	A kind of Caribbean cherry, found in juices and snow cones
Achiote	Annatto seed
Adobo	A seasoning of ground peppercorns, oregano, garlic, salt, olive oil, and lime juice
Ajonjolí	Sesame seeds
Asopao	A kind of stew or thick soup made with rice and either chicken, seafood, or meat
Amarillos	Plantains fried until yellow-brown, soft, and sweet
Bacalaítos	Cod fritters
Chayote	A vegetable that looks like a wrinkled pear and is similar in taste to a squash
China	An orange
Cuchifrito	A batter-fried snack
Empanadillas	Turnovers
Frituras	Fritters
Gandinga	A stew made with pork tripe, kidneys, and liver
Gandules	Pigeon peas
Guarapo	Sugarcane juice
Guineo	A banana (not a plantain)
Jueye	Crab
Lechón	Roast pig
Mallorcas	A buttery bread covered in powdered sugar; the Puerto Rican danish
Pana or **Panapén**	Breadfruit
Pasteles	A kind of wrap filled with meat
Pastelón de carne	A meat pie
Pegado	The hard, crunchy rice scraped off the bottom of the pot
Pionono	A fried plantain cake stuffed with ground beef
Piragua	A snow cone
Quesito	A cream-cheese-filled sweet pastry
Sancocho	A stew made with root vegetables and meat
Salmorejo	A thick, tomato-based soup made with crabmeat; spicier than normal Puerto Rican fare
Sofrito	A seasoned sauce typically made with onions, garlic, peppers, and coriander
Surullo/ Sorullito	Fried cornmeal in the shape of mozzarella sticks
Tembleque	A local dessert made with coconut, vanilla, and cornstarch
Tostones	Plantains baked into a hard patty
Yautia	Taro

A piragua (snow cone) vendor

The most famous of these libations is, of course, the piña colada; but it is the tip of the mixed-drink iceberg. As famous as it is, the piña colada is considered old hat in many trendy bars and lounges.

Rum has enjoyed a hip resurgence through the *mojito,* a Cuban drink known for the clumps of mint leaves lying at the bottom of the glass. Other mixed drinks made with rum include *coquito,* which is the local take on eggnog, and Planter's Punch, made with pine-apple, lemon, lime, and orange juices and served over cracked ice. Some popular classic mixed drinks get the rum (not bum) treatment. Don't be surprised if your Bloody Mary is mixed with rum, and sangria usually features a splash of rum. The rum and sour often replaces the whiskey sour, rum vultures the gin in rum and tonic, and you can order a rum collins . . . you get the idea.

Premium rums are on the rise, and Puerto Rico's best include Reserva Añeja, Bacardi Select, Don Q Gran Añejo, and Ron del Barrilito Three Star. These are not the rums found in the average rum and Coke, but rich liquors best savored neat. On the flip side, there's *ron caña,* which isn't actually rum but a similar liquor made from sugarcane: It's the local equivalent of moonshine.

I could (and others have done so) write a book about Puerto Rican rum. Instead, I'll turn to another choice. The local beer, Medalla, is light and cheap, and found everywhere (either a dangerous or fantastic combination, depending on your perspective). Most popu-lar brands of beer are available as well. Drinking alcohol is a social custom on the island. Even among the younger crowd, it's an aid to enjoying an evening rather than the main ingredient in a mission to get hammered. Cocktails are popular, hard liquor not as much. If you don't drink alcohol, you can enjoy a variety of fresh fruit juices, as well the island's excellent coffee.

RECREATION: PICK YOUR PASSION

You can find a beach anywhere in the Caribbean. But after you've gotten your tan and gone for a swim, then what do you do? Puerto Rico's lengthy and exuberant answer to this ques-tion is one of the reasons it stands head and shoulders above all the other islands, and many countries, south of Florida. The choice of recreation here is enough to satisfy the appetites of the lazy or the wild, the spectator or the participator. Puerto Rico makes full use of its terrain, resources, and ecology to offer a full range of activities. Most of these are covered in detail throughout this book. Here, I've summarized in broad strokes the differ-ent options you have to entertain yourself while you're on the island.

Over and Under Water

Obviously, the biggest attraction is the beach. There are all kinds of beaches and beach activities in Puerto Rico; above the surface, you can find great spots for surfing, suntan-ning, privacy, shell collecting, parties and events, or simply unique experiences (like the black-sand beach on Vieques). Once you dip under the water, a new world awaits you. Whether you're snorkeling or diving, the reefs, islets, sunken hulls, and the combination of Caribbean and Atlantic waters bring a stunning variety of marine life to the island. The local waters offer a visual spectacle that rivals the best dive destinations on the planet.

Certain beaches are hot spots for a specific activities. For example, the places to go for aquatic sports like parasailing or kite boarding are Ocean Park and Punta Las Marías. For

Sunset at Esperanza, Vieques

people-watching, the Condado, Isla Verde, and El Escambrón beaches all draw crowds, especially during the peak seasons. If you want to go to a beach that also serves up great fried snacks, head to Piñones and Luquillo. For more remote beaches, you have only to hop in a car (or a *público*) and head out of San Juan to reach your destination. One note of clarification about the beaches of Puerto Rico: The Spanish word for "beach" is *playa,* and most of the beaches you encounter will bear this name. However, you'll also find several *balnearios* (public beaches). Unlike the more secluded spots, these beaches typically offer more amenities (such as lifeguards) and post the hours they're open. The other term you'll see a lot is *cayo,* which means "islet" or "key." Some of the most beautiful and isolated stretches of sand are found in Puerto Rico's *cayos,* but they are accessible only by boat.

West, to Porta Del Sol

The western coast of Puerto Rico is called Porta Del Sol (Sun Gate), and it boasts some of the best beaches on the island. You can almost pick a city along the coast at random and you won't be disappointed. Some of the more popular destinations are

Ballenas Beach and Bay	A beach and bird lover's paradise.
Domes Beach	Its breaks attract surfers from all over the globe.
Playa Boquerón	Rising out of the water at this beach is a statue of the pirate Roberto Cofresí, who was sheltered by the people of the village because he shared his booty with them.
Playa Crash Boat	Wildly popular with surfers and scuba divers.

Mar Chiquita (Little Sea) in Manatí, near San Juan

Playa El Combate	A local favorite, with spectacular sunsets.
Playa Jobos	Known for great surfing.
Playa Shacks	Famous for its **Blue Hole** snorkeling area.
Puerto Hermina	Small and secret (so secret, it was known as a smuggler's cove for pirates).
Puntas	A cluster of small beaches in the city of Rincón, separated either by natural barriers or word of mouth.
Spanish Wall Beach	A relatively isolated place, it's a short hike from Domes.
Surfer's Beach	Self-explanatory.

Also on the West Coast is one of Puerto Rico's three bioluminescent bays (or biobays)—**Bahía La Parguera.** While most believe that the bay has lost much of its potency due to, among other things, damage from excessive use by motorboats, a visit here is still an eerily beautiful experience; take a kayak tour on a moonless night to get the most out of it.

Closer to home (or San Juan, at least) if you're traveling west is the city of Manatí. Here you'll find one of my favorite little beaches on the island: **Mar Chiquita,** which means "Little Sea." The rough waters of the Atlantic are becalmed by twin arms of rock that stretch out from the land, creating a horseshoe of water and sand. Surfers will prefer the wicked breaks in **Los Tubos** (The Tubes).

East, to Fajardo
The **Seven Seas Beach** near Fajardo is so called because, seen from above, it is said that
you can count seven different shades of blue-green in the water. Fajardo is also the gateway
to Puerto Rico's most popular islands: Vieques and Culebra, and home to a fantastic bioluminescent bay, which I can attest is worth the trip from San Juan. One look at the
beaches here and you might never want to return to the main island.

Offshore
For Puerto Rico's best beaches, you might need a car and a boat. Culebra and Vieques
islands have gained worldwide renown for the quiet majesty of their beaches. Careful
underdevelopment, especially on Culebra, has ensured that the beaches retain their natural beauty. Other islands aren't as famous. Near Guánica lies a tiny, remote place called
Gilligan's Island, which lives up to its rather hokey name. Even farther away (about 50
miles off the coast of Mayagüez) lies **Mona Island,** which has 5 miles of unspoiled beach.
Mona Island is also home to a benign colony of iguanas, so many, in fact, that Mona has
been compared to the Galapagos Islands.

　　Actually, Puerto Rico lays claim to a veritable archipelago of islets, and, just as you
would in the Florida Keys, you can hire a boat and go find your favorite. Some are close to
shore; others are devoid of beach; and a few aren't open to the public at all. **Desecheo,** for
example, is a natural wildlife reserve; **Monito** has no access by boat; and **Cayo Santiago** has
an exclusive resident community of monkeys, who are there to be researched and not visited. Each of these spots has excellent diving, and boats do go there.

　　Many of these stretches of sand and palm are privately owned. Technically, this shouldn't
mean anything to you; according to Puerto Rican law, all beaches are public property, up

Boats off Palominitos

until the sand meets the vegetation and buildings, if there are any. But in Puerto Rico, people do their own thing and guard their land against trespassers. Legal or not, there's a chance you'll be harassed if you are discovered on a seemingly deserted beach bearing a PRIVATE PROPERTY sign.

You don't have to be *in* the water to enjoy it. From kayaks to catamarans, Puerto Rico will give you every chance to skim the surface of the ocean. You can take a Jet Ski tour of Old San Juan or charter a yacht and go exploring. The best boating on the island is in Fajardo, the sailing capital of Puerto Rico. With its forest of masts and populous marinas, the city looks like something you'd find along the Mediterranean coast.

Day sails from Fajardo are especially popular because they are a fun, relaxing way to explore nearby *cayos* like **Icacos**, **Diablo**, **Palominos**, and **Palominitos.** From any of these spots, you'll have access to turquoise waters and reefs that teem with life. With food and drink part of the package, this is a wonderful day away from the metropolitan delights of San Juan, and in the winter, you can even go whale-watching.

From San Juan, Culebra, and Vieques, there are wonderful boating, kayaking, and luxury yacht excursions that transport you to places that will take your breath away: the glowing lagoons of bioluminescent bays, uninhabited tropical islets, or simply out in open water. You can even visit nearby St. Thomas and see how another Caribbean island compares to Puerto Rico.

Over and Under Ground

Typically, in the Caribbean most of the fun is centered on the water; in Puerto Rico, when you leave the beach, you're just getting started. The diverse terrain includes almost every kind of ecological setting: rain forest, beach, limestone cliff, volcanic rock, cave, ocean, lagoon, and river. Add all of the constructed development to the natural bounty and you'll understand why it's extremely difficult to get bored here.

If city life is your focus, there are enough bars, lounges, and clubs in San Juan to keep you dancing until your feet fall off. Locals enjoy going out late into the night. Two good places to start searching for the best parties are the popular restaurants and hotels, which often book live bands and have special events on weekends. Other venues for live music and dancing are cultural and tourism-driven promotions that take place weekly. Once you leave the capital, and especially once you get to Vieques and Culebra, entertainment options are more limited.

Puerto Rico offers all of the basic recreational activities available in a major American city: bowling alleys, pool parlors, movie theaters, malls, and the like. Especially outside San Juan, horseback riding is a popular pastime, whether on green pastures or along the beach. Puerto Rico has some of the finest golf courses, attached to the finest hotels and boasting the finest views, in the Caribbean. And hikers will love the trails through El Yunque rain forest, which stays cool even on the hottest days; or the less-heralded Guánica Dry Forest, an international biosphere reserve with over 700 plants species, some of which don't exist anywhere else on Earth.

It's not just the plants and marine life that border on the fantastic; bird-watchers from around the globe flock to Puerto Rico (forgive the pun) to catch a glimpse of one of over 250 species, many of them endangered, "speciality," or endemic to Puerto Rico. In addition to El Yunque, national wildlife refuges in Cabo Rojo, Guánica, Culebra, and Vieques are sanctuaries for bird and birder alike.

The golf course at Wyndham El Conquistador

Nine Holes by the Sea

With up to 200 inches of annual rainfall each year, El Yunque rain forest is the wettest land in Puerto Rico. That kind of moisture is great for tropical forests, and superb for golf courses. Nearby are some of the best:

Bahía Beach Golf Course
787-256-5600
www.bahiabeachpuertorico.com

The 18-hole course closest to San Juan, this one is right on the beach. Accessible to the public with advance tee times. Open daily 7 AM–8 PM.

Coco Beach Golf & Country Club
787-888-7002
www.cocobeachgolf.com

A full-scale club, including 36 holes, a putting green, and a driving range. Open daily 6:30 AM–7 PM.

Westin Río Mar Beach Golf Resort & Spa
787-888-6000
www.westinriomar.com

The resort has two courses, both open to nonhotel guests. The River course was designed by Greg Norman. Open daily 6:30 AM–6:30 PM.

And then there's all that other stuff you may not have expected to find here: For fans of "extreme" sports, there's rock climbing, rappelling, free jumping—you know, activities many of us always wanted to try but never did. Not all of the action takes place above-ground: The Río Camuy cave system, on the western part of the island, is one of the largest in the world, and it's the only one with an underground river running through it. You can do it the easy way (take a trolley down into the bowels of a massive sinkhole), or the exhila-rating way (rappel through the belly of the caves), or the slightly insane way (spelunking in areas not open to the public).

Over and Under: Gambling

Gambling is legal where regulated and authorized by the local government, and is the exclusive domain of hotels. It's a popular draw for tourists, but it is not the only betting done on the island. If cards are your thing, the most popular game in Puerto Rico is black-jack. Establishments offering roulette, Caribbean stud poker, baccarat, craps, Let It Ride, and slot machines are also ready to take your money and, on occasion, give you some.

The Spanish have bullfighting; the Puerto Ricans opted for cockfighting, which has been legal since 1933. It's widely practiced, especially in the island's interior towns. The sport has thrown into relief some underlying differences between American and Latin cul-tures. The U.S. Congress in 2002 passed legislation to curb what it considers cruelty to animals (and many Puerto Ricans are in favor of the legislation). However, the Spanish have long held bullfighting as a sacred tradition, and cockfighting is pervasive throughout South America.

Cockfighting is one of the most popular spectator sports and betting venues in Puerto Rico. Held in *gallísticos* (circular pits with a matted stage), matches draw thousands and are often televised. Bantams are bred specifically for the sport, and special spurs made of metal or bone are fitted over the birds' natural spurs. While these matches are bloody affairs, they are not always fatal. If you are so inclined, you don't have to venture far to see cockfighting: **Club Gallístico de Puerto Rico** in Isla Verde, near some of the biggest hotels, holds fights every Saturday.

For a more benign animal sport (although some people argue that it is almost as inhu-mane as bullfighting and cockfighting), you can go to the racetrack and bet on the horses. Horse racing (and horseback riding as well) has a faithful following and a long tradition on the island. **El Comandante**, a racetrack in Canóvanas, near San Juan, hosts races on Monday, Wednesday, and weekends. It's also home to the annual Clasico del Caribe, a big racing event that draws jockeys and horses from many countries. If you can't make it to the track, you can place your bets at one of the many *agencias hipicas* (betting agencies) throughout Puerto Rico.

SO WHAT'S WRONG WITH THIS PLACE?

I know what you're thinking: There must be *something* wrong with this island. I've painted a rosy picture, albeit one that I feel is accurate. Still, Puerto Rico does have negative aspects: drugs, unemployment, corruption, traffic, the homeless, and crime head the list. Of these, crime (specifically nonviolent crime) impacts tourists most.

The drug trade drives crime in Puerto Rico. Drug use is rampant, and it's one of the biggest problems facing the island. Drugs are widely available because Puerto Rico is a major pit stop between South America and the United States. Its proximity to Colombia and other major drug producers opens Puerto Rico's borders to hoards of small, private charter planes. In addition, with its heavy traffic at the ports, the island is vulnerable to ships carrying their precious illegal cargo north. Plenty finds its way to the local streets. The FBI and Drug Enforcement Administration (DEA) have offices on the island, but their presence isn't nearly enough to stem the tide.

What does this mean for the tourist? In truth, not as much as you'd think. Violent crimes involving tourists are rare, even if petty theft is not. To be a victim of violent crime, you have to be in the wrong place at the wrong time and seek out the wrong places, such as clubs known to attract, say, a rougher *raggaetón* rap crowd; shantytowns like La Perla on the northern edge of Old San Juan; and low-income neighborhoods. Tourist areas are well monitored by the police and are usually safe. If you are the victim of a crime, you can call 911 in an emergency.

Puerto Rico's sagging economy has many causes and consequences. The *Puerto Rico Herald* described it in 2005 as suffering from "stagflation"—economic malaise due to zero growth, high inflation, reduced salaries, and raging unemployment—the factors that also undermined the U.S. economy in the 1970s. Also in 2005, an economic study determined that San Juan was the most expensive city in Latin America. The island is in a complex and uncertain economic position, and a clear path to greener pastures has yet to be mapped out.

How does Puerto Rico's struggling economy affect the tourist? The most immediate effect I saw, to my surprise, was a growing number of homeless people and beggars. Although harmless, vagrants on the street might scream at no one in particular, and this can be alarming. I've also never been approached so many times for money as I was in 2006. The economy and homelessness are, of course, linked to unemployment, which has been a historic problem on the island. Puerto Rico has consistently suffered staggering unemployment rates, sometimes reaching as high as three times the national average. At press time, they were languishing in the double digits.

You'll also feel the pinch in your wallet. Puerto Rico is an amazing vacation destination, but it's not cheap; and San Juan in high season is an expensive city to enjoy. Once you leave the capital, the prices go down, but tourist destinations always charge premium prices. The islands of Vieques and Culebra can be surprisingly expensive as well.

Major Happenings throughout the Year

In their respective chapters, I've covered weekly and annual events in each of the three main destinations featured in this book. What follows is a summary of the big bashes and events occurring either in a specific city or throughout the island.

Festival Casals de Puerto Rico (Casals Festival)
Past dates have varied, but the 2007 festival was held from February to March.
www.festcasalspr.gobierno.pr/index2.html

February 2006 marked the 50th anniversary of the Casals Festival, an annual tribute to cellist Maestro Pablo Casals. Although Casals was not Puerto Rican (he was born in Spain), he moved to the island in 1957, where he organized the Puerto Rico Symphony Orchestra as well as this musical event. The festival has drawn great masters including conductors

Leonard Bernstein and Zubin Mehta, and fellow cellist Yo-Yo Ma. Held in the Centro de Bellas Artes Luis A. Ferré (Luis A. Ferré Performing Arts Center) in Santurce, the event consists of a series of concerts stretched out over several weeks.

Carnival de Ponce (Ponce Carneval)
Week preceding Ash Wednesday (February)

Puerto Rico's answer to Mardi Gras is an explosion of color, parties, and masks. And, true to the local custom of marking religious occasions by having a good time, it is strategically held just before Lent. The Ponce Carnival, which began in the 18th century, has a rich history. The true stars of the show are the *vejigantes* (referring both to the papier-mâché masks as well as the people wearing them), which bring Puerto Rico's costumed folk legends to life. The masks range from the typical to the spectacular.

Puerto Rico Online

Literature on Puerto Rico is readily available and plentiful; for the most up-to-date information, however, surf the Web. Of the many sites covering the island, the best is **www.goto puertorico.com,** the official site of the Puerto Rico Tourism Company. You can research just about everything you'll need for your trip and download regional travel planners that are very handy. Another good resource is **www.meet puertorico.com,** the official site of the Puerto Rico Convention Bureau. Other useful Web sites include

www.puertoricoisfun.com

www.solboricua.com

www.puertoricowow.com

www.whattodoinpr.com

http://welcometopuertorico.org

www.experience-puertorico.com

The festival has a deeply symbolic meaning: The *vejigantes* represent benevolent spirits, who, through a good deal of *bomba y plena* and general revelry, banish evil demons. So if you get whacked about the head with a *vejiga* (an air-filled cow bladder), which doesn't hurt, it's most likely because you're under suspicion of harboring a mean spirit. The *vejigantes* run around smacking people at their whim; however, your chances of getting whacked rise exponentially if you are accompanied by an attractive young woman wearing revealing clothing. There, now you've been warned.

The festival culminates on the Tuesday before Ash Wednesday with the Entierro de la Sardina (Burial of the Sardine), a custom imported from Spain. Featuring a mock funeral procession (it's not a fish in the casket, it's actually a dummy) led by drag queens and fake mourners, this ceremony honors the approaching month-long prohibition against eating meat. The hapless dummy is set on fire as devastated mourners wail hysterically, enacting a metaphorical burning away of the sins of the flesh. The festival is an absolute blast and an example of Puerto Rico at its nutty, festive best. It's a free event, but a tough ticket nonetheless. Ponce is packed for this annual tradition, and it's wildly popular with the locals.

Puerto Rico Tourism Fair
March
787-287-0140

Puerto Rico's towns and cities gather to display their tourist attractions and let you know why you should include them in your travels. A fun, varied event that draws crowds of over 100,000 each year. Held in Ponce and San Juan.

Christmas display at Plaza Colón in Old San Juan

Danza Week
May
787-841-8044

Danza doesn't mean "dance," but a specific style of music and dance that is close to the heart of many Puerto Ricans. For one week in May, this formal musical expression, which is similar to the waltz, takes center stage in Puerto Rico. The event, sponsored by the Institute of Puerto Rican Culture, includes demonstrations in period dress, concerts, and a parade. The weeklong festivities take place in San Juan and Ponce, with a final concert performed by the San Juan band.

Puerto Rico Heineken Jazz Fest
June
787-294-0001 (for tickets)
www.prheinekenjazz.com

Held annually in the open-air Tito Puente Amphitheater in the Hato Rey district of San Juan, the Heineken Jazz Festival is among the premier events in jazz worldwide, attracting renowned artists in addition to local legends. Honoring Latin flavor in jazz music, it's a four-day musical party that includes several headliners as well as jazz workshops for musicians. You can buy CDs of each year's performances; the proceeds fund academic scholarships.

Puerto Rico Salsa Congress
July
787-470-8888
www.puertoricosalsacongress.com

A Puerto Rican Christmas

Puerto Ricans go all out for Christmas: The season is one long string of parties, concerts, religious ceremonies, family reunions, and general revelry. The parranda (a group of carolers) sometimes gather as early as November to spark their Christmas spirit, and continue belting out songs until mid-January. To give you an idea of why Christmas is a great time to be on the island, below is a chronology of events. (Not every family practices everything, of course, but these are the most popular traditions of the season . . . and Puerto Ricans don't mess around when it comes to Christmas.)

Nine Days to Noche Buena (Christmas Eve)
For the nine days preceding Christmas Eve, the Catholic Church conducts misas de aguinaldo, Masses held at dawn and highlighted by the singing and music of aguinaldos (traditional Christmas songs). On the night of the December 24th, called Noche Buena, families and friends get together for the Christmas feast. There's no turkey or honeyed ham here, this is Christmas, Puerto Rico–style. Traditional dishes like lechón (roast pork) with arroz con gandules (rice 'n' beans) are the norm. Instead of a Yule Log, you'll probably eat tembleque (a dessert made with coconut, cornstarch, vanilla, and cinnamon). Bypassing traditional eggnog, a Puerto Rican family will serve their version of the drink, called coquito (coconut nog). After dinner, it's customary to attend midnight Mass, called Misa de Gallo (Rooster's Mass), which can feature live reenactments of the Nativity scene.

La Fiesta de Los Santos Inocentes (Festival of the Innocent Saints)
    December 28 marks La Fiesta de Los Santos Inocentes. This occasion remembers the day Herod, fearing the arrival of Jesus, sent his soldiers to slay the firstborn from every family in and around Bethlehem. Rather than a somber, melancholy affair, the festival is usually characterized by children dressing up as soldiers and playing tricks on each other. This isn't as popular now as it once was, but the town of Hatillo, for one, still commemorates it.

Old Year, New Year
Año Viejo (Old Year) is the Spanish term for New Year's Eve. Like most of the world, this is when Puerto Rico parties hardest. There's no ball-drop, but there is a great deal of noise: fireworks (technically illegal, but who's bothering?), cheers, cars blaring horns, and the sounds of parties reverberate throughout the island. On the stroke of midnight, a custom that continues in Spain today is also followed here: The locals scarf down 12 grapes for luck. Other superstitions include scattering sugar outside your house to attract good luck, and throwing a bucket of water out the window to rid yourself of all the bad things that happened in the old year and wipe the slate clean for the new one.

Three Kings and a Father
One of the unexpected benefits of being under American and Spanish rule is the development of two gift-giving days during Christmas. Puerto Ricans ackowledge Santa Claus by exchanging presents on December 25, but they also hand them out on January 6, **El Día de los Tres Reyes Magos** (Three Kings Day). The "milk and cookies for Santa" tradition in the United States has a cute cousin here: It's customary for children to put grass in a box at the foot of their beds, food for the camels of the three kings who have come to visit them. The undisputed king of Three Kings Day is the small, southern town of Juana Diaz, whose tres reyes travel all over the island before returning home in a triumphant procession.

Octavitas
By all accounts, the Octavitas tradition is dying out in Puerto Rico, but some still cling to this extended eight days of revelry and family visits. Octavitas begins after January 6, elongating the season until the middle of the month for a truly marathon holiday.

Any function advertised as "The most important salsa event on the planet" deserves some attention, and if you enjoy dancing and Latin music, you can't miss this one. In 2006, the Puerto Rico Salsa Congress marked its 10th year with its usual pageantry of exhibitions and nightly dances. It attracts some of the best salsa bands and performers on the . . . well, on the planet, including, in 2006, Eddie Torres, the Palladium Mambo Legends, and Tito & Tamara. Scores of people come from near and far to enjoy the visual spectacle, mingle and meet fellow "salsaficionados," and take lessons.

Barranquitas Artisans Fair
Mid-July
787-857-0530

Barranquitas, a town in the mountainous interior of Puerto Rico, hosts this annual event, the oldest crafts fair on the island. The expo attracts more than a hundred local artisans from all over Puerto Rico to Barranquitas. Collectors and lovers of Puerto Rican arts and crafts are immersed in exhibitions displaying the best the island has to offer. The festival is augmented by frequent concerts.

San Juan International Billfish Tournament
August–September
787-722-6624
www.sanjuaninternational.com

One of the world's longest-running and most honored game-fishing events, the San Juan International draws fishermen from around the globe. The tag-and-release competition lasts a week and is known for abundant blue marlin fishing during the day (there's a "Blue Marlin Alley" off the coast of San Juan) and parties at night. Held at the Club Náutico in San Juan, in Miramar.

Fiesta de la Música Puertorriqueña
November–December
787-724-1844

Organized by the Institute of Puerto Rican Culture, this annual event celebrates Puerto Rican music and culture at various venues throughout the island. The festival occurs during the weekends and features traditionally garbed dancers and a range of music, from *bomba y plena* to the philharmonic orchestra.

Bacardi Artisans' Fair
First and second Sunday in December
787-788-1500

Held at the Bacardi rum distillery in Cataño, this is the largest artisans' fair in the Caribbean. Over the years, it has grown to include live folklore and pop music (including performances by stars such as Celia Cruz and Marc Anthony), amusement rides for kids, and a popular troubadour competition.

4

OLD SAN JUAN

Revel in the Past

INTRODUCTION TO SAN JUAN AND THE SURROUNDING AREA

San Juan, the largest city in the Caribbean, comprises many diverse neighborhoods, clustered together into three main areas: the Old City, the beach and resort strip, and the surrounding communities.

The historic and cultural heart of the city is **Old San Juan**. First-time visitors tend to spend the great majority of their time within the walls of the old city, which boasts the principal landmarks of the island. Next to Old San Juan is **Puerta de Tierra**, a tiny strip of land that joins the peninsula to the rest of the island. Historically a slum, this area is now home to the island's military, naval, coast guard, and government buildings.

Puerta de Tierra leads into **Condado**, which is known for its beaches, architecture, hotels, casinos, restaurants, and fashion. It has lost some of its former glamour, but massive investment in this district in recent years may restore its popularity. Its neighbor, **Ocean Park**, sports one of the best and most active beaches on the island. However, this area has avoided the large-scale hotel and resort development that has cropped up in Condado and in **Isla Verde**, which lies directly to the east. On the opposite coast from Condado is **Miramar**, an upscale residential neighborhood. Just south of the beaches is **Santurce**, known for its arts and culture as well as local flavor.

Three other neighborhoods round out the capital city of San Juan. **Hato Rey** is the prime business sector, as well as home to the largest shopping center in the Caribbean. **Río Piedras** boasts two major points of interest: the University of Puerto Rico and the botanical gardens. **Puerto Nuevo** is a middle-class residential community.

Beyond these distinct neighborhoods, the surrounding communities continue the sprawling metropolis. **Bayamón, Carolina, Cataño, Guaynabo,** and **Trujillo Alto** incorporate suburban aspects of life in the Caribbean's busiest capital.

Old San Juan, La Ciudad Amurallada (The Walled City), encapsulates Puerto Rico's history, identity, and culture better than any other part of the island. For good reason, this is where the cruise ships dock, where tourists spend most of their time if they want to simply soak in the atmosphere and culture of Puerto Rico, and where the locals go for a fun night out. Sloping cobblestone streets, myriad architectural styles, and all the colors of the Caribbean make it a beautiful city that transports visitors to a bygone era, but Old San Juan (Viejo San Juan in Spanish) is also the nexus of the island's shopping, dining, and entertainment.

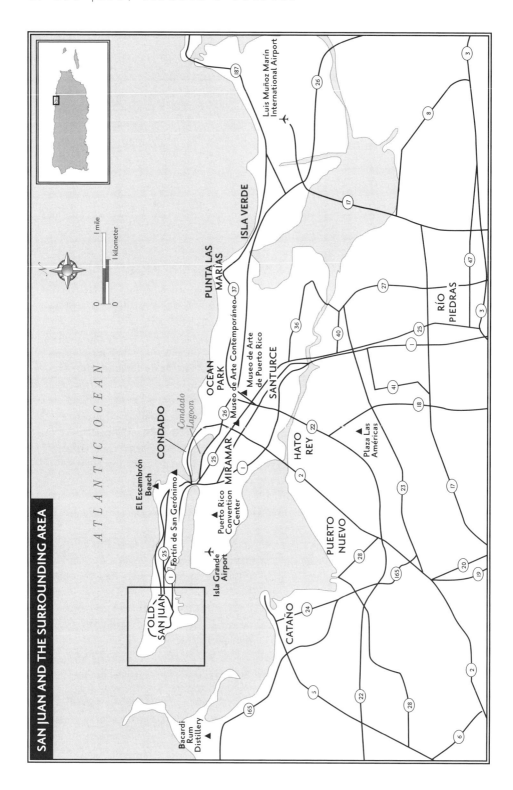

SAN JUAN AND THE SURROUNDING AREA

OLD SAN JUAN

ATLANTIC OCEAN

Bacardi Rum Distillery

Isla Grande Airport

Puerto Rico Convention Center

El Escambrón Beach

Fortín de San Gerónimo

CONDADO

Condado Lagoon

MIRAMAR

OCEAN PARK

PUNTA LAS MARÍAS

ISLA VERDE

Museo de Arte Contemporáneo

Museo de Arte de Puerto Rico

SANTURCE

HATO REY

Plaza Las Américas

RÍO PIEDRAS

PUERTO NUEVO

CATAÑO

Luis Muñoz Marín International Airport

1 mile
1 kilometer
0
0

Viejo San Juan comprises seven square blocks, and in two days you can leisurely cover most of it. Buses run the length and breadth of the city, a free trolley is available for tourists, and you can find taxis outside the larger hotels and in the main plazas—but they all diminish the fun of exploring the place on foot.

A walk in Old San Juan is a journey to a quixotic land where the treasures of the past meet the luxuries of the present. Most of the buildings are quaint-looking structures huddled along narrow roads and painted in tropical hues that sometimes clash horribly with the cars careening down the street. The rainbow of colors provides a delightful reminder that you're in the Caribbean, while the Colonial architecture, cobblestone streets, and wrought-iron balconies are reminiscent of an ancient European settlement. Plazas adorned with fountains and sculptures, cafés and shops, will tempt you all day as you stroll, and almost every corner reveals at least one interesting place to visit.

While the old city caters mainly to tourists, it's also home to thousands of Puerto Ricans. As a result, there's a pleasant blend of quiet residential life, local hangouts, must-see attractions, and thriving social venues in Old San Juan. The people are extremely friendly and tend to have a genuine curiosity for tourists. You're not likely to hear English spoken among Sanjuaneros (as the residents of San Juan are sometimes called), and this adds to the feeling that you're far away from home. It's an interesting experience to wander through Old San Juan, admiring structures that were built before Jamestown was settled, hearing Latin music pumping out of cars, and reading Spanish road signs, but then to pull out those familiar dollar bills to pay for a Medalla—the local beer—or a *piragua* (passion fruit) from a vendor with a portable cart. But this is the essence of the magic of Old San Juan: the intoxicating feeling of being in several places, and several epochs, at once.

San Juan Gate

The old city is unlike anything in the United States or the Caribbean, and visitors have access to a full menu of activities within its stout walls. At the foot of the city lie massive docks, which are bare and uninteresting unless you're onboard a cruise ship and have to embark or disembark. So, you might want to start your trip at **La Casita** (787-724-4788), the Puerto Rico Tourism Company's information center. Located in the Plaza de la Dársena, immediately off Pier 1, the information center provides literature and maps of Puerto Rico, well marked with all of the major points of interest, dotted-line itineraries, and trolley stops in case you get tired.

You can also cross the plaza and head west to beautiful Paseo La Princesa, a wide, tree-lined promenade flanked on one side by the *muralla* (city wall). Here you'll find the lovely bronze Raíces

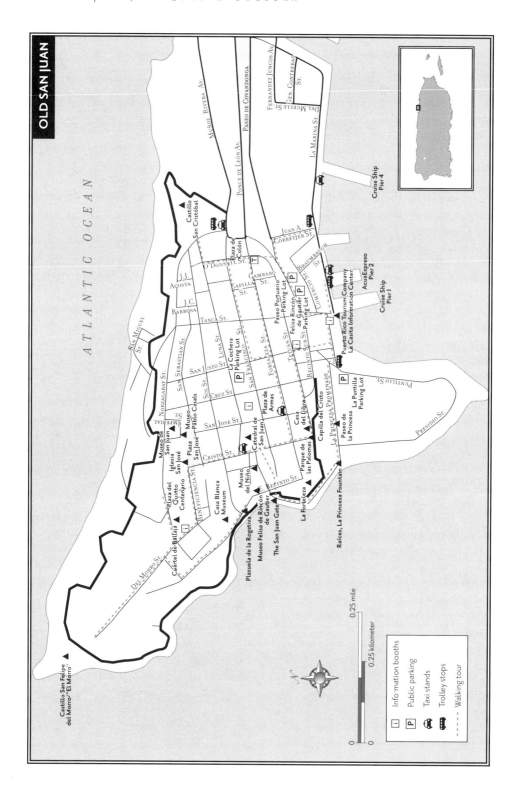

OLD SAN JUAN

ATLANTIC OCEAN

Castillo San Felipe
del Morro/"El Morro"

Castillo
San Cristóbal

Plaza de
Colón

JUAN A
CORRETJER ST.

FERNANDEZ JUNCOS AV.

GEN CONTRERAS
ST.

DEL MUELLE ST.

LA MARINA ST.

PONCE DE LEÓN AV.

MUÑOZ RIVERA AV.

PASEO DE COVADONGA

Cruise Ship
Pier 4

AcuaExpreso
Pier 2

Cruise Ship
Pier 1

Puerto Rico Tourism Company
La Casita Information Center

O'DONNELL ST.

J.J.
ACOSTA

J.C.
BARBOSA

Capilla
St.

GAMBARO
ST.

Paseo Portuario
Parking Lot

Felisa Rincón
de Gautier St. Parking Lot

COMERCIO ST.

BRAUMBAUGH

SAN MIGUEL
ST.

TANCA ST.

SAN JUSTO ST.

SAN SEBASTIAN ST.

NORZAGARAY ST.

La Luna St.

La Cochera
Parking Lot

SAN FRANCISCO ST.

FORTALEZA ST.

Plaza de
Armas

RECINTO SUR ST.

TETUÁN ST.

PUNTILLO ST.

PRESIDIO ST.

Casa
del Libro

La Puntilla
Parking Lot

Sol ST.

CRUZ ST.

SAN JOSE ST.

IMPERIAL
ST.

Museo de
San Juan

Plaza
San José

Iglesia
San José

Museo
Pablo Casals

Catedral de
San Juan

Plaza del
Quinto
Centenario

BENEFICENCIA ST.

CRISTO ST.

Casa Blanca
Museum

Museo
del Niño

Capilla del Cristo

Paseo de
las Palomas

LA PRINCESA PROMENADE

Paseo de
la Princesa

Plazuela de la Rogativa

Museo Felisa de Rimcón
de Gautier

The San Juan Gate

La Fortaleza

RECINTO ST.

Raíces, La Princesa Fountain

Cuartel de Ballajá

DEL MORRO ST.

0.25 mile

0.25 kilometer

ℹ️ Information booths

🅿 Public parking

🚕 Taxi stands

🚋 Trolley stops

----- Walking tour

Street in Old San Juan

(Roots) Fountain, which celebrates the cultural and ethnic roots of Puerto Rico, and the Antigua Cárcel de La Princesa ("La Princesa Jail"), a former prison of great notoriety that now houses the Puerto Rico Tourism Company's headquarters. From the docks and the tourism office, all of Old San Juan lies open to you.

FOUR HUNDRED YEARS IN THE MAKING

It's with good reason that the entire seven-block area of Old San Juan has been declared a National Historic Site. The city is home to Puerto Rico's oldest and most treasured historical monuments, and the first ones on your list should be the two forts. Perched atop a hill on the northwest corner of the walls overlooking the ocean is the magnificent El Morro, the fortress that made Puerto Rico such a formidable military stronghold. Less than a mile away lies San Cristóbal, a second fort of even grander scale. But these magnificent structures are merely the grandest representations of a fascinating heritage that spans over 400 years.

Old San Juan is full of a diverse array of museums and galleries that house collections of arts, crafts, archaeological findings, and records of the people who make up Puerto Rico. While the largest and most impressive museums lie outside the walled city, I've found that Old San Juan offers a wonderful collection of what I call "boutique museums": small, intimate tributes to art, literature, individuals, and eras. Check out a few if you have the time. They have a charm all to themselves.

Many of the more beautiful houses in the city were the residences of notable people in the island's history, including Ponce de León, whose family lived in La Casa Blanca (The White House) for over 250 years. Typical of a Spanish settlement and a deeply Catholic city, Old San Juan boasts many churches. The most prominent of these are the Catedral de San Juan and the Iglesia de San José, two of the oldest churches in the Western Hemisphere. In

The Mythology of Old San Juan

Like most historic cities, Old San Juan conceals its own legends. Two of the more famous ones are a sculpture, *La Rogativa* (The Procession), and *Capilla del Cristo* (Chapel of Christ). *La Rogativa* commemorates a religious procession in 1797 that was said to turn away a British attack, when Sir Ralph Abercromby mistook the faithful for Spanish reinforcements. (All indications are that it was the stout defenses at Forts San Gerónimo and San Antonio, rather than the procession, that repelled the British. Still, the procession did take place, giving birth to a stirring memorial and a proud tale.)

The tiny chapel at the end of Cristo Street honors the miracle of a young man who, along with his horse, fell over the edge of the cliff on which the chapel was later built. As they plunged to their deaths, the man prayed to a Catholic saint to save him. The saint obliged, but the horse died. (In reality, both died, and the chapel was put there to prevent further accidents.)

La Rogativa   *Capilla del Cristo*

addition, the oldest executive mansion and one of the oldest theaters in the New World are found within the walls of the city.

In the plazas and quiet corners of Viejo San Juan, you'll often find lovely tributes to the city's past. Sculptures, fountains, and monuments commemorate important events, depict Puerto Rican myths, and celebrate key historical figures. Some of the more beautiful and evocative works include the *Raíces Fountain*, *La Rogativa* sculpture, and the unique *Tótem Telúrico*, a ceramic-and-granite totem representing the earthen origins of the people of the Americas. The monument was erected in 1992 to mark the 500th anniversary of Columbus's discovery of the New World.

Raíces, La Princesa Fountain

AT PLAY IN THE OLD CITY

When the sun sets, Old San Juan gets energized. After dark, anyone who loves to eat, drink, and dance will find new reasons to cherish the city. Puerto Rico is famous for its liquor. The Bacardi rum company is 15 minutes from the city and offers tours of its distillery. Rum-based cocktails are the island's specialty, and the most illustrious of them all, the piña colada, is a proud Puerto Rican creation. On Fortaleza Street is a well-known restaurant called La Barrachina, which claims to be the birthplace of the famed drink. (This is actually a matter of some debate, as many believe the Caribe Hilton was the first to make the cocktail; a representative of Don Q Rums informed me that, while La Barrachina indeed created the piña colada, the drink only became famous through the Hilton.) Numerous establishments vie for the title "Best Piña Colada," and it may be prudent to visit several of these contenders before making a decision.

Hips Don't Lie

To say that Puerto Ricans like to dance is like claiming the Earth enjoys rotating on its axis; it's in their blood. In San Juan, a number of venues feature live bands that play salsa and merengue while locals and tourists alike dance the night away. Don't feel shy or offended if a stranger whisks you onto the dance floor at any given moment.

For the younger crowd, the hypnotic *raggaetón* beat has swept beyond Puerto Rico and the Caribbean, reaching mainstream radio stations all over the globe. The music comes with its own dance form, which Puerto Ricans have christened *perreo*. Let's just say it's a youthful, primal, and seductive form of musical expression.

Bars and lounges are easily found in Old San Juan, some resembling your favorite college haunt and others dressed up in cool, sophisticated elegance. A new and popular trend these days is the restaurant-bar-lounge. Several of Old San Juan's better restaurants change themes after the kitchen closes (some keep the kitchen open), turn up the music, and keep the night going. You'll find people lining up outside a restaurant after midnight, waiting to get past the bouncers and into the late-night ambience. Dragonfly, Fratelli, and Blend, all on Fortaleza Street, are just a few solid choices for a full night out.

Dancing and music are big in Puerto Rico, and both reflect Puerto Rico's common cocktail of cultures and identities. *Bomba* and *plena* are distinctly Puerto Rican blends of percussion, music, singing, and dance. Salsa is pervasive throughout the island, but so is *raggaetón*, a highly charged fusion of rap, hip-hop, and Latin rhythms.

Ostra Costa

The nightlife in Old San Juan is just as varied. Whether you prefer twirling to the sound of a live band in a smoky room, or a trendy club blasting the latest hits, the city will provide. Two other factors help to make Old San Juan a hopping, popping scene—for the most part, a night of dancing won't cost

Aguaviva

Panorama Bar and Latin Grill at Hotel Milano

you an arm and a leg and, because clubs don't have a mandatory closing hour, they often stay open until six or seven in the morning.

Paradise on a Plate

Dining in Old San Juan encompasses the traditional and the avant-garde. You can eat a simple and hearty meal in a canteen-style eatery or sample nouveau Puerto Rican dishes at one of the fancier restaurants on Fortaleza Street. Visitors should at least try the local food, which is delicious, infused with tropical ingredients and flavors and, unlike other Caribbean cuisine, not at all spicy. Not to be missed is the dizzying variety of finger foods— such as *frituras* (fried snacks) and *pastellitos* (turnovers)—as well as two mainstays of local cooking, *arroz con pollo* (rice and chicken) cooked with coconut milk, and *mofongo*, the unofficial national dish of Puerto Rico. *Mofongo*, available everywhere, is a mound of fried, mashed green plantain stuffed with meat, vegetables, or seafood. It's very tasty, but after a few days of sampling different varieties, it's possible that you'll never want to see *mofongo* again. If you reach this breaking point, don't worry, Old San Juan also features several choices to tempt a global palate, including Japanese, Thai, Indian, and several international fusion establishments.

By and large, restaurants in Puerto Rico take great care in their decor and setting. The personality and atmosphere ranges from Colonial and rustic to canteen-style to hip and trendy. Several cafés offer outdoor seating where you can soak in the gorgeous weather while you eat. More than a few mimic the brightly colored walls of the city and decorate with beautiful examples of native arts and crafts. And some, like the Panorama Bar & Latin

Fortaleza Street

Grill atop the Hotel Milano, boast terrific views. Dining out tends to be a noisy, lively affair, and remains a favorite pastime for locals and tourists alike. Indulge yourself and enjoy it.

BUYER BE AWARE: A SMORGASBORD OF SHOPPING

Shopaholics will be hard-pressed to maintain any amount of discipline in the old city, but before I work you up into a lather, there is some bad news: Puerto Rico's days as a "tax-free" haven are over. As of November 15, 2006, a 7 percent sales tax was imposed citywide. Of course, customers have been paying an excise tax (which was factored into the price and thus invisible to the consumer) for ages, so the difference is minimal. But the psychological and marketing edge that came with the "tax-free" tag is now gone, and it will be interesting to gauge its effect on revenue from tourism in the near future.

Now for the good news. Products that are made in Puerto Rico are generally of good quality, and several major brand names have factory outlets nestled among the historic sites in Old San Juan. In fact, the heart of the shopping district is within steps of the San Juan Gate, the last remainder of the five massive doors that once provided entry to the walled city. On Cristo and Fortaleza streets, you'll find everything from desiccated butterflies to Harry Winston jewelry. San Francisco Street is another main thoroughfare for tourists, with shops lining the road.

Once again, the juxtaposition of North and South America can be found in a shopping expedition. You might find yourself hopping from the Ralph Lauren Polo factory store on Cristo Street to Olé, a local shop where you can pick up Puerto Rican handmade artifacts, Panama hats, and other memorabilia. After perusing the crafts and souvenirs on Fortaleza Street, you can check out the art galleries and fashionable clothing stores on San José and Cristo streets, or explore Tanca and Tetuan streets for kitschy trinkets. The arts and crafts are especially hard to resist, and Old San Juan is peppered with shops selling masks, ceramic wall hangings of the city's brightly colored buildings, hand-carved religious icons, and other unique souvenirs.

Those of you who come to Puerto Rico for its natural beauty may not tarry long in Old San Juan. Still, with all that it offers to so many people, the old city is in many ways the most enchanting and entertaining part of any visit to Puerto Rico. If you truly want to get a feel for what this island is all about; if you want to leave the present for a few hours; or if you simply feel like strolling through an immaculate, well-groomed, and picturesque corner of San Juan, then this is the place for you.

LODGING

Bóveda Rentals
787-725-0263
www.boveda.info
209 Cristo Street, San Juan 00901

Many people know of Bóveda as a souvenir shop, but few know about the short-term rental apartments available in the same building as the store. Located on Cristo Street, it's a great place to be in the old city. There are two apartments. The Garden Suite, designed for budget-minded couples, is actually a suite within an apartment (the rest of the apartment stays empty, but employees might pass through), furnished with a desk, kitchen, and private bathroom. The Gallery Suite is a larger, better-appointed space over-looking the street. The rooms don't accommodate children under age 10. $–$$.

La Caleta Apartment Rentals
787-725-5347
reservations@thecaleta.com
11 Caleta de Las Monjas, Old San Juan 00901
Realtor office address: 151 Calle Clara, Old San Juan 00901

If you want to live like a local, your best bet might be to take up residence at 11 Caleta de Las Monjas. La Caleta has over 30 properties for rent, with a three-night minimum stay required (but they can be flexible). The choice ranges from studios at a bargain price (some under $50 a night in low season) to three-bedroom apartments. Equipped with kitchenettes or full kitchens—depending on the property—and laundry machines, this is a terrific budget alternative for people planning an extended stay in Puerto Rico. Granted, you won't enjoy the luxuries of a major hotel, there are no elevators, and you'll need to carry your own luggage, but these are clean, well-kept, furnished apartments, some with balconies facing scenic views of Old San Juan. $–$$.

Chateau Cervantes
787-724-7722
www.cervantespr.com
329 Recinto Sur Street, Old San Juan 00901

Blink and you might pass it by, but that would be a shame. The unobtrusive facade of Chateau Cervantes hides one of Old San

Junior Suite living area at Chateau Cervantes

Juan's newest and most polished gems. Even after you open the double-doors, you'll wonder if you came to the right place; the lobby is practically nonexistent, and the downstairs level is almost completely occupied by the hotel's restaurant. But this is part of the charm of Chateau Cervantes, which takes the boutique hotel concept into an elite class of its own. The hotel is small, with a mere 12 suites that ooze luxury and style. But it's the meticulous pampering of their guests that elevates Chateau Cervantes to something special. Consider the limousine pickup from the airport and personalized in-room butler service. The lushly appointed suites are designed by Nono Maldonado, a local designer of considerable fame. Rooms have high ceilings, marble-tiled bathrooms, soft lighting, and a blend of classic and modern furniture. The two-room master suites have a kitchenette and bar. The Presidential Suite is just fabulous, occupying an entire floor and featuring a private garden terrace, whirlpool, and steam room. All rooms have flat-screen TVs and wireless Internet access. Facing a busy street, this is nevertheless an oasis in Old San Juan. Its downstairs restaurant, Panza, is quickly gaining a reputation as one of the city's best. Chateau Cervantes is one of the most expensive destinations in town, but there's also nothing quite like it in all of Puerto Rico. $$$$.

The Gallery Inn
787-722-1808
www.thegalleryinn.com
204–206 Norzagaray Street, Old San Juan 00901

Imagine that an old friend of yours, who is an artist of some renown, has invited you to her home for a few days. This best describes the feeling of staying at the Gallery Inn, a warm, intimate hotel on the top of the hill of Old San Juan. The 300-year-old house is stuffed with sculpted busts, statues, paint-ings, and other artwork by owner Jan D'Esopo, and one room chronicles the colorful lives of Jan and her husband, Manuco. Each room at the inn is different, and the entire house is open to guests. It's a fantastic place to explore. Cockatoos and macaws, led by Social Director Campeche (a salmon-crested Moluccan cockatoo), are part of the house's personality. As you stroll through the music room, the studio, or up to the deck to enjoy spectacular views of the ocean, you'll truly feel like you're in someone's home rather than a hotel. The staff is friendly and engaging; at a wine and cheese reception, guests and hosts get to know each other. If you're lucky, you may even be in residence during an impromptu concert in the romantic, candlelit music room, where well-known classical musicians sometimes drop by to entertain and enchant. This is an altogether different place to stay, and it's not for everyone. There are no fancy amenities at the Gallery Inn, no elevators, sliding key cards, or room service. There's an absolute absence of formality, but also an absolute emphasis on making you feel like an old friend. $$–$$$$.

Hotel El Convento
787-723-9020
www.elconvento.com
100 Cristo Street, Old San Juan 00901

Located across the street from the famed San Juan Cathedral is another historic landmark, one that rents rooms. El Convento is a majestic building, a 16th-century convent converted into a luxury hotel that breathes the spirit of Viejo San Juan. Its 58 rooms and suites surround an open-air, leafy courtyard that houses a bar, a restaurant, and dining tables. There's an outdoor pool and a Jacuzzi, an excellent restaurant, and an elegant banquet hall. Although the nuns who lived here 400 years ago most likely didn't enjoy rich decor and excellent service, guests should note that the rooms lack state-of-the-art amenities and are smaller than those in the average AAA four-diamond hotel. But these are minor drawbacks that lend an old-fashioned charm to a hotel that Condé Nast named one of the world's best places to stay. $$$$.

Hotel Milano
1-877-729-9050; 787-729-9050
www.hotelmilanopr.com
307 Fortaleza Street, Old San Juan 00901

You can't get any closer to the action than the Milano, which is situated right on Fortaleza Street. This is a cozy hotel with simply furnished, well-kept rooms, amiable staff, and the charm and personal attention of its owner, Juan San Emeterio. One of its main draws is the Panorama Bar & Latin Grill, an excellent rooftop restaurant that offers fine local food in addition to a beautiful view of the city and San Juan Bay. If you can, try to reserve a room with a view of downtown Old San Juan. $$.

Da House
787-366-5074
www.dahousehotelpr.com
312 San Francisco Street, Old San Juan 00901

"Where are you staying?"
"Me? I'm at Da House, man."
And that's where you'll be if you check into Da House, the newest hotel in Old San Juan. A project of the Nuyorican Café, Da House is meant to be everything the café is: bohemian, urban, and affordable, and inspired by art, culture, and music. The building has an artistic soul; it used to be a seminary where traveling artisans would take up residence when they came to Old San Juan. Today, each floor has a different artistic theme, and the 27 rooms are priced to accommodate those who create and appreciate art but haven't (yet) made mil-

lions in the business. Some rooms have a patio, and all guests can enjoy a rooftop terrace with fantastic views of the city. The finishing touches are still being put on Da House, including an Internet café serving pastries and snacks. $–$$.

Howard Johnson Plaza de Armas
787-722-9191
www.hojopr.com
202 San José Street, Old San Juan 00901

One of two Howard Johnson hotels in the greater metropolitan area, you can't beat this one for location. Smack in the center of the old city, right off the Plaza de Armas square, Howard Johnson is an economically friendly alternative with basic rooms, free continental breakfast, and high-speed Internet access. Some suites come with refrigerator, sofa bed, and—if you ask for it—a balcony overlooking the plaza. $–$$.

The Sheraton Old San Juan
1-866-653-7577; 787-721-5100
www.sheratonoldsanjuan.com
100 Brumbaugh Street, San Juan 00901

Step off a cruise ship or walk along the docks, and you can't miss the elegant, concave face of the Sheraton. The grand lobby, sweeping double staircase, and warm colors evoke the Colonial architecture of the old city; but in every other way, it's a modern hotel with top-class amenities. With 240 rooms, it's the largest hotel in the walled city. The accommodations are spacious and typical of Sheraton quality, and many have ocean views. For entertainment and relaxation, look above and below the sleeping quarters. In the lobby, the only casino in Old San Juan offers blackjack, poker, roulette, craps, and slot machines. A gorgeous rooftop pool gives guests wonderful views of San Juan Bay. The hotel also has two ballrooms and several meeting rooms. $$$.

S.J. Suites Hotel

787-725-1351
www.sjsuites.com
253 Fortaleza Street, Old San Juan 00901

It doesn't look like much on the outside (actually, there's nothing more than an elevator and a staircase on the street level—the lobby is one flight up), but S.J. Suites is an affordable all-suite hotel that puts you right on trendy Fortaleza Street, just steps from great restaurants, bars, and lounges. The rooms here are comfortable but basic, and come with a free continental breakfast. $$–$$$.

DINING

311

787-725-7959
www.311restaurantpr.com
311 Fortaleza Street, Old San Juan

Trois Cent Onze ("311" in French) doesn't mess around. With the closing of the celebrated La Chaumière, the mantle of "best French food in San Juan" may very well rest here. The food is purely French, with all the classics (a terrific bouillabaisse, filet mignon with cognac and green peppercorn sauce, duck foie gras) and minimal attention to the flavors of the Caribbean. As much as you'll enjoy the food, you'll equally love the elegant decor, with its Moorish tiles, high ceilings, and romantic dining room. For a special treat, book a Vintner's Dinner, in which the chef pairs food and wine. Open Monday through Friday noon–3 PM for lunch, and Monday through Saturday 6–11 PM for dinner. $$$.

Aguaviva

787-722-0665
www.oofrestaurants.com/aguaviva
364 Fortaleza Street, Old San Juan

Aguaviva

Aguaviva is ocean-blue cool, from the jellyfish ceiling lamps, to the delectable raw bar, to the watermelon sangria. This restaurant does creative things with seafood, and you'll appreciate them for it. Their ceviches are simply inspired, and a tasting menu lets you sample all six, which are completely different from each other (my favorites were the tuna and salmon cured in tequila, and the grouper with coconut and lime). Food Network groupies have to sample the Nuevo Paella, made with seared jumbo scallops. This dish went all the way to *Iron Chef America*, where it competed against Mario Batali's preparation. (Don't ask who won; it's better to just appreciate the talent.) During lunch hours, the menu includes a range of excellent sandwiches, including a surprisingly tasty calamari sandwich. It's one of the best places to eat in Puerto Rico. Open Monday through Wednesday 6–11 PM, Thursday through Saturday 6 PM–midnight, and Sunday 4–10 PM. $$–$$$.

Barrachina

787-721-5852
www.barrachina.com
104 Fortaleza Street, Old San Juan

The birthplace of the piña colada is the primary claim to fame at this sidewalk café (check out their Web site for a voucher for a free one), but not the only reason to go there. The restaurant is at the end of an arched alley and is beautifully decorated with native art. You can enjoy a number of tasty cocktails and sample from an extensive menu of Puerto Rican and Continental cuisine. The restaurant isn't cheap, but the food is good, and the staff is friendly. During high season, the restaurant sometimes hires a man with a megaphone to urge passersby to walk in, which is a little annoying. Open daily: Sunday through Tuesday, and Thursday, 10 AM–10 PM; Wednesday 10 AM–6 PM; Friday and Saturday 10 AM–11 PM. $$$.

Barú

787-977-7107
www.barupr.com
150 San Sebastián Street, Old San Juan

If you're the kind of diner who loves to try a little bit of everything, come to Barú. This stylish, longtime stalwart of the dining scene in Old San Juan offers a wide variety of tapas-style plates that are meant to be shared and explored. The restaurant does a great job of giving local ingredients Mediterranean and Asian accents, coming up with creations like shrimp skewers flamed in orange liqueur, resting on a mound of *yucafongo* (*mofongo* made with yucca) and shiitake risotto with goat cheese. Their crunchy yucca chips, served with a jerk mango dip and almond-encrusted goat cheese, are a nice way to kick off the evening. If you can, try to get a seat on the outdoor patio. Open Monday through Friday 6 PM–11:45 PM, weekends 6 PM–12:45 AM (the bar stays open until about 2 AM). $$.

Blend

787-977-7777
309 Fortaleza Street, Old San Juan

The name is appropriate; here, *blend* implies not just a mix of ingredients and flavors but also style, ambience, music, and venue. There are different sections to the restaurant including a bar in front; an intimate dining area, adjacent to a live DJ booth; and a lounge area in the back. Blend invites the customer to experience a full night out, from evening cocktails to dinner to club, in one location. On the whole, it's a neat idea; but my impression is that Blend is still figuring out how best to pull it all together (e.g., when to turn up the music to transition from restaurant to club). The menu is creative and always changing, but a little inconsistent. Some dishes are excellent, like the Halibut Three-Way (a cut filet prepared with three accompaniments), while others leave you waiting for the lounge scene to kick in. Blend is open daily, except Monday, at 5:30 PM and closes at midnight Tuesday through Wednesday, at 2 AM on Thursday, and around 3 AM on weekends. $$.

La Bombonera

787-722-0658
259 San Francisco Street, Old San Juan

One of the most popular breakfast joints on San Francisco Street is La Bombonera, an old-fashioned coffee shop where tourists rub elbows with locals at the long counter and order a sugarcoated *pan de Mallorca* to go with an excellent cup of coffee made in an antique Cuban coffeemaker that's no longer available outside Cuba. These toasted delicacies (called by some "Puerto Rico's danish") are available with cheese, ham and cheese, ham and egg, or simply with butter. They're better than most breakfast sandwiches, and cost just a few dollars. There's an extensive menu of Puerto Rican food here as well, but the majority of the clientele come for the

Mallorcas. It's an ideal spot for breakfast or lunch while you're in the old city. Open daily 7:30 AM–8 PM. $–$$.

The Brick House
787-559-5022
359 Tetuan Street, San Juan

The self-styled home of "Gringo-Rican" cuisine serves up comfort food, a surprisingly good *mofongo,* and some of the best chicken wings around. The place will remind you of your local bar, wherever you live. But the food is better than at most bars, and the Brick House has enough events and specials running to make it a hopping destination from early afternoon to late into the night. Their "Cheap and Easy" brunch menu has all giant portions and hearty food (great steak and eggs), and on "Super Sports Sunday" you can catch NASCAR, and football and basketball games. Open Monday through Friday 11 AM to closing (which might be closer to dawn than to dusk), Saturday and Sunday 11 AM–3 PM for brunch, and 4 PM to closing for dinner and after-hours partying. $–$$.

El Burén
787-977-5023
www.elburenpr.com
103 Cristo Street, Old San Juan

Just across from the Hotel El Convento, El Burén is an unpretentious place known as much for its creative gourmet pizzas (named after the streets of Old San Juan) as for its excellent *mojito* (they use brown sugar instead of syrup) and sophisticated entrées like a rum-glazed tuna carpaccio and a shrimp fettuccine with a Cointreau, cinnamon, and orange juice reduction. Or, you can try their signature salads; my favorite is the tropical spinach salad with mango, papaya, mozzarella cheese, and a passion fruit drizzle. Along with the good-quality, affable staff and outdoor patio, people love the reasonable prices.

Open Monday from 4 PM to midnight, and Tuesday through Sunday from noon to midnight. $$.

Divino Bocadito
787-977-0042
www.divinobocadito.com
252 Calle Cruz, Old San Juan

There are lots of Spanish–Puerto Rican hybrid restaurants in San Juan, but this is the real deal, straight from Spain and not a *mofongo* in sight. If you've ever been to Madrid, this will bring you right back to the typical *tasca* (tavern) *Española,* where you get tasty tapas, hearty classics, and very reasonably priced, authentic paellas (including one with *arroz negro,* "black rice," that's cooked in squid ink—a dish I haven't seen outside Spain). If you come for the food, you'll almost certainly stay for the show. On Thursday and Saturday, you can catch Flamenco dancing at 8 and 9 PM, respectively. On Wednesday night there are Sevillana dance classes, and Sevillana shows every half hour on Friday. Divino Bocadito offers the most affordable night out in Spain, if you can't actually travel to Spain, that is. Open Wednesday through Sunday 6 PM–midnight. $$.

Dragonfly and Dragonfly Too
787-977-3886
www.oofrestaurants.com/dragonfly
364 Fortaleza Street, Old San Juan

Dragonfly is the current "in" place to see and be seen in Old San Juan. It's not just the Latin-Asian fusion with some mouth-watering selections, including a creative sushi menu. It's not just the dimly lit, lounge-like ambience. It's also a general vibe, an aura of sophisticated cool that has made it wildly popular with just about everybody. It's the house rule that anyone, male or female, arriving in shorts will be promptly outfitted with a sarong before they're shown to their table. Oh, and it's the delicious creations you've never heard of before, like Peking duck nachos drizzled with wasabi sour cream and the Asian marinated *churrasco* steak with shoestring potato "dragonfries." For starters, you can share a plate of pork and plantain dumplings with an orange *mojo* sauce, or try one of their specialty rolls: The criollo roll is a true original, filled with a mini crab turnover with avocado and *mofongo* tempura. For dessert, Dragonfly presents the orgasmic milk chocolate *pot de crème* as its popular star. If you're at one of the two bars, try the sweet, gingery Dragon Punch for a highly Asian-accented cocktail. Dragonfly is not just a restaurant; it's almost a culinary right of passage for the hip, cool, and hungry. Open for dinner Monday through Wednesday 6–11 PM, Thursday through Saturday until midnight. $$–$$$.

La Fonda del Jibarito
787-725-8375
www.eljibaritopr.com
280 Sol Street, Old San Juan

Step into this colorful canteen and you might well feel like you're a regular working-class Sanjuanero stopping by for lunch. The restaurant is named after the Jíbaros, the farmers who live in the mountains and are integral to the social fabric of Puerto Rico. La Fonda del Jibarito recalls the simple life with minimal decor and food served cafeteria-style at one end of the restaurant. The place has a special, down-to-earth appeal, especially for tourists who are sick of fancy restaurants. This is the place to be for delicious, home-style Puerto Rican cooking, with typical dishes including whole fried snapper, fried pork chunks and, of course, *mofongo*. Open daily 11 AM–9 PM. $.

Fratelli
787-721-6265
www.ristorantefratelli.com
310 Fortaleza Street, Old San Juan

Fratelli is a favorite with the young, hip crowd that tends to gravitate toward Fortaleza Street at night. This elegant, airy restaurant is predominantly Italian, serving up all the classics: antipasto misto, carpaccio *di manzo,* rich pasta and risottos, and osso bucco. What I like best are the criollo twists that make the Italian dishes sing a tropical tune. The excellent tuna carpaccio, for example, is presented with an avocado truffle relish. The *al cartoccio* is a braised baby halibut filet wrapped in a plantain leaf. And their *mare e monti* (surf and turf) combo is a little different as well: a hunk of lobster sitting on a grilled filet mignon, all served over a bed of lobster risotto. For dessert, try the crème brûlée, flambéed at your table, or the tiramisu with homemade whipped cream. Open Monday through Saturday noon–2:30 PM for lunch; Tuesday and Wednesday 6–10:30 PM, and Thursday through Saturday 6 PM–midnight, for dinner (the bar stays open till late). $$–$$$.

Restaurante Mirabueno
787-723-0984
102 Tanca Street, Old San Juan

Located on a less commercial, less trafficked corner of Old San Juan, Mirabueno is an attractive restaurant serving up Spanish and Puerto Rican food. A variety of rooms and dining areas provide several choices in atmosphere. The mood changes perceptibly—from the bar, which dominates the entrance, to the main dining hall to the lovely patio with a unique, modern fountain, and on to an intimate private room. The restaurant's specialty is its variety of *cazuelas de arroz* (rice casseroles), which you can order with banana, shrimp, salmon, or crabmeat. There's also a mix-'n-match menu of meat, fish, or shellfish served paired with your choice of tropical sauces, from a typical *sofrito* to a mustard and passion fruit medley. A live band (piano, violin, guitar, and bongos) will serenade you

Thursday through Saturday evening 8–10 PM. Open daily 11 AM–midnight. $$.

La Ostra Cosa

787-722-2672
154 Cristo Street, San Juan

You have to love the disclaimer, "We are not responsible for increments of passion. Please direct your claims to your partner." Love is in the air, and seafood on the plate, at this cute, funky restaurant in the heart of the old city. The menu is arranged according to aphrodisiacal potency, and includes oysters (naturally), a very good citrus sole ceviche, green-lip mussels steamed in beer and garlic saffron, and fresh grilled prawns. Don't shy away from "Alien," a dish named for the arrangement of Alaskan king crab legs seasoned with herbs and served with a champagne butter. The courtyard dominated by a huge quenepe tree takes you away from the madding crowd, allowing you an intimate lunch or dinner during which you're free to ply your companion with a variety of suggestive foods. Open daily noon–10 PM. $$.

Panza

787-289-8900
www.cervantespr.com
329 Recinto Sur Street, Old San Juan

Panza, the restaurant of the ultrachic Chateau Cervantes Hotel, carries through the Don Quixote theme brilliantly. The menu presents prefaces (appetizers), essays (tapas), and contents (entrées), all tying together to deliver an inspired culinary novel. The dishes appear to be old classics, until you examine them in detail and discover the subtle changes that make Panza so special. The lobster bisque, for instance, is flavored with coconut; the crunchy *taquitos* (small tacos) are made of taro and filled with twice-cooked duck. The most well-read chapters in the menu include Three Verses of Tuna (a delicious

Panza

combination of plantain-encrusted spicy tuna roll, tuna over black vinegar and sherry seared tomatoes, and a coffee-glazed filet), and a magnificent sable filet in a sesame miso broth over cauliflower truffle puree, with a tomato and porcini compote. The menu changes often, but I hope they keep this last creation, because it was the single best dish I ate in Puerto Rico. The dessert, of course, is the epilogue (*psst:* If they have it, ask for the multilayered, multiflavored, multitextured caramelized *pain perdu* with pineapple marmalade, coconut sorbet, and candied pistachios.) With its intimate space, gracefully simple decor, and exceptional cuisine, Panza is one of San Juan's newest stars. Poor Sancho Panza never ate this well. Open Monday through Saturday 12–3 PM for lunch and 6 PM–midnight for dinner. $$$–$$$$.

The Parrot Club

787-725-7370
www.oofrestaurants.com/parrotclub
363 Fortaleza Street, Old San Juan

Celebrating its 10th anniversary in 2006, this hip, rowdy, colorful restaurant is a stalwart of Nuevo Latino cuisine. With indoor and outdoor seating, live music, and a festive atmosphere, the Parrot Club is a favorite among Puerto Ricans and tourists alike. But its popularity stems beyond the ambience. A wide selection of flavorful drinks (try the Parrot Passion, a cool mix of passion fruit, orange, Bacardi Limón, and triple sec) make it a local hot spot. It's considered *la casa del mojito* (the house of the *mojito*) for its wide selection. And the varied Cuban-criollo menu's not too shabby either. Try the open-faced *arepa*, a cornmeal patty with *ropa vieja* (shredded beef with peppers), avocado, and sour cream, or the blackened tuna in a dark rum sauce with orange essence and mashed yucca, to get a feel for the creative, tasty food. (If you're there for the weekend brunch, try the breakfast twist to the open-faced *arepa*, served with a poached egg and hollandaise sauce.) There's live music every Tuesday, Thursday, and Saturday, and a romantic outdoor patio in the back. Open for dinner Sunday through Wednesday 6–11 PM, Thursday through Saturday 6–midnight; open Monday through Friday for lunch 11 AM–4:30 PM, and for weekend brunch noon–4 PM. $$.

El Patio de Sam
787-723-8802
www.elpatiodesam.com
102 San Sebastián Street, San Juan

Just off San José Plaza, El Patio de Sam is more than the dark, rustic bar you see from the outside. Beyond the bar and enclosed restaurant space is a warm, sunlit patio where you can dine on flavorful Puerto Rican specialties, triple-decker sandwiches, and massive half-pound burgers. (The very good *asopao* is not on the menu, but you can ask for it.) There's a full menu of inventive cocktails (the most popular are

the Lady Killer, which is part gin, peach schnapps, Cointreau, and passion fruit juice; and the Borinquen, which is a mix of Barcardi 151 Rum, passion fruit, orange juice, lime, and grenadine) and fresh fruit frappés. El Patio, a 60-year-old tradition in Old San Juan, has a colorful history. Owned by a onetime jockey–turned–bicycle salesman, the restaurant has grown from humble beginnings to become one of the more well-known hangouts in the old city. The kitchen also serves next-door **Nono's**, a two-floor bar that's always busy on the weekends. Open daily noon–11 PM, with the bar staying open until 2 AM on Friday and Saturday. $–$$.

El Picoteo
787-723-9020
www.elconvento.com
100 Cristo Street, Old San Juan

Old San Juan offers a full range of international cuisine, and one of the best in the city is this Spanish tapas restaurant and bar, located in the picturesque Hotel El Convento. With easy access from the road, El Picoteo is a frequent stop for locals and tourists from all over the city. In addition to the pleasant backdrop of the hotel courtyard, the Spanish food here is excellent, even by the standards of this author, who has lived in Spain for several years. The tapas, hot and cold, include Spanish standbys such as garlic shrimp, potato salad, and warm goat cheese, and the paella is the real deal. Open daily from noon to midnight. $$–$$$.

Sofia
787-721-0396
355 San Francisco Street, Old San Juan

This culinary homage to Sofia Loren is the newest star of the Oof family (which spawned Dragonfly, the Parrot Club, and Aguaviva). Photographs of Sofia, along with colorful Murano blown-glass panels, graces the walls of this stylish Italian restaurant, which serves all of the classics and avoids the fusion route. The atmosphere is relaxed and casual and the rich food is served up in large portions. To satisfy a big appetite at lunch, you can't beat the *polpette alla parmigiana,* a massive meatball, mozzarella, and tomato open-faced sandwich, or one of their grilled paninis. The brick oven pizzas are in the original Neapolitan style. For pasta, try what some call the best spaghetti carbonara on the island; or, if you want something different, check out the *bucatini* with meatballs (the thick, hollow pasta lets you slurp up the meat sauce as you eat). Sofia also has a selection of *spuntini* (the Italian version of tapas), including mini risottos and asparagus wrapped in breaded prosciutto with a white bean dip. Try to save room for dessert, specifically the amazing ricotta cheesecake with a thin trail of honey truffle. There's live music Thursday through Saturday night, and the bar features creative cocktails (like a basil blueberry *mojito* and an Italian sangria made with Prosecco sparkling wine and pineapple). Open for lunch Monday through Friday 11:30 AM–4 PM; open for dinner Monday through Wednesday 6–11 PM, and Thursday through Saturday 6 PM–midnight . Open continuously 11:30 AM–11 PM on Sunday. $$–$$$.

ATTRACTIONS, PARKS & RECREATION

Castillo de San Felipe del Morro (San Felipe del Morro Castle)
787-729-6754
501 Norzagaray Street, Old San Juan

El Morro, officially the Castillo de San Felipe del Morro, is Old San Juan's most recognizable and impressive landmark. A visit to this imposing fortress takes you immediately back in time and gives you a true appreciation of how formidable Puerto Rico was as a military stronghold. Indeed, in over 400 years, El Morro has withstood several attacks, and fell only once. As you approach it, you cross a wide green expanse, where, in 1598, a land

Castillo San Felipe del Morro

La Fortaleza

assault by the Earl of Cumberland finally broke through the Spanish resistance. It's hard to believe that, at one point, the U.S. Navy converted this lawn into a golf course. This open field was fortunately restored to its original look, and today you'll find people picnicking and flying kites here, within El Morro's shadow.

The word *morro* means "promontory," and this fort sticks out into the entrance of San Juan Bay. Across the water lies another, smaller fort known as **El Cañuelo**, which was El Morro's partner in the island's defense. Enemy ships seeking a way into the bay had to sail through a deadly gauntlet of crisscrossing cannon fire from the two citadels. El Morro is divided into six levels, comprising dungeons, barracks, passageways, and storerooms. As you walk along its ramparts, you can squeeze into one of the signature *garitas* (sentry boxes) jutting out from the walls. Open daily 9 AM–5 PM. $.

La Fortaleza (The Fortress)
787-721-7000, ext. 2211
www.fortaleza.gobierno.pr
Recinto Oeste Street, Old San Juan

The oldest governor's mansion in the Western Hemisphere is also one of the grandest. La Fortaleza, which means "The Fortress," was completed in 1540 during a massive construction effort to secure the island's defenses. It fell twice, to the Earl of Cumberland in 1598 and to the Dutch commander Boudewyn Hendrick in 1625. In 1846, it was remodeled, given the elegant pale blue and white facade you see today, and converted for full-time use as the governor's home. Also known as **El Palacio de Santa Catalina** (Santa Catalina

You Say "Tomato," I Say "Fort"

There are no true forts in old San Juan: El Morro, La Fortaleza, and San Cristóbal are all castles; small ones, perhaps, but castles nonetheless. Incorrectly labeled as forts by the U.S. government, they have come to be known as such.

Palace), the mansion has housed 170 governors of Puerto Rico. Its tiled roofs, patios, galleries, arches, and wrought ironwork are classic examples of Spanish architecture, but the fortress also houses a poignant marker of the passing of Spanish dominion on the island. An old mahogany clock stands along one of the corridors in La Fortaleza. Before he vacated the premises, the last Spanish governor paused in front of it and struck its face with his sword, stopping time to note the very last moment of Spanish rule in the New World. Guided tours are offered every weekday, except holidays. Open 9 AM–4 PM on weekdays. Free.

Castillo de San Cristóbal (Saint Christopher Castle)
787-729-6777
Norzagaray Street, Old San Juan

Built on a hill, Castillo de San Cristóbal is the largest of San Juan's forts, and the largest fort built by Spain in the New World. The huge structure rises almost 150 feet above sea level and dominates the northeast edge of the old city. While El Morro kept watch over the oceans, San Cristóbal guarded the land approach to Old San Juan. The castle was completed in the 1785, covering 27 acres and cleverly designed according to the "defense-in-depth" model. Essentially, this meant several layers of defense; the castle was little more than a network of fortifications; if an enemy breached one wall, they faced several other, stouter defenses. One look at the fort's layout demonstrates the ingenious design. San

Castillo de San Cristóbal

Casa Bacardi visitors center at the Bacardi Rum distillery

Cristóbal was tested in its infancy, when Sir Ralph Abercromby's 60 ships and over 3,900 troops failed to capture the city because they were unable to penetrate beyond its land defenses. From its battlements, the Spanish fired the first shot of the Spanish-American War in 1898. Throughout the centuries, the fort has been modified many times, but the most incongruous of these enhancements are the concrete World War II bunkers installed by the U.S. Army in 1942. Open daily 9 AM–5 PM. $.

Bacardi Distillery
787-788-8400
www.casabacardi.org
Road 165, Km 6.2, Cataño

Okay, so it's not actually in Old San Juan, but the Bacardi distillery (Casa Bacardi) is one of Puerto Rico's most visited sites, and many tours to the factory depart from the old city. While most tour companies charge you for transportation, the Bacardi tour itself is free and comes with a complimentary drink. The tour of the world's largest rum distillery is a mix of Epcot and alcohol. Leisurely paced trams take you to the various rooms of Casa Bacardi, where you learn about the history of the distillery, participate in hands-on and nose-on exercises that will either give you a greater appreciation of rum or make your head swim, and finish off, of course, at the gift shop. During high season, tours can fill up early if you make your own way to the distillery, you might want to call ahead. Open M Saturday 8:30 AM–5:30 PM (last tour at 4:15), and Sunday 10 AM–5 PM

Catedral de San Juan (San Juan Cathedral)
787-722-0861
www.catedralsanjuan.com
151–153 Cristo Street, Old San Jan

Catedral de San Juan

Majestic Catedral de San Juan is the most beautiful and significant religious landmark in Puerto Rico. The church you see today has been through a lot. The original chapel built here in the 1520s was promptly destroyed by a hurricane. It was looted in 1598 and suffered the wrath of another hurricane in 1615. Major restorations were completed in 1917. Much like St. Patrick's Cathedral in New York City, Catedral de San Juan is the site of many high-society weddings. The cathedral tour has a few highlights, some of them a little eerie: In 1908, the remains of Ponce de León were removed from Iglesia de San José (San José Church) and relocated to the cathedral, where they currently lie *on* a marble tomb. And there's a wax-covered, glass-encased mummy of Saint Pio, a Roman martyr here as well. Some beautiful stained-glass windows are still intact, but most of the cathedral's original finery has been stripped away through the ravages of time and invaders. Tours are given daily 8:30 AM—4 PM. Donations welcome.

El Paseo del Morro

The San Juan Gate
End of San Juan Street, Old San Juan

In the 1630s, the Spanish constructed the massive walls that would protect the southern flank of Old San Juan. The city wasn't completely fortified until the 18th century, when the northern walls were constructed. Five gates were built to allow access to Old San Juan, and the San Juan Gate, the only breach along the walls facing the harbor, became the main entrance to the city. Today, the gate's massive, painted wooden door is an icon of Old San Juan. The best time to visit is in the early evening, while the sun is on its way down, so you can enjoy the lovely walk from the gate. (Take this stroll during the day, and you'll roast in the sun.) Called **El Paseo del Morro** (El Morro's Passage), the path snakes along the edge of the island, beneath the city's formidable walls.

Iglesia de San José (San José Church)
787-772-0861
Plaza San José (On Morovis Street between Norzagaray and San Sebastián streets), Old San Juan

The second-oldest church in the Western Hemisphere, Iglesia de San José is a rare example of Spanish Gothic architecture in the New World. Built in the 1530s, it was originally a Dominican monastery and chapel. Within its stark white walls lie a 16th-century crucifix and a 15-century altar imported from Spain. The church was the original burial place of Ponce de León and still houses his coat of arms. The tomb of José Campeche, one of Puerto Rico's most acclaimed painters, is also here. In front of the church is a small plaza that has become a popular meeting place for young Sanjuaneros. In the center of the plaza is a bronze statue of Ponce de León, cast from cannons captured from the British in 1797. The church is currently under extensive renovation and is closed to the public. Admission may still be free when the church reopens.

Iglesia de San José

Parque de Las Palomas (Pigeon Park)
Tucked away at the end of Cristo Street, just steps from the Capilla Del Cristo, is tiny Parque de Las Palomas. True to its name, this is a paradise for pigeons, and the thousands of plump birds that come here are its main draw. The park, which lies atop the city wall, abuts a large, sloping stone wall with dozens of pigeonholes cut into it. For a dollar, you can buy bird seed and watch the pigeons swarm toward the food as you scatter it. The park also offers wonderful views of San Juan Bay and overlooks Paseo La Princesa. It's a popular spot for children in a nice, secluded pocket of the city. Open 24/7. Free.

A Night Out on the Town

Not two minutes ago, we were tourists. But now we play the role of prisoners walking along San Sebastián Street, where prisoners of long ago were led, in shackles, to the city jail (now City Hall) and, maybe, to the gallows. As we walk, our guide, Debbie, tells us the romantic legend of the prisoner and the executioner's daughter.

It's all part of the fun on the "Night Tales in Old San Juan" tour, brainchild of **Legends of Puerto Rico** founder Debbie Molina. Her infectious passion for Puerto Rico and its history, and her extensive research, are what make this tour so appealing; that, and the privilege of entering landmark historic buildings at night, when they are closed to the public. The tour covers 2 miles and lasts approximately two hours (with several stops to let you rest and listen to your guide). Along the way you'll hear tales of love, pirates, war, and myth in the old city. Debbie also points out locations where movies were shot and, if you're lucky, she will even sing Noel Estrada's lilting anthem, "En Mi Viejo San Juan," for you. Amid the street lamps and under the stars, the nighttime experience best captures the romantic history of the Puerto Rican people and their island. The tour makes several stops at some of San Juan's best-known monuments, and even the most educated history buff might learn a thing or two about the life and times of a colonial outpost. This is a unique way to see, and appreciate, Viejo San Juan.

"Night Tales in Old San Juan" tour

CULTURE

Institute of Puerto Rican Arts and Culture

787-724-5949

Plaza del Quinto Centenario, Old San Juan

Students of Puerto Rican art and culture come to the institute to learn about the island's arts and crafts. The building, one of Puerto Rico's oldest landmarks, used to be a hospital for indigents, and before that was a Dominican convent. It currently showcases the work of local artisans. A notable exhibit explores the revived craft of *mundillos,* tatted fabrics made from a type of lace found only in Puerto Rico and Spain. Visitors can also catch a glimpse of Puerto Rico before the Spanish arrived through a model of a Taíno village and a fine collection of pottery, stone tools, and other pre-European artifacts. Open 9 AM–4:30 PM Wednesday through Sunday. Free.

La Casa del Libro

787-723-0354

255 Cristo Street, Old San Juan

www.lacasadellibro.org

Among the unique museums in Old San Juan is this quaint homage to the printed book. Located at the end of Cristo Street, La Casa del Libro (The House of the Book) is dedicated to the book as art. In addition to exhibiting its collection of over 7,000 rare and special books, the museum educates visitors on the history of printing and bookmaking. There's a vast collection of literary treasures: handwritten and hand-illustrated manuscripts; a document signed by Ferdinand and Isabella regarding Columbus's second journey and considered the oldest printed document in the Americas; a copy of James Joyce's *Ulysses* illustrated by Matisse; a single page from a Bible printed by Gutenberg on his revolutionary press, in 1450; a copy of *Don Quixote* printed in 1605 (its first year of publication); and 370 books printed between 1450 and 1500, the first 50 years of the Gutenberg press and the dawn of the printing age. This is the largest collection of *incunabula,* as these books are called, in Latin America. Open Tuesday through Saturday, except holidays, 11 AM–4:30 PM. Free.

Museo Casa Blanca

787-725-1454

One San Sebastián Street, Old San Juan

Casa Blanca (White House) has no current connection to local government, though it was built by Juan Ponce de León in 1521. It is erroneously known as Ponce de León's home; he died before he could take up residence here. His son-in-law rebuilt the house two years later, after a hurricane had destroyed it. Ponce de León's family lived in Casa Blanca for over 250 years. Today it is a museum, commemorating the lives of Puerto Rico's founding family and serving as one of the most ancient monuments to the island's history. La Casa Blanca preceded El Morro and La Fortaleza as a military structure, and was the first fort built of stone on the island. The tour takes you through the main rooms, providing a good overview of the simple, rustic lifestyle of centuries past. If she's available, ask Sheila Proenza to be your guide. Open Tuesday through Sunday 9 AM–noon and 1–4:30 PM. $.

The kitchen at Museo Casa Blanca

Museo de las Américas

787-724-5052
www.museolasamericas.org
End of Norzagaray Street in the Cuartel de Ballajá, Old San Juan

The Cuartel de Ballajá (Ballajá Barracks) was the quarters of Spanish soldiers who lived on the island in the 1800s. It later housed American soldiers, and served as a military hospital during World War II. Today the three-story building houses the Museo de las Américas (which occupies only the second floor of the Cuartel). The museum lives up to its name, showcasing changing exhibits of traditional arts, crafts, archaeological findings, and artifacts from North, South, and Central America, as well as the Caribbean. There are three permanent collections: the African Heritage, the Indian in America, and Popular Arts in America. In addition, collections throughout the year focus on modern art, artifacts, and photography. Each exhibit is tucked away in a separate room within the barracks. The staff are happy to explain the collection. Open Monday through Friday 10 AM–4 PM, Saturday 11 AM–5 PM. Guided tours are available on weekdays at 10:30, 11:30, 12:30, and 2. Free, except for the Indian in America exhibit ($).

Museo del Niño (Children's Museum)

787-722-3791
www.museodelninopr.com
150 Cristo Street, Old San Juan

If you've brought the kids, it would be a crime to deprive them of this experience. Museo del Niño provides a wonderland for kids to play and learn. The three-story museum is designed with the child in mind. There is a tiny kids' town (no adults allowed), a child-sized re-creation of a typical Puerto Rican plaza, and separate areas where children can learn on computers, dress themselves up in a mock wardrobe, and learn what recycling is all about. There's even an area where they can learn about mosquitoes. But the pride and joy of the museum is the Health Hall, which includes giant exhibits on a healthy diet and the basics of the human body. The star here is "Stuffee," a giant Muppet-like figure who zips open to reveal all the main organs of the human body. Another favorite for groups is the mini TV studio, where children report the news in front of news cameras and an audience of other kids. Their reports are shown on screens behind them. Open Tuesday through Thursday 9 AM–3:30 PM, Friday 9 AM–5 PM, Saturday and Sunday 12:30–5 PM. $.

Museo de San Juan
787-723-4317; 787-724-1875
150 Norzagaray Street, Old San Juan

Given the impressive history of San Juan, you'd expect this museum to house a significant collection of art and artifacts. It's not as grand in scale as its name implies, however, and consists mostly of paintings, photographs, and some archaeological objects. Still, the permanent collection in Oller Hall offers a visual journey from the origins of the city to the present day, and a theater runs a recurring film about the city called *San Juan: Ciudad de Todos* (San Juan: Everybody's City). The paintings include works from Puerto Rican masters José Campeche and Francisco Oller. Open Tuesday through Friday 9 AM–4 PM, Saturday and Sunday 10 AM–4 PM (closed noon–1 for lunch). $.

Museo Felisa Rincón de Gautier
787-723-1897
51 Caleta de San Juan, Old San Juan

If Margaret Thatcher ever decides to establish a museum chronicling her life, she might want to visit Old San Juan to see how best to do it. This unusual homage to one of the leading female figures in the history of Puerto Rico and the Caribbean is hidden away in a quiet corner of the old city. It's worth discovering, if only to learn about the remarkable life and career of a woman you might never have heard of but who was nevertheless a powerful force in the feminist movement. In 1946, just 26 years after women were given the right to vote in the United States, Felisa Rincón de Gautier became the first woman to be elected mayor of San Juan; it was a post she would hold for 22 years. Her accomplishments earned her the title "Woman of the Americas" in 1954 from the Union of American Women; it's one of over 130 commendations she has received from governments and institutions. Easily the most impressive exhibit in the museum, which used to be her home, are the plaques that cover two stories of wall space. Open Monday through Friday 9 AM–4 PM. $.

Museo Pablo Casals
787-723-9185
101 San Sebastián Street, off San José Plaza, Old San Juan

Classical music lovers may want to check out the life and works of Pablo Casals, Puerto Rico's preeminent maestro. On display are Casals's cello, piano, original manuscripts of his music, and various commendations he received. Also on display are hundreds of

The Galleries of Old San Juan

You don't have to be a connoisseur to appreciate beautiful art, and you don't have to be a collector to appreciate a beautiful art gallery. Throughout Old San Juan, you'll find lovely galleries displaying some of Puerto Rico's best art. Whether you're looking for a new centerpiece in your home, or simply exploring what the old city has to offer, the following places are worth a stop.

Galería Botello

787-723-9987
www.botello.com
208 Cristo Street, Old San Juan

The arched hallway of Galería Botello leads into a lovely oasis of a patio where, to the melody of a soft, gurgling fountain, you can admire Angel Botello's distinctive paintings and sculptures, as well as works by artists from Latin America. Also enjoy displays of beautiful, antique *santos*. Open Monday through Saturday 10–6.

Galería Sánchez

787-929-4663
www.galeriasanchez.com
320 Fortaleza Street, Old San Juan

A small space on Fortaleza Street, what this gallery lacks in size it makes up for in stunning landscapes by Erick Sánchez. Also on exhibit are beautiful expressionist and abstract works. Open Sunday through Thursday 11–6, Friday and Saturday noon–8 or 9.

Galería Sin Título

787-723-7502
157 Luna Street, Second Floor, Old San Juan

Besides its very cool name, Galería Sin Título (Untitled Gallery) boasts an eclectic collection of contemporary art with a particular emphasis on drawing, photography, and conceptual expressions. It also hosts theater and drama clinics. The gallery features a global mix of up-and-comers as well as established artists. Open Wednesday through Saturday 11–5.

Obra Galería

787-723-3206
www.obragaleria.com
301 Cruz Street, Old San Juan

Obra Gallery is a tastefully designed tribute to art, with a leather ottoman, a stunning view of San Juan Bay, and tasteful, modern decor. The gallery has revolving exhibits of some of the best-known contemporary artists, including Basquiat, Nick Quijano, and portraitist Jesus María del Rincón. Open Tuesday through Saturday 11–5.

Siena Art Gallery. See Souvenirs, Gifts & Books.

recordings, videotapes, and vintage posters from the Casals Festival, an internationally renowned classical music event held annually in Puerto Rico for more than 50 years. You can listen to recordings and watch taped performances in the music room on the second floor. Open Tuesday through Saturday 9:30 AM–4 PM. $.

NIGHTLIFE

El Batey

787-725-1787
101 Cristo Street, Old San Juan

In the city of ultrachic lounges and hip hangouts, El Batey is something of an anomaly. Located on serene and quaint Cristo Street, it sticks out like a sore, grungy thumb. El Batey didn't break the bank on decor: Graffiti are scrawled all over its bare walls (you can request a marker to add your own imprint on the place), the lampshades consist of business cards, and the dilapidated wooden bar is covered with autographs of the young and not-so-famous. The pub looks as if it belongs near a college campus rather than an ancient cathedral, but nobody in Old San Juan is complaining. El Batey is legendary both for its throwback ambience and its fantastic relic of a jukebox. Open daily after 8 PM. $.

Blend
787-977-7777
309 Fortaleza Street, Old San Juan

You can start your night early with dinner at Blend; come in afterward to enjoy the "Best Bar in San Juan"—two years running. Hang out in the funky lounge with a cool cut-glass waterfall dominating the length of one wall; or you can visit the lounge in the VIP room. A live DJ cranks it up after hours and plays a variety of lounge music. One nice thing about the lounge is that it's a comfortably large area with high ceilings. Open daily except Monday at 5:30 PM, closing at midnight from Tuesday to Wednesday, at 2 AM on Thursday, and around 3 AM on weekends. $$.

Club Lazer
787-725-7581
www.clublazer.com
251 Cruz Street, Old San Juan

Over 20 years young, Club Lazer is one of the centers of *raggaetón*, hip-hop, and dance music in Old San Juan. The three-level club features pockets of space where the atmosphere changes, giving you a variety of options to suit your mood as the night grows long. The dance floor is lit by laser lights, which give the club its name. There's a VIP lounge and a more accessible lounge that is bathed in red velvet in the lowest level of the club. An open-air rooftop terrace provides a relaxed change of scenery, and on certain nights you can buy *pinchos* (skewers) from the barbecue. Be prepared to enjoy a long night, and wear your flashiest stuff if you want to blend in. On some nights, people don't stop until they see the sun, and then they run home. Once a month, the club hosts a special night, be it a booty-dance competition or an amateur MC night. The club has hosted DJs and music icons such as DMX, from the United States. Doors open at 10 PM Friday through Sunday. $$.

Colmado Bar Moreno
787-724-5130
365 Tetuán Street, Old San Juan

Sofo might be the trendiest neighborhood in Old San Juan, but directly below it is a place where trendiness just doesn't fly. Colmado Bar Moreno is a liquor/general store that converts into a *reggaetón*-blaring, no-frills bar at night. This is the place to come for cheap drinks. Customers line up at the counter, buy their drinks, and then take them outside to the tables in the small plaza across from the bar. You can't take bottles out, but drinks are served in plastic cups. Open daily until midnight.

Dragonfly and Dragonfly Too

787-977-3886
www.oofrestaurants.com/dragonfly
364 Fortaleza Street, Old San Juan

After the kitchen closes, one of the hottest restaurants in town becomes one of Old San Juan's coolest lounges. People dressed in their nighttime best linger around one of the two bars or pack in the small lounge to chill out (no dancing here). In the hip gloom and dark red and black decor, it's easy to sit back and enjoy the night. Open Monday through Wednesday 6 PM–11 PM, Thursday through Saturday until midnight, but the lounge stays open until 1 or 2 in the morning. $$.

Fratelli

787-721-6265
www.ristorantefratelli.com
310 Fortaleza Street, Old San Juan

As the clock stretches past 11, Fratelli restaurant morphs into a late-night hangout, with lines outside and the action centered on the bar. The music is turned up, playing a mix of *raggaetón,* salsa, merengue, and other rhythms into the wee hours. Wednesday is Champagne Night. Open till 1 or 2 AM. $–$$.

Kú Lounge

787-722-6949
www.kudetarestaurant.com
314 Fortaleza Street

Kudeta restaurant, the inspiration for the name Kú Lounge, has closed and is reopening as something else; but the lounge, which is above the restaurant and has a separate entrance, isn't going anywhere. One of the most popular destinations for the young, fashionable crowd, the multilevel hot spot invariably draws lines of pretty people at night. Walk up the stairs to enter a cool space with funky chandeliers, tasty tapas, talented DJs, and suede banquettes likely to be full when you get there. Bottle service and VIP rooms are on the third floor. Open Sunday through Wednesday 7 PM–11 PM, Thursday through Saturday 10 PM–5 AM. $$.

Marmalade

787-724-3969
www.marmaladepr.com
317 Fortaleza Street, Old San Juan

Another restaurant that doubles as a nighttime hot spot, the lounge at Marmalade is a bright, eminently stylish place that draws chattering throngs of well-dressed young hipsters. The space is very artistic, dominated by a long wavy table in the center that is matched by a wavy ceiling lantern. Retro couches line the walls. Come for the sophisticated food and stay for the drinks and great music. After 10, this place starts to jump. Opens every evening at 6 PM and closes at midnight Monday through Thursday, at 2 AM Friday and Saturday, and at 10 PM Sunday. $$.

Nono's

787-725-7819
100 San Sebastián Street, Old San Juan

On the corner of Cristo and San Sebastián streets, Nono's is a longtime favorite. This two-level bar is a simple place, with a bar on the first floor, pool tables on the second. Try the daily drink specials. Burgers and other fare are prepared in kitchen at **El Patio de Sam** next-door. Set in a Colonial building, the bar opens out toward Plaza San José, letting you drink in the night and the atmosphere of the old city as you savor your beer. Nono's opens daily at 11 AM and stays open until 4 AM.

The Nuyorican Café

787-977-1276
www.nuyoricancafepr.com
312 San Francisco Street, Old San Juan

Tucked in an alleyway, Callejón de la Capilla, the Nuyorican Café can be easily spotted—it's the place with all the people pouring into and out of its doors. Unassuming from the outside, the bar is a raucous, smoky, musical gem. Music is the lifeblood of the place. Live performances are frequent and so popular that the bands sell their records at the bar (the cover charge is typically $5). Live jazz and salsa, salsa dancing classes, theater, and open-mike poetry are some of the events you might catch at the Nuyorican, a great place to mingle with artists and young Sanjuaneros. Open 7 PM–2 AM every day. Free to $, depending on the evening's entertainment.

Pink Skirt

787-725-1205
301 Fortaleza Street, Old San Juan

Walk in at 10 or 11 at night and the place is deserted. Pink Skirt is a strictly after-hours lounge, restaurant, and bar. It's a fun, offbeat hole-in-the-wall that serves up tasty and creative Asian-fusion fare (try the Kamikaze Burger). The action gets going after midnight, and after 2 AM you'll have to wait in line to squeeze in. Intensely funky decor (check out the poofy spiral couch), intensely friendly people (who have no qualms about rubbing up against you), intense techno and hip-hop music. On weekends, it has been known to stay open until as late as 8 AM. $$.

Pool Palace

787-725-8487
www.poolpalacepr.com
330 Recinto Sur Street, Old San Juan

Pool hall, sports bar, restaurant, games, and dancing: The Pool Palace offers all of the above. The 15 Brunswick pool tables are the main draw, but miniskirted, slick clubbers are a magnet, too, and keep the dance floor going. Since the Palace is open all day, it makes for a nice afternoon if you need a change from touring historic sites. The action heats up at night, though, especially during one of the club's many special events. Open 11 AM–midnight or 1 AM during the week, and up to 3 AM on weekends. $–$$.

La Rumba

787-725-4407
152 San Sebastián Street, Old San Juan

From Thursday to Saturday, La Rumba is the place to dance to live salsa and Afro-Cuban music. You might be surprised to learn that it's one of the few spots in Old San Juan that caters to salsa lovers—the club, lounge, and bar scene has become much more popular than salsa. Still, the dance floor is usually crammed with people, and the bands are terrific. Most of the people on the dance floor know what they're doing, but newcomers are welcome, and it's not hard to find a partner who can show you the ropes. Features live music every night. Open 8 PM–3 AM. $.

Señor Frog's

787-977-4142
104 Comercio Street, Old San Juan

Spring-breakers and college students from all over Mexico and the Caribbean know the familiar hunting cry of Señor Frog's—loud music, live bands, karaoke, raucous crowds, girls dancing onstage, and just about everybody urging you to have fun, try one more drink, and maybe do something you've never done before. The Puerto Rico branch, just behind the Sheraton, is no different. There's a full menu here for lunch and dinner, but there are better places to go for food. For a boisterous party, though, you're in good hands. Open 10 AM–1 AM. $$.

SHOPPING

Apparel, Footwear & Accessories

Cappalli

787-289-6565
206 O'Donnell Street, Old San Juan

Across from Plaza Colón, you'll find one of Lisa Cappalli's two boutiques in San Juan. A frontrunner of women's fashion in San Juan, Lisa designs the full range of women's clothing, including a children's line, casual wear, formal wear, and bridal gowns. She's known for lots of lace and for her attention to detail. Every piece is handmade, and many items have started trends (I'm told a Cappalli lace blouse hangs in almost every Puerto Rican woman's closet). Lisa describes her products as timeless, sensuous, very sophisticated, and above all, feminine. She forgot to mention that they are more affordable than many designer pieces. Her customers—which consist of a broad local and international clientele—agree with her assessment. Chances are, you will too. Open Tuesday and Wednesday noon–7 PM, Thursday through Saturday noon–9 PM, and Sunday noon–5 PM. $$–$$$$.

Chavin Cotton

787-721-5338
www.chavincotton.com
255 Tanca Street, Old San Juan

For something a little different, drop by Chavin Cotton for a range of all-natural, 100 percent cotton clothing made in Peru. With the exception of a few black items, there are no dyes or coloring in the products, leaving the fabric a soft, off-white color. Chavin sells tops, dresses, and skirts for women. Open daily 10 AM–7 PM. $$.

Clubman

787-722-0757
www.clubmanpr.com
363 Fortaleza Street, Old San Juan

The Brooks Brothers of Old San Juan, Clubman carries quality men's business attire. In addition to ties and suits, they're well known for their large stock of reasonably priced *guayabera* shirts. Open Monday through Saturday 10 AM–7 PM, Sunday noon–5 PM. $$–$$$$.

Custo Barcelona

787-722-1212
www.custo-barcelona.com
152 Cristo Street, Old San Juan

This small outpost of an internationally recognized brand has a selection of funky, youthful clothes for women. Their patterned tops, especially, have a modern, urban style to them, and are among the brand's signature pieces. It's a different look from what you'll find in the more well-known stores. Open Monday through Saturday 10 AM–6 PM, Sunday 10 AM–5 PM. $$–$$$.

Punta Pie

787-725-1769
www.puntapie.com
304 San Francisco Street, Old San Juan

There aren't many shoe stores in Old San Juan, but for stylish, distinctive footwear, let your feet guide you to Punta Pie. They sell predominantly women's shoes made in Brazil and Colombia, but they offer some men's shoes as well. The designs range from elegant to funky, and the look and feel of the store is straight out of Soho. Punta Pie is somewhat exclusive—only 12 pairs of each shoe are available—and the prices match the quality and design. Open Monday through Saturday 9:30 AM–7 PM, Sunday 11 AM–5 PM. $$$.

Outlet Alley

While the bulk of the shops in Old San Juan center around jewelry and gifts/souvenirs, several major labels have set up outlet or factory stores, all on Cristo Street. Here are some names you'll recognize:

Coach
787-723-7285

Dooney & Bourke
787-289-0075

Guess
787-977-1550

Polo Ralph Lauren
787-722-2136

Reebok
787-977-2116

Jewelry

Argenta
787-722-3936
249 San Francisco Street, Old San Juan
Hector Giovanni is pleasant and engaging, and one of the few licensed jewelers and gemol-
ogists you'll come across in these parts. His collection includes silver jewelry, precious and
semiprecious stones (check out his collection of larimar—a blue gemstone unique to the
Caribbean—and amber pieces), watches, and Swarovski crystal. Argenta is also the exclu-
sive supplier for Elle Jewelry in the Caribbean. Open daily 10 AM–7 PM. $$–$$$$.

Bared
787-725-7005; 787-725-4832
Corner of Fortaleza and San Justo streets, Old San Juan

There are three Bared stores in Old San Juan, and 13 additional branches around the island.
This Bared occupies two floors of a beautiful landmark building. On the first floor, you'll find
designer jewelry, fine crystal, and well-known, high-end brands of watches. The second
floor features a bridal collection. Baccarat, Breitling, Bulgari, Cartier, and Lalique give you an
idea of the selection, and the prices. Open Monday through Saturday 10 AM–7 PM. $$$$.

Demel
787-725-5171
267 San Francisco Street, Old San Juan

Demel specializes in fine Italian jewelry, mostly set in silver. The store itself is beautiful,
and the collection is of very high quality. Open Monday through Saturday 11:30 AM–5 PM,
Sunday 11:30 AM–4:30 PM. $$$$.

Joyería Riviera
787-725-4000
247 Fortaleza Street, Old San Juan

Joyería Riviera is one of the flagship stores in San Juan. Located in a 200-year-old man-
sion, it carries collections by designers from all over the world. The shop is also the largest
distributor of Rolex watches on the island. Prices start at around $150 and reach into the
tens of thousands of dollars. Open daily 10 AM–6 PM. $$$–$$$$.

Michael Lawrence Studios
787-725-9509
202 San Francisco Street, Old San Juan

Here you'll find a collection of fine jewelry, art, and antiques housed in a historical build-
ing. There are some lovely, custom-designed pieces, and the store offers a "buy one get
one free" promotion on selected items. The staff will happily meet your particular tastes if
what you'd like isn't readily available ("We can get anything in the world," they tell me). In
addition to jewelry, you can buy tobacco and a wide range of spirits, including bottles of
wine not found anywhere else on the island. Antiques and art are on the second floor.
Open daily 9:30 AM–6 PM. $$–$$$$.

Samina

787-723-1027
152 Fortaleza Street, Old San Juan

From watches to Faberge-style eggs to fine porcelain, Samina stocks a diverse array of high-end jewelry and collectables. Their gold-cast porcelain and blown-crystal figurines are imported from Italy, and they specialize in diamonds, Tahitian pearls, Austrian opals, and tanzanite. Most of their gems are set in 14 or 18 carat gold. Open daily 9 AM—7 PM. $$$–$$$$.

Souvenirs, Gifts & Books

Bóveda

787-725-0263
www.boveda.info
209 Cristo Street, Old San Juan

Bóveda is a departure from the typical Old San Juan gift shop. You can find everything from postcards to paper lanterns, and items from Ireland to Japan. There's a huge variety, and something for every budget. Their colorful and wide-ranging jewelry includes items made from coral, marble, porcelain, bone, gemstones, and sea glass. Open daily 10 AM—6 PM. $–$$$$.

La Casa de Las Casitas & Handicraft

787-723-2276
250 Cristo Street, Old San Juan

Paul and Milagros Kelly are among the most helpful store owners in San Juan, offering a range of arts and crafts, *vejigante* masks, creative wall hangings, accessories, handmade hammocks (the one hanging in the store against a huge photo of a beach is a persuasive sales tool), and even a clean restroom for travelers looking for a souvenir *and* a bathroom break. Open daily 10 AM—6 PM. $–$$$$.

Cronopios

787-724-1815
255 San José Street, Old San Juan

This is one of the nicest bookstores in town—any town. The patio within the store, with its natural light and trickling fountain, is a sanctuary where you can sample music CDs. The collection includes books in Spanish and English. Open daily 9 AM—7 PM. $–$$.

El Galpón

787-725-3945
154 Cristo Street, Old San Juan

At this well-known arts and crafts store on Cristo Street, Gustavo Lerner stands ready to help customers select the best *vejigante* mask, *santo* figurine, *guayabera* shirt, or Panama hat. The small space is stuffed with handmade artifacts, photographs, and hand-rolled cigars. Masks of all shapes and sizes cover the walls. Open daily 10 AM—6 PM. $–$$$$.

Máscaras de Puerto Rico

787-725-1306

105 Fortaleza Street, Old San Juan

La Calle (the street) is a corridor leading off bustling Fortaleza Street into the miniest of mini-malls. The most prominent shop here is Máscaras de Puerto Rico, one of several places in Old San Juan where visitors can find the *careta* (mask), of the *vejigante*. Along the walls is a wonderful collection ranging in price from $20 to over $2,000. There are generally two styles: oval-shaped ones made out of gourd or coconut shells, and elaborate papier-mâché creations. Other knickknacks crafted by artisans from all over the island are also available. Open daily 10 AM–6:30 PM. $–$$$$.

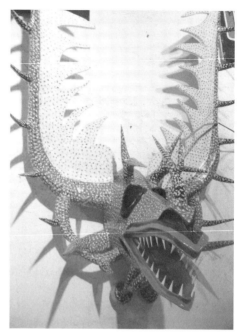

Máscaras de Puerto Rico

(By the way: If you travel farther into La Calle, you'll come across other little stores selling leather goods, clothing, arts and crafts, and accessories. At this point, if the 15-foot walk has tired you, you can rest at **Café El Punto** for a coffee or fresh fruit shake, and maybe sample something from the small Puerto Rican and Chilean menu. Then it's onward for another 2 or 3 feet before you reach the end of the road and **Treasure Coins, Gems and Antique Decoratives**, which specializes in ancient and worldwide coins.)

Mi Pequeño San Juan

787-977-1636

www.ducart.net

107 Calle Cristo Street, Old San Juan

Located directly across from the Hotel El Convento, this family-owned store specializes in handmade reproductions of the buildings of San Juan. With their tropical colors and detailed work, the ceramic replicas serve as adorable wall hangings. Open Monday through Saturday 10 AM–6 PM, Sunday 11 AM–5 PM. $–$$$.

Mi Rincón

787-723-1412

251 Cristo Street, Old San Juan

This tiny treasure of a shop has one of the more interesting collections of locally made artifacts and artwork. Everything is handmade and nothing is mass-produced. The artistically treated photographs of Old San Juan landmarks is the creation of the store's charming owner, Cuca Del Rincón. Her name gives the store a cute double meaning (*mi rincón* means "my corner"). Along with the photographs, you'll find a few unique items, including ornaments, decorative art, and souvenirs. Open daily 11 AM–6 PM. $–$$$.

Olé

787-724-2445

105 Fortaleza Street, Old San Juan

Located in the heart of Old San Juan's main shopping strip, Olé offers a hodgepodge of old photographs, miniature carvings of saints and the three kings, Peruvian Christmas ornaments, handmade puppets, and other arts and crafts. But the main draw is the wonderful collection of Panama hats that sell for as little as $20 or as much as $1,000, depending on the quality of the weave. Once you've found the hat style that best fits you, you can hang back while one of the friendly staff fits the hat to your head and finishes it off with a decorative band of your choosing. Open Monday through Saturday 10 AM–6 PM, Sunday 10 AM–5 PM. $–$$$$.

The Pampered Pet

787-721-1370

203 San Justo Street, Old San Juan

If you want to buy your pet a souvenir, head straight to the Pampered Pet, which stocks everything from treats to fancy beds. The store's two- and four-legged staff are excellent (Calypso, the black lab, is a bit lazy, however). The only pet store in Old San Juan has pioneered teaching proper pet care in the city for 18 years. Owner Wilma Valle has been on TV

Mi Rincón

and in the media numerous times, and has done her part to ensure animals are well treated and integrated into the family. The Pampered Pet also has live animals ready for adoption, and they'll get any breed you want. The store takes care of transportation (to the U.S. mainland) and all the necessary details to make sure your newest best friend reaches you safely. Open Monday through Saturday 10 AM–6 PM, Sunday 11 AM–5 PM. $–$$$.

Patchouli
787-725-3447
152 Cristo Street, Old San Juan

Patchouli prides itself on being a locally owned and run souvenir store featuring nothing but Puerto Rican artists. Their products include a range of ceramic vases and candleholders depicting Old San Juan's buildings, Puerto Rican music, ethnic clothing, and my favorite, back massagers that double as turtle figurines. You can also create your own jewelry and buy a stuffed toy for the kids. Open daily 10 AM–6 PM. $–$$$.

Santos *at Siena Art Gallery*

Puerto Rican Art & Crafts
787-725-5596
www.puertoricanart-crafts.com
204 Fortaleza Street, Old San Juan

True to its name, you'll find a little bit of everything Puerto Rican at this store. The ceramics, masks, artwork, jewelry, *santos,* and wall hangings are all handmade on the island. You can also buy snacks, condiments, and coffee. Open Monday through Saturday 9:30 AM–6 PM, Sunday noon–to 5 PM. $–$$$.

Siena Art Gallery
787-724-7223
www.sienaartgallery.com
253 San Francisco Street, Old San Juan

While Siena is primarily an art gallery, I've listed it here for the wonderful collection of *santos* (carved saints) the store has for sale. These are more detailed and intricate than the ones you'll find in most other stores, and each is marked with the name and region of the artisan who created them. You'll pay more for these pieces, but the workmanship is easily worth more. Open Monday through Saturday 10 AM–7 PM, Sunday noon–5 PM. $$–$$$$.

FOOD PURVEYORS, LIQUOR & CIGARS

Casa Don Q

787-977-1720
Ochoa Building #500, in front of Pier 1, Old San Juan

This small museum and store has photographs and memorabilia, and a beautiful display of everything to do with Don Q rum and the Serrallés Distillery, where the magic started. Most people ignore all this and head straight to the onsite bar for a free sample of a Don Q rum variety. You can buy bottles of everything under the Don Q brand, including clear Don Q Cristal, the most popular drink on the island, and Don Q Gran Añejo, one of the top five aged rums in the world. Open in high season Monday through Wednesday 11 AM–8 PM, Friday through Sunday 9 AM–6 PM. In low season, open daily except Thursday 9 AM–6 PM. Free–$$.

The Cigar House at The Doll House

787-723-5223; 787-725-9604
www.thecigarhousepr.com
255 and 258 Fortaleza Street, Old San Juan

It's hard to imagine two more incongruous partners than cigars and dolls, but there it is. Actually, the odd name originates with the dolls once sold here, but the store is better known these days for having the largest selection of cigars in Puerto Rico. Cigar aficionados will love the 500-square-foot, walk-in humidor, and the global variety, which includes Padron Anniversary 1926, MonteCristo, Romeo y Julieta, and the most expensive, El Zino Platinum Crown Series. (They're also the exclusive retailer for Davidoff on the island.) In addition to cigars and cigar accessories, the store sells hats, souvenirs, and novelties. Open daily 9:30 AM–6:30 PM. $–$$$.

Casa Don Q

"Romantic Sunsets" is a good name for this free weekly event, which takes place against the backdrop of the city's ancient walls and San Juan Bay. As the sun sets on the last day of each week, Paseo La Princesa comes alive with strolling couples, families, and tourists out to breathe in the just-right ocean breeze. Stalls line the road, selling food, drinks, and arts and crafts. At the end of the promenade, like a masterpiece in a museum gallery, stands the majestic *Raíces* fountain, with little kids frolicking in its spraying waters. A stage with musical shows draws a crowd, and couples dance in the night air to the sound of a live band. This is a wonderful moment to steal a little pocket of time with a loved one. If you've built up an appetite, I recommend the snacks sold at the last kiosk on the left before the fountain. Also, keep an eye out for the guy selling fresh oranges, which are peeled and cored, making them easy to eat. 5:30—7 PM. Free.

La Casita Festival
Every Saturday
Plaza de la Dársena

Not quite a full-blown festival, this is nonetheless a nice way to hear live music for free. Held in the afternoon, it can be a break from all the culture you've been soaking in. From here, you can meander down the Paseo La Princesa or head up to Fortaleza Street for dinner. Considering its location directly on the docks, it also provides a musical farewell for cruise ship passengers in town just for the day. 5:30 —7 PM. Free.

Día de Los Tres Reyes (Three Kings Day)
January 6
Throughout the city and Puerto Rico

December 25 may be the most celebrated holiday in the Catholic world, but Puerto Ricans give Christmas stiff competition with their reverence for Three Kings Day. The three kings are important icons here, and their place in society goes so far as to supplant Christmas as the time-honored gift-giving day. Gifts are traditionally exchanged on January 6, the day the three kings arrived to visit Jesus; and Puerto Ricans honor the occasion with festivals, music, and dancing. The activities culminate in a procession depicting the three wise men riding camels into Old San Juan. If you've brought the family, grab the kids and run to La Fortaleza, the governor's mansion, where free gifts are handed out to children throughout the day. Free.

Fiestas de San Juan Bautista
Third week of June
Parades and processions throughout the city

The Fiestas de San Juan Bautista (Festivals of Saint John the Baptist) take place each year in June, culminating on June 23. They are a celebration in honor of the city's patron saint, but they're also an occasion when religion takes a back seat to partying. The event is popular among Sanjuaneros because it's the only time crowds can go to the beach at night in a safe environment. Once they reach the sea, revelers perform "cleansing" rituals, which consist mainly of jumping backward into the water seven times, for good luck. Sanjuaneros joke that each jump should be followed by a beer. Free.

Fiestas de San Sebastián (Festivals of Saint Sebastian)
January 19–21
San Sebastián Street, Old San Juan

Perhaps the biggest party in all of San Juan takes place during the Fiestas de San Sebastián. This is another event in which religious fervor is doused by celebrations, revelry, arts and crafts shows, stalls, massive crowds, and alcohol. Sebastián Street gets jam-packed, and the carnival atmosphere is a major attraction for San Puerto Ricans and tourists. Free.

LeLoLai Festival
787-721-2400
www.gotopuertorico.com
Throughout the year
Various venues in Old San Juan

Developed by the Puerto Ricon Tourism Company, the LeLoLai Festival is a year-round program designed to allow visitors to experience Puerto Rican culture, music, and dance. This colorful, vibrant, and entertaining event consists of weekly shows held throughout San Juan that showcase the Spanish, Indian, and African heritage of the people. The name "LeLoLai" is derived from the sound made by the guitar and the *cuatro,* a smaller, local cousin of the guitar. $.

Noches de Galerías (Night of the Galleries)
First Tuesday of every month, February through May and September through December
787-723-7080
Various galleries in Old San Juan

For art loves, this is a can't-miss experience. Noche de Galerías is a special event designed to promote the arts in Puerto Rico. About 20 galleries and museums throughout Old San Juan throw open their doors in the evening. Visitors out for an evening stroll can enjoy a free glass of wine as they explore Puerto Rico's best art displays. While you're at it, you might be further entertained by traveling minstrels, who come out to add some extra flavor to the goings-on. An extremely popular event, it's a delightful way to spend an evening in the old city. What makes it even more fun is that after the galleries close, people tend to stay out to go barhopping and club hopping. 6–9 PM. Free.

Panza Truffle Festival
November–December
787-724-7722
At Panza restaurant, 329 Recinto Sur Street, Old San Juan

A new arrival to the gastronomic calendar of events, the truffle festival brings the Piedmont tradition to Puerto Rico. White truffles from Alba, among the most highly prized foods in the world, are featured in a menu tailored to bring out their rich flavors. Each dish is paired with an excellent wine. At $250 per head, the cost might seem exorbitant; but consider that 1.2 kilograms of the fungi recently sold for more than $100,000 in Hong Kong. The menu changes every year, but one inaugural festival included an herbed cheese

and egg soufflé with sliced white truffles and homemade egg *tagliolini* tossed in truffle butter sauce and served with sliced white truffles. White truffles are considered by some
to be the food of the gods, and this event is as unique as it is decadent. Reservations
required. $$$$.

SoFo Culinary Festival
Held in June and November–December each year
Fortaleza Street, Old San Juan

So-Fo (South Fortaleza) is the tongue-in-cheek name for the trendy cluster of restaurants
on the southern end of Fortaleza Street. Exactly where SoFo begins seems to be a matter of
opinion, but twice a year (typically in June, and November through December) its culinary
might is celebrated with the wonderful SoFo Culinary Festival. Fortaleza Street is closed off
and converted into a promenade, and participating restaurants set up tables, food displays,
and demonstrations outside. (At press time, the Parrot Club aimed to produce over 1,000
mojitos in one hour for the upcoming festival.) It's a fun way to sample different foods from
some of Puerto Rico's best restaurants while enjoying a festive outdoor atmosphere. The
event typically takes place over several days from 6–11 PM. Free.

Teatro de los Niños (Children's Theater)
Third Sunday of each month
Paseo La Princesa

As you can see, Paseo La Princesa is a popular destination. Many mini-fêtes and events
take place here throughout the year, and the cutest of them might well be the Children's
Theater. Held in the afternoon, the theater features games, live music, clowns, puppet
shows, and other delights for kids and the kid in all of us. 4–5 PM. Free.

5

From Puerta de Tierra to Isla Verde

White Beaches and Blackjack

If Old San Juan is the cultural and historical center of the island, the stretch of beachfront that begins in Puerta de Tierra and ends in Isla Verde is home to the island's biggest, flashiest resorts, coziest oceanside inns, and most sought-after boutique hotels. The neighborhoods that invite you to gamble in the hotels and gambol in the water are Puerta de Tierra, Condado, Ocean Park, Punta Las Marías, and Isla Verde. Located eastward from the old city, they bring a different personality and appeal to San Juan.

The coast along Puerta de Tierra

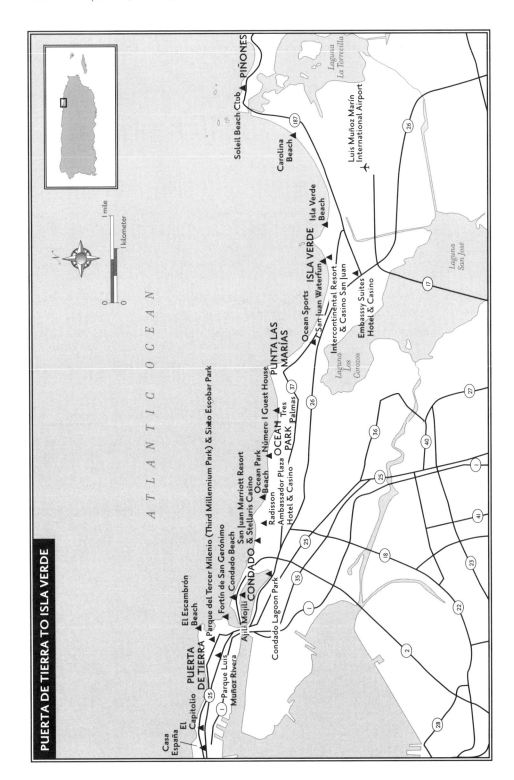

PUERTA DE TIERRA TO ISLA VERDE

ATLANTIC OCEAN

Casa
España
El
Capitolio
PUERTA
DE TIERRA
Parque Luis
Muñoz Rivera
El Escambrón
Beach
Parque del Tercer Milenio (Third Millennium Park) & Sixto Escobar Park
Fortín de San Gerónimo
Condado Beach
Aiti Mojili
CONDADO
San Juan Marriott Resort
& Stellaris Casino
Ocean Park
Beach
Radisson
Ambassador Plaza
Hotel & Casino
Condado Lagoon Park
Número I Guest House
OCEAN
PARK
Tres
Palmas
PUNTA LAS
MARIAS
Ocean Sports
San Juan Waterfun
ISLA VERDE
Isla Verde
Beach
Carolina
Beach
Soleil Beach Club
PIÑONES
Luis Muñoz Marín
International Airport
Intercontinental Resort
& Casino San Juan
Embasssy Suites
Hotel & Casino
Laguna
Los
Corozos
Laguna
San José
Laguna
La Torrecilla
Laguna

25
1
25
35
1
25
26
37
36
40
25
18
1
41
23
22
2
28
187
26
17
27

PUERTA DE TIERRA—THE GATEWAY

Puerta de Tierra (literally "Earth Gate") is the small strip of land that connects the old city to the rest of the island and kicks off the resort strip. This is also the seat of Puerto Rico's government. El Capitolio—where Puerto Rico's Senate and House of Representatives meet—the Supreme Court, and the offices of the U.S. Navy and Coast Guard are located here. Most of these buildings are closed to the public, but El Capitolio is open for tours. Puerta de Tierra is also a residential community with a much less glamorous history than that of Old San Juan.

It's ironic that today Puerta de Tierra is home to the island's government, serene parks, and landmark hotels. For hundreds of years, it was far from a destination of choice for

wealthy and influential Puerto Ricans. It used to be a slum located just beyond the Santiago Gate (the only gate that faced the land to the east, hence "Earth Gate") that led into the walled city. Consisting of mainly non-European immigrants and former slaves, Puerta de Tierra was an ostracized community, physically and economically cut off from Old San Juan. While the area was critical to the defense of the city, Puerta de Tierra remained a tiny, impoverished settlement until the walls came down and the city expanded in the latter half of the 19th century. Only in the last 100 years has major development elevated the neighborhood to its present status.

With the expansion of government facilities into the area in the 1920s came the construction of parks and, a few decades later, a new concept in urban planning: the residential condominium. Two of San Juan's landmark hotels—the Normandie and the Caribe Hilton—moved in at this time and immediately made the area more attractive to tourists. Puerta de Tierra was helped greatly by its most marketable asset: El Escambrón, one of the best beaches on the main island of Puerto Rico.

Puerta de Tierra has come a long way. Still, hotels and beaches aside, it's a working-class neighborhood far from the tourist trail, and not the best place to be after dark. Yet its story is that of the underdog who overcame all obstacles.

LODGING

Caribe Hilton

1-877-GO-HILTON; 787-721-0303
http://hiltoncaribbean.com/sanjuan
Los Rosales Street, San Geronimo Grounds,
Puerta de Tierra, San Juan 00901

Although its location places you within easy reach of the wonders of Old San Juan and the beaches of Condado and Isla Verde, the Caribe Hilton does its very best to tempt you into staying put. This big hotel dominates the tip of Puerta de Tierra and offers its guests an array of dining and entertainment activities. It is the only hotel in Puerto Rico with a private beach, which overlooks El Escambrón Balneario. Between the beach and the open-air lobby is a sprawling, multilevel swimming pool with a terrific poolside bar. A tropical garden and bird sanctuary are also on the premises. After a game of tennis on a lighted court, you can relax at Olas Spa and Health Club. The hotel has six full-service restaurants and a nightclub-bar-lounge. A shopping arcade lines one wall of the lobby.

The rooms are furnished in a tropical theme, with prices depending on size and view. For big spenders, luxury villas offer one- and two-bedroom suites with terrace, full kitchen, and views of the ocean, Condado Lagoon, and San Gerónimo fort. A $50 day pass is available for nonguests who want to enjoy the hotel's facilities. $–$$$$.

Normandie Hotel

787-729-2929
www.normandiepr.com
499 W. Muñoz Rivera Avenue, Puerta de Tierra, San Juan 00901

The story of the Normandie is almost as cool as its design. Built in 1942 to resemble an ocean liner, the hotel was a labor of love built by Puerto Rican–born engineer Félix Benítez Rexach for his wife, Lucienne (Moineau) Dhotelle. The couple met aboard the SS Normandie, en route from France to New York City, and fell in love during the voyage. Years later, when the ship sank, Rexach decided to build a hotel that resembled the Normandie as a monument to his love. He did his job well, and today the

The lobby at the Normandie Hotel

Normandie Hotel stands alone, a master-piece of the art deco style, rising gracefully into the sky. Its interior carries through the nautical theme with porthole-style win-dows; an angular, elongated lobby floor unlike that in any other hotel; and a "prow," which houses the popular N Lounge. The Normandie also boasts a full-service spa, 24-hour gym, 24-hour lobby bar, business center, and small art gallery, as well as a gift shop. Guests also have immediate access to the white sands and waters of El Escambrón. Its 174 rooms have a modern and clean design, and the Normandie offers 24-hour in-room food and beverage serv-ice. Recently bought by the Ritz-Carlton group, the Normandie will be revamped and spruced up but will retain its name and its romantic history. $$–$$$.

DINING

Atlántico Pool Bar & Grill

787-721-0303, ext. 6207
http://hiltoncaribbean.com/sanjuan
At the Caribe Hilton, Los Rosales Street, San Geronimo Grounds, Puerta de Tierra, San Juan

Atlántico is one of the best poolside lunch spots you'll find in San Juan. The gorgeous, meandering pool laps against one of two bars where you can get a variety of tropical drinks from bartenders juggling bottles à la "Cocktail." One of these libation artists, Hiram Avila, won the gold medal in the 2006 Bacardi Grand Prix in Italy for his Caribbean Melon (a mixture of Bacardi rums, and pomegranate and watermelon juices). So you know these guys know what they're doing. The fare is basic (sand-wiches, burgers, corn *surullitos*) and the setting very casual. At Atlántico, it's all about the location, the sun, and the occa-sional iguana relaxing with the guests. Open Sunday through Thursday 10 AM–6 PM, Friday and Saturday 10 AM–7 PM. During high season, the pool bar stays open until 9 PM. $–$$.

Atlántico Pool Bar & Grill at the Caribe Hilton

El Charro
787-724-6148
402 San Agustín Street, Puerta de Tierra, San Juan

You won't find El Charro in too many travel books. This undiscovered, quaint little Mexican restaurant is just a short taxi ride from the Caribe Hilton and Normandie hotels, and it's a great change of pace from more touristy venues. This is an authentic Mexican restaurant, not a Tex-Mex joint. The *refritos* (refried beans) are homemade and delicious; the tacos are served traditionally, on a round, open tortilla; the burros are tasty and plump. The menu is all in Spanish, but those familiar with fajitas, tacos, and margaritas will have no problem navigating through it, and the friendly staff, led by owner Keyla de Angeles, is happy to assist. El Charro is a slice of local life, catering primarily to local patrons and members of the Senate and House of Representatives, out for drinks and a hearty meal after a long session. The decor is funky, rustic, and fun. Check out the large altar to the Virgin Mary, hanging above the staircase, and the arts and crafts on the walls. Open Monday 11:30 AM–3 PM, Tuesday through Thursday 11:30 AM–9 PM, and Friday 11:30 AM–midnight. Closed on weekends. $.

El Escambrón Beach Club Restaurant
www.escambron.com
787-724-3344
In Parque Nacional del Tercer Milenio (Third Millennium Park), off Highway 25, Puerta de Tierra, San Juan

El Escambrón Beach Club is a true beachfront restaurant that serves fresh seafood, great *mofongos,* and steaks. It's within walking distance from the Caribe and Normandie hotels, and a perfect lunch or dinner spot if you're spending the day at the beach. The club also hosts weddings and meetings. Open Monday through

Thursday 11:30 AM–10 PM, Friday and Saturday 11 AM–11 PM, and Sunday 11 AM–10 PM. $$.

El Hamburger
787-721-4269
402 Muñoz Rivera Avenue, Puerta de Tierra, San Juan

Just east from El Capitolio is a canteenlike shack with zero decor, and, of course, hamburgers at their grilled best. The patties are small in diameter but thick and juicy. It's a fun, noisy place to hang with the locals late into the night, and it's an escape from hotel restaurants if you need a break from fancier menus (and prices). Open daily 11 AM–12:15 AM, and until 3 AM on Saturday. $.

Madrid–San Juan
787-729-7171
http://hiltoncaribbean.com/sanjuan
At the Caribe Hilton, Los Rosales Street, San Geronimo Grounds, Puerta de Tierra, San Juan

While other Spanish restaurants tend to keep their menus close to the mother country, Madrid–San Juan celebrates the culinary delights of both cultures. With its hanging hams, rather formal dining room, and colorful artwork, this is one of the fanciest restaurants in Puerta de Tierra. The tapas menu is huge and includes a few local dishes like *bacalaitos* (cod fritters) and conch salad. There's live Sevillana dancing on Tuesday night, from 8 to 10 PM, and live music Wednesday through Saturday from 6:30 PM to closing. Open Sunday through Thursday noon to midnight, Friday noon–1 AM, and Saturday 6 PM–1 AM. $$$–$$$$.

Palmeras
787-721-0303
http://hiltoncaribbean.com/sanjuan
At the Caribe Hilton, Los Rosales Street, San Geronimo Grounds, Puerta de Tierra, San Juan

The Caribe Hilton's flagship restaurant, Palmeras is known for a diverse menu that keeps things new. Every night features a different theme, and the Friday-night seafood buffet is a local favorite for its all-you-can-eat crab legs, oysters, mussels, and grilled-before-your-eyes fish filets, jumbo shrimp, and chunks of lobster tail. The restaurant has a large dining space with poolside views and an open kitchen station staffed with a team of chefs, where the dinner specials and brunch take center stage. The decor changes with the menu, carrying through the theme of the evening. Sunday brunch at Palmeras is a family event, and Sanjuaneros arrive early to take care of the spit-roasted *lechón a la barra* (roast pig) that awaits them in the kitchen station, surrounded by smiling chefs, and the *frituras* station. Add the extensive salad bar and dessert station that accompanies each buffet; the friendly, attentive staff; and the personal touches Palmeras provides (a free cake is served for birthdays

Iguana at the Caribe Hilton

and other special events), and it's small wonder that Palmeras has a loyal following. Open daily 6 AM–11 PM. $$–$$$$.

ATTRACTIONS, PARKS & RECREATION

El Escambrón

The biggest attraction in Puerta de Tierra is the *balneario* El Escambrón. This public beach has lifeguards, parking, a nearby restaurant, and, more important, calm, clean waters that have earned it the prestigious "Blue Flag" status. The voluntary Blue Flag program rewards the high quality of a beach's water, safety, and sanitary services, and environmental management and education. El Escambrón is the closest beach to Old San Juan and can get very busy on the weekends. $ (for parking).

Fortín San Gerónimo

This small defensive battery located near the Caribe Hilton once protected San Juan from land attacks. It was completed in 1788 and immediately tested in 1797 when the British invaded. Heavily battered, it was rebuilt and served as a military post into the 20th century. It has fallen into disrepair, but there are plans to renovate the landmark. At press time, its interior was closed to the public; but you can walk up to the fort and take in great views of Condado across San Juan Bay.

El Escambrón

Parque Nacional Muñoz Rivera
787-449-5672
www.parquesnacionalespr.com/munoz_rivera_par.asp
Avenida Ponce de León, Puerta de Tierra, San Juan

This park (not to be confused with Parque Nacional Luis Muñoz Marín, which is miles away) is a broad, rectangular space where people come to picnic, jog, and take the kids to the playground. Two other parks are adjacent to this one: **Parque Nacional del Tercer Milenio** and **Parque Sixto Escobar,** the stadium that hosted the Pan-American Games in 1979. Open 24 hours. Free.

CULTURE

El Capitolio, the seat of Puerto Rico's government

El Capitolio (The Capitol)
787-721-6040
Avenida Ponce de León, Puerta de Tierra, San Juan

El Capitolio is the seat of the government of Puerto Rico. Constructed in the 1920s, the building, with its great dome, was modeled after its larger cousin in Washington, DC. The Senate and the House of Representatives meet here during the week. The giant rotunda features the original Constitution of Puerto Rico, ratified in 1952, and the island's coat of arms. This isn't a "must-see" stop during your first visit to Puerto Rico, but it's a beautiful building. Located just outside Old San Juan, it offers great views of the city, Castillo de San Cristóbal, and the ocean. Free tours are offered by appointment.

La Casa de España

787-724-1044
Avenida Ponce de León, Puerta de Tierra, San Juan

One of the most breathtaking structures not just in Puerta de Tierra, but in all of San Juan, La Casa de España evokes the majesty of Spanish architecture. Built in 1932 as a private club and civic center, the building now has a restaurant and hosts cultural events throughout the year that allow you a glimpse of its ornate Andalusian patios, graceful arches, and fountains. The club also hosts Flamenco and Sevillana dance classes twice a week. You have to pay one month's dues to participate, but as these are only $20 and $50, respectively (for as many classes as you want for that month), the price of admission is worthwhile. The classes are two hours long, and are held Monday and Wednesday from 6:30 to 8:30 PM. $$–$$$.

NIGHTLIFE

N Lounge

787-729-2929
www.normandiepr.com
499 W. Muñoz Rivera Avenue, San Juan

Located on the "prow" of the Normandie Hotel, the N Lounge is near the top of the list of places to hang out at night in San Juan. The lounge emulates the rest of the hotel in its design and theme, the decor predominantly white and nautical, following the curved arc of the building (the outdoor terrace is a delight). There are resident and guest DJs. It's not a large space, and it can get packed on weekends. Open Monday through Saturday 6 PM–2 AM.

Oasis

787-721-0303
http://hiltoncaribbean.com/sanjuan
At the Caribe Hilton, Los Rosales Street, San Geronimo Grounds, San Juan

Continue past the reception desk at the Caribe Hilton and you'll reach Oasis, a spacious bar and lounge with a cool, calm atmosphere. By lounge standards, Oasis is practically cavernous, and the soaring arc of windowed wall overlooking the pool and the ocean augments the illusion of open space. There's live music every night, but the bar is busiest, and most fun, during weekends. It's also a great place to watch your favorite sports events, with flat panel screens throughout the bar providing a good view no matter where you sit. You can order lunch and dinner as well at the bar. Open Sunday through Thursday, noon–1 AM, Friday and Saturday noon–3 AM. $.

WEEKLY & ANNUAL EVENTS

Wine Festival
April–May
787-721-6040
At Casa de España, Avenida Ponce de León, San Juan

There are three reasons to take part in this annual celebration of wine. The first is the chance to visit Casa de España, an architectural treasure of a building (see page 137). The second, of course, is to enjoy a wide selection of wines. Finally, proceeds go to the upkeep and maintenance of the facility. $$$.

CONDADO—CHIC BOUTIQUES AND FANCY TREATS

Cross the Dos Hermanos bridge from Puerta de Tierra and you'll find yourself on Ashford Avenue, the main thoroughfare that runs through Condado. This is the fashionable district of San Juan. Condado (which means "county") is known for its high-end boutiques. Condado Lagoon and the Atlantic Ocean surround a thin peninsula dominated by hotels and luxury condominiums. The neighborhood is home to many San Juan celebrities and millionaires and, in general, caters to a more upscale clientele than the rest of the island. With its beachfront condos and art deco architecture, it has often been compared to Miami's South Beach (one building even goes so far as to bear the name *Miami*).

Condado has been linked to wealth for over a century but has in the last decade experienced a decline in popularity and pizzazz. Millionaires built homes here in the early 1900s (among them the Vanderbilts). In the 1950s, government-sponsored resort hotels began popping up in the neighborhood, and Condado enjoyed a glitzy reputation as Puerto Rico's premier tourist district. Those days have come and gone, but private business and government have joined forces to usher in a rebirth of Condado. Multimillion-dollar restorations of many top hotels in the area (among them the long-defunct La Concha and Vanderbilt) have been carried out for close to a decade. Along with refurbishments and updates to hotels, a general cleanup of the area is underway to reaffirm Condado's reputation as a playground for the wealthy. It's also the safest neighborhood in the city.

Because of its long-standing social status, Condado is one of few areas in all of Puerto Rico where you may encounter snooty looks from the staff at high-end, and even not-so-high-end, boutiques. You don't have to pay top dollar to stay here, however. Some hotels are pricey, but there is also a full range of moderately priced ones, with some true bargains in the mix. Many of these hotels are steps from Condado Beach, so it's no surprise that tourists still love this part of the island. A large stretch of beach is nearby, casinos abound, and Old San Juan is a short cab ride away. In addition to the shops, the neighborhood has a great selection and variety of restaurants.

LODGING

Acacia Seaside Inn

1-800-946-3244; 787-727-4153
www.acaciaseasideinn.com
Eight Taft Street, Condado, San Juan 00911

Sister to the acclaimed At Wind Chimes Inn and closely following its model, Acacia is a new arrival to the Condado scene. The finishing touches on this three-story hotel are currently being added, and at press time it was scheduled to be fully operational sometime in 2007. The rooms and suites are pleasant and light, and most have balconies with partial views of Condado Beach, which is just steps away. The hotel also has a pool and rooftop terrace, and guests have full access to all At Wind Chimes Inn amenities, only a half block away. Like its sister hotel, Acacia is a great bang for your buck. $–$$.

At Wind Chimes Inn

1-800-WINDCHIMES; 787-727-4153
www.atwindchimesinn.com
1750 McLeary Avenue, Condado, San Juan 00911

Sculpture on Ashford Avenue

The lounge area in Wind Chimes Inn

Hands down my favorite place to stay in Condado, At Wind Chimes Inn is an intimate refuge that's small in size but big on charm. Removed from the bustle of Ashford Avenue, the inn is a beautifully restored Colonial Spanish villa, its white walls, terra-cotta tiles and floors, and serene location instantly inviting. Inside, the friendly staff go out of their way to assist you. The 22 rooms have 10-foot ceilings, air-conditioning, and cable TV, and some come with a kitchenette. The hotel has a small pool with a natural rock waterfall, and, hidden away at the back, a "tiki boat bar" that serves breakfast, lunch, and light dinners, as well as a mean sangria. You can sit at the bar or walk up the stairs to relax in the pleasant lounge. The beach is only a block away; also close by is a bus stop that will take you to Old San Juan for less than a dollar. For the amenities, this is one of the best bargains you'll find. $–$$.

El Canario Inn
787-722-3861
www.canariohotels.com
1317 Ashford Avenue, Condado, San Juan
00907

One of a trio of hotels under the El Canario banner (El Canario by the Lagoon and El Canario are also in Condado), this moderately priced hotel gets the nod over the other two. Service is spotty, as are the opinions of other guests (one disgruntled visitor proclaimed the place "a dump"), but you do get a complimentary breakfast and a fashionable neighborhood at a budget rate. $–$$.

Casa del Caribe
1-877-722-7139; 787-722-7139
www.casadelcaribe.net
57 Caribe Street, Condado, San Juan 00907

Those on a budget should strongly consider Casa del Caribe if they plan to stay in

Condado. Located a block from the Stellaris Casino at the Marriott, a great stretch of beach, and a neighborhood park, it's an ideally situated bed & breakfast inn that lets you enjoy the best of Condado without paying resort hotel prices. Boutiques and restaurants are a short walk away. The rooms are basic but spacious, air-conditioned, and pleasant, and the atmosphere is casual and friendly. Another rarity for Condado: free parking (which can be an adventure). $.

Condado Plaza Hotel & Casino
1-866-317-8934; 787-721-1000
www.condadoplaza.com
999 Ashford Avenue, Condado, San Juan 00907

The first hotel you'll come across as you enter Condado is one of the largest ocean-front properties in the area. It's also among the hotels in San Juan undergoing extensive remodeling and upgrading of the lobby, restaurants, shops, and guest rooms. The rooms, especially, have been transformed from the typical Caribbean look to a chic, richly colored decor that is modern and eye-catching. Many have private balconies, and the tower rooms have wonderful views of the old city, the ocean, and Condado Lagoon. The hotel also has a large ocean-front pool, tennis courts, and a popular casino. $$–$$$$.

Hotel El Portal
787-721-9010
www.hotelelportal.com
76 Condado Avenue, Condado, San Juan 00907

Closer to Baldorioty de Castro Avenue, the expressway leading to San Juan, than to the beach, El Portal is removed—in more ways than one—from the bustle and glamour of Ashford Avenue. The decor and style of the hotel won't blow you away, but maybe the budget prices will. Rooms are basic but have all the necessary amenities; your stay comes with a complimentary continental breakfast; and the sundeck provides wonderful views of Condado Lagoon. $.

San Juan Marriott Hotel & Stellaris Casino
1-800-464-5005; 787-722-7000
www.marriott.com
1309 Ashford Avenue, Condado, San Juan 00907

The Stellaris Casino is one of the most popular casinos on the island. The hotel's large, inviting pool, set among palm trees, is fantastic and leads directly to one of the best stretches of beach in Condado. And the Marriott is joining the renovation revolution, remodeling its rooms to include flat-screen TVs, the "Marriott Revive" bedding package, and new decor that retains a Caribbean theme. With over 500 rooms and more than 10,000 feet of meeting space, it's an easy-to-spot landmark. $$–$$$$.

Radisson Ambassador Plaza Hotel & Casino San Juan
1-888-201-1718; 787 721-7300
www.radisson.com/sanjuanpr_ambassador
1369 Ashford Avenue, Condado, San Juan 00907

Flashy, this isn't. The Radisson Ambassador has spacious rooms with balconies and all the amenities of a large, modern hotel. The decor is nothing to rave about, and there are certainly better restaurant options outside the hotel. The Radisson's best draws are probably the rooftop pool and the large casino. $$–$$$.

DINING

Ajili Mojili
787-725-9195
1006 Ashford Avenue, Condado, San Juan

Just the name tickles the tongue, doesn't it? Ajili Mojili, an institution in Condado, is a

Ajili Mojili

beautifully decorated, ideally situated restaurant by the sea. From the waiters, clad in suspenders and sombreros, to the indoor patio with its faux terra-cotta tiled roof, to the can't-miss, artfully prepared food, this is a wonderful Puerto Rican experience. The food celebrates everything criollo: Local ingredients rule in the kitchen, and local specialties take on a sophisticated edge. Dishes like *mofongos rellenos* (available with succulent skirt steak, shrimp, roast pork, and other fillings), plantain-breaded shrimp, *tortilla cuchi-cuchi* (a crunchy, munchy, garlicky mix of halibut, yucca, and plantain), and an assortment of fritters all celebrate the island's culinary roots. The restaurant leaves Puerto Rico for its wine, offering an extensive international selection, and has a few signature cocktails (including all manner of flavored *mojitos*). For a romantic date, a special occasion, or simply a lovely night out, Ajili Mojili offers among the best cuisine, atmosphere, and service on the island. Open daily noon–3 PM (Friday and Sunday until 4 PM) for lunch; open Monday through Friday 6–10 PM, and Saturday and Sunday 6–11 PM, for dinner. $$$–$$$$.

Bangkok Bombay

787-721-1470
58 Caribe Street, Condado, San Juan

I'm usually wary of kitchens that specialize in two different cuisines; fortunately, I came here anyway. One of the newest restaurants in Condado, Bangkok Bombay won't stay quiet for long. The pairing works because the restaurant offers distinct Thai and Indian menus rather than exploring a fusion of the two. The classic Tom Yum Goong, for example, doesn't hold back on the chili peppers; and the peanut-heavy Massaman Curry is the real thing. On the Indian side, try the excellent Tikka Masala or Tandoori Lamb Chops. The decor is more Thai than Indian; it's tasteful and romantic, with statues adorning the walls, a very pleasant entrance and seating area, and oil-lit lamps. On a busy night, you'll hear the continuous sizzle and pop of the still-flambéing dishes float past. Those with a sweet tooth can begin their meal with a B&B martini (served with a lychee) or end it with a warm, syrupy Gulab Jamun. If you want a change, this is an excellent, and authentic, departure from the Caribbean. Open for lunch Monday through Friday noon–3 PM; open for dinner Monday through Thursday 6–10 PM, Friday 6–11 PM, Saturday 5–11 PM, and Sunday noon–10 PM. $$–$$$.

Cielito Lindo

787-723-5597
1108 Magdalena Avenue, Condado, San Juan

Cielito Lindo has many locals screaming "Olé!" as they quaff strong margaritas and feast on authentic Mexican fare like mole, cheese and chicken enchiladas and, of course, tacos galore. The decor is that of a humble Mexican cantina, and in fancy Condado, Cielito Lindo is beloved all the more for its low-key pleasantry. Open Tuesday through Thursday 11 AM–8:30 PM, Friday and Saturday 11 AM–10 PM. $$.

East

787-721-8883
At Hotel El Portal, 76 Condado Avenue, Condado, San Juan

The line of cars cramming into the Hotel El Portal (off Ashford Avenue) are not all for the hotel; a healthy majority are waiting for the valet at East to relieve them of their vehicles so they can go enjoy some of the best sushi in the city. East sticks to the basics and doesn't fiddle around too much with the Caribbean theme (okay, so there is a coconut eel roll, but that's it, really). All the usual suspects are on the menu, along with inventive rolls. The decor and service are typical of Japanese restaurants—a minimum of flair, a sushi bar at one end, and a prompt, attentive staff. Lunch or dinner, it gets packed fast. Open Monday through Friday noon–3 PM for lunch, 5–11:30 PM for dinner, and Saturday and Sunday 1–11:30 PM. $$.

La Patisserie de France
787-728-5508
1504 Ashford Avenue, Condado, San Juan

Amid all the fancy restaurants and rich food, it's good to know there's a place to go for a quick breakfast (croissants, pastries, and coffee) or a light lunch (salads and sandwiches). La Patisserie is nothing special—but sometimes, that's exactly what you need. Open Monday through Thursday and Sunday 7 AM–7 PM, Friday and Saturday 7 AM–9 PM. $.

Ramiro's
787-721-9049
http://netdial.caribe.net/~ramiros
1106 Magdalena Avenue, Condado, San Juan

Ramiro's is beyond an institution in Puerto Rico. Talk to anyone, from seasoned tourists to the oldest families, and they will tell you about their most recent visit to the restaurant (I don't say "last" because most come back for more). The food is best described as inventive Puerto Rican and Spanish. Among the favorites on the menu are the paillard of lamb with spiced barbe-cue and guava sauce, and the fish, which is bought fresh every day. The Ramiro brothers have served as chefs at dinners for the king and queen of Spain, and you might feel a bit royal, too, as you leave their restaurant. Open for lunch Monday through Friday noon–3 PM, Sunday until 3:30 PM; open for dinner Monday through Thursday 6:30–10 PM, Friday and Saturday 6:30–11 PM, and Sunday 6–10 PM. $$$–$$$$.

Urdin
787-724-0420
1105 Magdalena Avenue, Condado, San Juan

This is one of my favorite dining spots in Condado, not just for its delicious, inventive food, but for the quiet, intimate charm of the restaurant. There's a little bit of funk and a little bit of flash in Urdin, a small restaurant tucked amid a cluster of well-known local eateries. The menu might be best described as "Latin fine dining," but Urdin is a departure from *mofongos* and *arroz con pollo.* Try the halibut over a banana chutney and white wine sauce, or the duck cooked two ways (roasted in a tamarind jus and wrapped in a crepe), to get an idea of how Urdin plays with local ingredients to create something unique. For dessert, the *crema catalana* (the Spanish version of crème brûlée), served in an iced coconut shell, is fantastic. Open Monday through Saturday noon–3 AM, Sunday from noon to midnight. $$–$$$.

YerbaBuena
787-721-5700
www.yerbabuenapr.com
1350 Ashford Avenue, Condado, San Juan

If you want a throwback to how Condado used to be at its hippest, hoppingest zenith, salsa your way to YerbaBuena, a tribute to Cuba and early South Beach. The food is a blend of tasty, dressed-up Cuban and Puerto Rican favorites, and the atmosphere manages to stay festive and casual at all times. The bar is a great place to hang out, listen to live Cuban music on the weekends, and drink your fill of *mojitos* (YerbaBuena introduced the drink to Puerto Rico). Open Tuesday through Thursday 6 PM–midnight, Friday and Saturday 6 PM–2 AM, and Sunday 5–11 PM. $$.

Zabó Creative Cuisine
787-725-9494
14 Candina Street (entrance at Ashford Avenue), Condado, San Juan

Zabó lives up to its name. The menu globe-trots, often stealing ingredients from one country and marrying them to another. Examples? Try the Mexican Hummus, made with *pico de gallo* and guacamole, and served with blue corn chips; or guava-glazed spareribs with fried yucca and an Asian-themed green papaya salad. The restaurant, set in a beautiful villa, has an elegant but casual ambience. Open for dinner Tuesday and Wednesday 6–10 PM, and Thursday through Saturday 7–11 PM. $$–$$$.

ATTRACTIONS, PARKS & RECREATION

Casinos
Unlike Old San Juan, which only has one casino (and Puerta de Tierra, which doesn't have any casinos), Condado offers several places to cash in your savings or cash in your chips. All of them are open at least until 4 AM, and if you like to casino-hop, you can easily visit more than one in a night. Here's a neighborhood directory:

Condado Plaza Hotel & Casino
787-721-1000
999 Ashford Avenue, Condado, San Juan

The Diamond Palace Hotel & Casino
787-721-0810
55 Condado Avenue, Condado, San Juan

Radisson Ambassador Plaza Hotel & Casino San Juan
1-888-201-1718; 787 721-7300
1369 Ashford Avenue, Condado, San Juan

Stellaris Casino at the Marriott Hotel
1-800-464-5005; 787-722-7000
1309 Ashford Avenue, Condado, San Juan

Other Recreation

Condado Beach
The graceful curve of Condado Beach has been attracting tourists to this area for decades. Regardless of what the hotels are doing, Condado will be popular as long as its beach continues to sparkle. This is a fashionable stretch of sand to occupy. While Ocean Park may

draw a more low-key, neighborhood crowd, Condado (along with Isla Verde) is the place to be seen. The beach is protected by a natural rock barrier that creates calm waters perfect for swimming and wading. There's a tiny section of the beach right at the entrance to Condado that gives you great views of the Caribe Hilton, Normandie Hotel, and Fortín de San Gerónimo.

Parque del Indio (Park of the Indian)
Ashford Avenue at Krug, Condado, San Juan

A quiet, small open space right on commercial Ashford Avenue, Parque del Indio provides direct access to the beach. It has two lovely sculptures, neat columns of palm trees, and a sandy area for kids. Open at all times.

Parque Nacional Laguna del Condado (Condado Lagoon National Park)
787-724-4430
www.parquesnacionalespr.com/laguna_par.asp

Laguna del Condado is part of the picturesque charm of this area. Bordering three neighborhoods (Puerta de Tierra, Condado, and Miramar), the lagoon and adjoining park are ideal for running, kayaking, and boating. You can rent kayaks on the perimeter of the lagoon along Baldorioty de Castro Avenue. Admission is free.

NIGHTLIFE

Divas International
787-721-8270
1104 Ashford Avenue, Condado, San Juan

One of the few gentlemen's clubs to be found in San Juan, the bright pink awning of Divas stands out in ritzy Condado. The club features topless women dancing onstage, and a private lounge. Opens daily at 8 PM; closes at 4 AM Sunday through Wednesday and at 5 AM Thursday through Saturday. $.

Kali
787-721-5104
1407 Ashford Avenue, Condado, San Juan

"We warm up at 2 in the morning and don't stop until the last person leaves." That's the partying call of the after-hours revelers at Kali, an Eastern-inspired lounge that's plunged in dark red hues and exotic decor. The party can go on until it's light out, and—even better—the kitchen stays open until about 4 AM, serving appetizers, ceviches, and main dishes (imagine feasting on a *churrasco* steak long past midnight). Open Tuesday through Saturday from 7 PM and "onwards" (as late as 6 AM). $$.

Migas
787-721-5991
1400 Magdalena Avenue, Condado, San Juan

Migas is another restaurant that blurs the boundary between dinner and nightlife. The cuisine—a blend of French, Asian, and Caribbean—is creative and fancy, but the decor makes the place even more special. The restaurant's dining room is artfully decorated with mirrors and paintings, and the separate bar and lounge area is cool and dimly lit, and boasts a terrific wine list to accompany gourmet tapas like a prosciutto sampler and braised short ribs in a balsamic reduction. The only knock on Migas might be the early (for San Juan) closing hours. Open Monday through Wednesday 6 PM–11 PM, Thursday through Saturday 6 PM–midnight. $$.

SHOPPING

Cartier
787-724-4096
1054 Ashford Avenue, Condado, San Juan

Cartier and Condado are perfect complements. Anchoring the ultraprestigious 1054 Ashford Avenue strip, the store sells its signature collection of jewelry, watches, and accessories. Open daily 9 AM–6 PM. $$$$.

Costazul Surf Shop
64 Condado Avenue, Plaza del Condado Mall, Condado, San Juan
www.costazulsurfshop.com
787-722-6154

Shops along Ashford Avenue

Not all the shops in Condado cater to the well-heeled crowd. Costazul, which also has a store in Old San Juan, is one of the area's premier shops for surfers and skaters. In addition to boards, you can buy popular brands of apparel, swimsuits, and beach accessories. You can also rent surfboards daily or weekly. Open Monday through Saturday 10 AM–6:30 PM, Sunday 11 AM–5 PM. $–$$$.

David Antonio
787-725-0600
69 Condado Avenue, Condado, San Juan

Long known for his classic men's line (including modern takes on the classic *guayabera* shirt), David Antonio also has an eclectic collection of women's clothing, especially his chiffon tunics. Open Tuesday through Saturday 10 AM–6 PM. $$–$$$$.

Furla
787-977-0045
www.furla.com
1302 Ashford Avenue, Condado, San Juan

Furla is best known for its well-made, fine leather handbags, and these are displayed prominently in the Italian store's Condado branch. The style, elegance, and prices are perfectly suited to the neighborhood. $$$–$$$$.

Mademoiselle
787-728-7440
1504 Ashford Avenue, Condado, San Juan

One of the nicest women's boutiques in Condado, Mademoiselle doesn't have a major brand name spelled across its window, but it carries a full line of well-known European labels. Mademoiselle stocks exclusive brands like BleuBlancRouge, Newman, and Gerard Darel—all in-vogue fashions from Italy, Spain, France, and Germany. The store is well known for its affable and professional service as well as its range of elegant ready-to-wear clothing and accessories for the modern woman. Open Monday through Saturday 10 AM–7 PM. $$$–$$$$.

Monsieur
787-722-0918
1126 Ashford Avenue, Condado, San Juan

A high-end men's boutique with sleek, contemporary designs. The store carries casual and formal clothing. Open Monday through Saturday 10 AM–6:30 PM. $$$.

Nono Maldonado
787-721-0456
1112 Ashford Avenue, 2A, Condado, San Juan

One of Puerto Rico's most prominent fashion designers, Nono Maldonado is known for his elegant men and women's fashions. He specializes in linen, and his line includes made-to-measure and ready-to-wear clothing for men and women. His men's linen shirts are a signature item. Open Monday through Saturday 10 AM–6 PM. $$$–$$$$.

Piada

787-725-4941
1302–6 Ashford Avenue, Condado, San Juan

Want to look fashionable while you're at the beach? Stop by Piada on the way. This small store, part of a cute strip mall in Condado, has a line of high-end casual clothing, lingerie, bathing suits, and beach accessories. Open Monday through Saturday 10 AM–6 PM. $$$–$$$$.

Louis Vuitton

787-722-2543
www.vuitton.com
1054 Ashford Avenue, Condado, San Juan

Louis Vuitton brings its world-famous luggage, handbags, and accessories—displayed like museum pieces in this elegant boutique—to the most prestigious shopping address on the island. Open Monday through Saturday 9:30 AM–5:30 PM. $$$$.

Ric Oggetti

787-723-3950
1302 Ashford Avenue, Condado, San Juan

This exclusive gift shop carries funky and ultrastylish curios and objects for the home. The store is unique in fashion-heavy Condado, but shopping here is just as fashionable. From cute and creative kitchen items with a distinctive Italian flair to a line of facial and bath products from L'Occitane, there's a little bit of everything at Ric Oggetti. The colorful, off-beat collection is worth a stop along your shopping excursion. Open Monday through Saturday 10 AM–6 PM, Sunday 11 AM–5 PM. $$–$$$.

Suola

787-723-6653
1060 Ashford Avenue, Suite 6, Condado, San Juan

A small, trendy boutique near the most exclusive shops in Condado, Suola sells the best in women's footwear. In addition to high-fashion shoes from designers such as Valentino, Sergio Rossi, Cesare Paciotti, and Car Shoe, Suola has accessories and women's bags. Open Monday through Saturday 10 AM–6 PM. $$$.

FOOD PURVEYORS, LIQUOR & CIGARS

Piu Bello

787-977-2121
1302 Ashford Avenue, Condado, San Juan

There's really nothing quite like ice cream on a hot day . . . while shopping for thousand-dollar luggage sets . . . a block away from a gorgeous beach . . . across the street from a casino. Piu Bello's creamy gelati and fruity sorbets, available in all kinds of tropical and traditional flavors, will have you resting your laurels in the pleasant outdoor café. If you're feeling decadent, try their ice cream concoctions, which range far beyond the banana split. Open 8 AM–1 AM.

Pure and Natural
787-725-6104
1125 Ashford Avenue, Condado, San Juan

A vegetarian- and vegan-friendly juice bar right in the heart of Condado. Open Tuesday through Saturday 11 AM–10 PM, Sunday and Monday until 8 PM.

GOOD TO KNOW ABOUT . . .

Ashford Presbyterian Community Hospital
787-721-2160
www.presbypr.com
1451 Ashford Avenue, Condado, San Juan

"El Presby," a full-service hospital, is the medical center closest to the main tourism zones.

Cybernet Café
787-724-4033
1128 Ashford Avenue, Condado, San Juan

Surf the Web, check your e-mail, and print anything you need while you wait for a strong cup of java or something light to eat. Open Monday through Saturday 9 AM–11 PM, Sunday 10 AM–11 PM.

Walgreens
787-725-1510
1130 Ashford Avenue, Condado, San Juan

This branch is centrally located and open 24 hours a day (great for a Tylenol after you stagger out of the casino or a nightclub).

WEEKLY & ANNUAL EVENTS

El Cruce a Nado Chavín
July–August
787-721-2800
At Condado Lagoon

Not quite the crossing of the English Channel, this event, named after a disabled female athlete, is a swim across Condado Lagoon. People of all ages participate in one of three routes that vary in difficulty. There's also a route for disabled swimmers. Free.

Entrance to Ocean Park neighborhood

OCEAN PARK AND PUNTA LAS MARÍAS—MELLOW IN THE MIDDLE

You could almost compare Ocean Park to Cinderella: the stepsister of the glitzier, more puffed up Condado and Isla Verde. You could even pull off the "last laugh" theme, because this is a lovely residential neighborhood with great local bars and restaurants, and pristine gated communities. If I were looking for a place to live in San Juan, Ocean Park would be on the short list. In the middle of the tourist bustle, it nevertheless has a quiet, laid-back serenity loved by people who don't want to see or be seen. The park that gives the neighborhood its name is large (if plain), and the beach is fantastic.

But Ocean Park is not just popular with Puerto Ricans. It's a great destination for travelers who crave beachfront property without the pomp of a resort hotel. You won't find Miami Beach or Cancún-style high-rises here. Instead, quaint guesthouses, bed & breakfasts, and private rentals lie nestled within this suburb. In general, lodging won't cost as much as in the more well-known areas of San Juan. And it has more of a beach-and-surf atmosphere than anywhere else in the city.

There's no perceptible difference between Punta Las Marías and Ocean Park. If anything, Punta Las Marías has more apartment buildings and more of a residential feel than its neighbor. The area is named for the crest of land that begins the crescent of the Isla Verde Beach strip, and it's known for the best windsurfing in the metropolitan area. Small wonder that this little corner of San Juan is a favorite for boarders and kite surfers; on weekends, if conditions are good, you're likely to see boards and sails stretched out across the sand.

LODGING

L'Habitation Beach Guest House

787-727-2499
www.habitationbeach.com
1957 Italia Street, Ocean Park, San Juan
00911

Most places that welcome the gay community describe themselves as "gay friendly"; L'Habitation calls itself "straight friendly." This tiny inn (10 rooms in total) is right on the beach, and it has a very casual atmosphere, unique decor, and an extremely loyal clientele. At bargain rates, a secluded address, and with continental breakfast thrown in, it's easy to see why. Regulars even store their stuff in the lobby for their next trip. If you want a room, book early. $.

Hostería del Mar

1-877-727-3302; 787-727-3302
www.hosteriadelmarpr.com
One Tapia Street, Ocean Park, San Juan
00911

Hostería del Mar is a budget option facing the Ocean Park beach and quite removed from the action. While its restaurant consistently gets rave reviews, opinions about the hotel itself are mixed. Oceanside rooms have amazing views, and every room comes with a kitchenette. The rooms here are on the small side, but then, it's a small inn. The common areas of the hotel are nicely decorated in a typical tropical, beachside theme. $–$$.

Numero Uno Guest House

1-866-726-5010; 787-726-5010
www.numero1guesthouse.com
One Santa Ana Street, Ocean Park, San Juan
00911

You might think the name, "Number One Guest House," is arrogant, but there's nothing cocky about this place; quite the opposite. Numero Uno is a cute little inn that's

View from the Numero Uno Guest House

as close to the beach as you can get. The rooms are bright and comfortable, all with mini bars and air-conditioning, and some offer lovely views of the ocean. Guests can have their continental breakfast right on the sand in the beachfront dining area. There's a Lilliputian pool, which most guests tiptoe around on the way to the beach. And then there's **Pamela's** (see "Dining"), one of the best restaurants in the neighborhood). $–$$.

El Prado Rentals

787-391-1976
www.elpradoinn.net/rentals.htm
Several locations in Ocean Park

You can stay at a grand hotel, boutique hotel, or guesthouse. Or, you could contact Monique Lacombe at El Prado and rent anything from a furnished one-bedroom apartment (with full kitchen) to a gorgeous villa in the Ocean Park district. All are within two blocks of Ocean Park beach and come with a private parking space. The accommodations are just half the story. This family-run business is all about service. When you make your reservation, they'll send you a map with driving directions to your apartment; someone is there to welcome you, no matter what time you arrive; your room will have fresh flowers as well as special amenities for late-night arrivals (a few items stocked in the kitchen so you don't have to run out the next morning) and honeymooners; and a welcome kit that includes area maps and places to go in the neighborhood. El Prado can accommodate large groups as well. There's a three-night minimum stay. $–$$$.

Tres Palmas Inn

1-866-372-5627; 787-727-4617
www.trespalmasinn.com
2212 Park Boulevard, Punta Las Marías, San Juan 00913

Tres Palmas (Three Palms) has it all: oceanside location (facing the Punta Las Marías beach); amenities (pool, rooftop terrace with Jacuzzi, complimentary breakfast); and price (very reasonable rates). And, yes, there is a cluster of three palm trees right in front of the hotel. The 18 units are basically furnished but all have air-conditioning and cable TV. Each unit also has an in-room safe, which many rooms in small hotels don't have. With its warm colors, manicured indoor landscaping, and open spaces, the inn has a warm, friendly, and casual charm. $–$$.

DINING

Che's

787-726-7202
www.chesrestaurant.com
35 Caoba Street, Punta Las Marías, San Juan

There are quite a few Argentinean restaurants in San Juan, but Che's advocates—and they are legion—boisterously proclaim it the best. All that loyalty enabled Che's to celebrate their 30th anniversary in 2006. And their *parrilla* (grill) is as good as ever. You can start with a tasty cream of aspara-

gus soup or one of their many salads, but believe me, the grilled fare will fill you up. Your choice of meat includes succulent beef short ribs, lamb, sirloin, skirt steak, sausage, pork, chicken . . . need I go on? If you are at all carnivorous, get moving to this temple of meat. Open Sunday through Thursday noon–11 PM, and Friday and Saturday noon to midnight. $$.

Dunbar's

787-728-2920
1854 McLeary Avenue, Ocean Park, San Juan

Dunbar's is a place of niches. Want a great bar? You've got three. Want to dance to a live band? Check. Want to enter a pool competition or a dart-throwing contest? Dunbar's has you covered. And I haven't even begun to describe the food. Look around at the pleasant, relaxed decor (wisdom and wisecracks line the walls, and hundreds of patrons beam at you from the walls and the diner-sized menu), and you might think that food is basic pub fare. You'd be right, and you'd also be wrong. Dunbar's is more than it seems. Not too many bars quote Jorge Luis Borges on their menu. The food ranges from finger-licking chicken wings (don't let owner John Belsky talk you into trying the suicide sauce; I fell for that) to a Kyoto scallop fried rice. Any doubts about quality should be dispelled when you see the "Chef's Hat" awards hanging on the walls. So bring your buddies for a few drinks; bring your date for an intimate dinner; bring the family for Sunday brunch. Above all, bring your appetite and your smile—maybe you'll get your picture taken. Oh, and one more thing: Call ahead, tell them where you're from, and you might—just might—see your nation's flag hanging outside the restaurant when you get there. Opens weekdays at 11:30 AM, Saturday at 5 PM, and Sunday at 10 AM. $–$$.

Kasalta

787-727-7340
www.kasalta.com
1966 McLeary Street, Ocean Park, San Juan

Puerto Ricans *love* bakeries, and Kasalta is an institution in Ocean Park that does triple duty as a bakery, café, and gourmet market. Along bare, cafeteria-style rows of tables along the windowed wall, you can sit down and enjoy a hearty breakfast, crispy *quesito,* strong coffee, a rich dessert, or a homemade soup to go with one of a wide range of sandwiches. Cheap, quick, and simple—every neighborhood should have one of these. Open daily 6 AM–10 PM. $.

Pamela's

787-726-5010
At Numero Uno Guest House, One Santa Ana Street, Ocean Park, San Juan

No matter where you're staying, it's worth coming to Numero Uno for one reason: the food and the ambience at Pamela's. This restaurant is worth the hype, with its innovative Caribbean cuisine, extensive wine list (including a large selection of wines by the glass and moderately priced bottles) hand picked by manager Max Dubuche, and a choice of pleasant indoor dining or tables on the beach. Chef Esteban Torres changes the menu (even the dessert menu) every six months, and there are daily specials. What never changes is the excellent quality, freshness, and mouthwatering combinations of flavors. Don't forget to leave room for dessert (if they still have it, try the *tres leches* parfait with house-made caramel, served in a glass) and their excellent coffee. Open daily, serving lunch noon–3 PM, tapas 3–7 PM, and dinner 7–10:30 PM. $$–$$$.

Pescadería Atlántica

787-726-6654
www.atlanticapr.com
2475 Loíza Street, Punta las Marías, San Juan

Indoor dining room at Pamela's

Ask Sanjuaneros to list their favorite sea-food joints, and chances are they'll mention this one. Pescadería Atlántica is known not just for its simply prepared, fresh, and delicious fish but also for its reasonable prices and warm ambience. This is a family-style restaurant, and since the owners are seafood distributors and importers, you know you'll get the freshest catch of the day. Many of the dishes are typically Spanish. The tapas menu has all the usual suspects, including *gambas al ajillo* (shrimp sautéed in garlic) and *angulas* (baby eels). You have your choice of seafood dishes, but you really can't go wrong with any of their *a la plancha* (on the grill) dishes—your choice of broiled fish and seafood. Open Monday through Saturday noon–10 PM. $$–$$$.

Pinky's
787-727-3347
51 Maria Moczo Street, Ocean Park, San Juan

How about a little bit of California in Puerto Rico? If you like fresh fruit smoothies (they fill your glass and leave the rest in the blender at your table), beyond-satisfying breakfasts (try the mammoth six-egg breakfast burrito), and great, fresh wraps (with lots of options for vegetarians), Pinky's is for you. It's one of the few places you can actually eat healthy. Plus, Pinky's delivers—straight to your hotel room, or even to the beach. Open Monday through Saturday 7 AM–8:30 PM and Sunday 7 AM–6:30 PM. $.

ATTRACTIONS, PARKS & RECREATION

Ocean Park and Punta Las Marías Beaches

Forget casinos, museums, and half-millennium-old buildings; people come here for one main reason: to enjoy the fantastic beaches, which are a paradise for those who love water sports. On any given weekend, you're likely to see windsurfers and kite surfers soar above the surf. Why here? A 4-mile-long barrier reef a half mile offshore contributes to the clean breaks and big swells that attract surfers from all over.

Ocean Park Beach

Parque Barbosa

The large expanse of green that gives Ocean Park the latter half of its name is Parque Barbosa, which faces the ocean and the beach. It's definitely more of a functional park than a touristy one; you'll see kids gathering after school on bleachers and joggers running around a track. One nice feature: Tennis courts are available for public use. Free admission.

NIGHTLIFE

Dunbar's
787-728-2920
1854 McLeary Avenue, Ocean Park, San Juan

With three bars in two levels, a separate pool hall, and a dance floor with a stage for live bands, Dunbar's is a swinging hot spot in laid-back Ocean Park. It's popular with people of all ages and tastes. There's a daily happy hour from 5 to 7 PM. At press time local bands were headlining the entertainment: Indigo on Thursday night, and Melissa y Madre Tierra on Friday night. Open till midnight Sunday through Thursday and till 1 AM on the weekends.

Mango's Café
787-727-9328
2421 Laurel Street, Punta Las Marías, San Juan

By day, Mango's serves burgers, wings, and other light fare. By night, the atmosphere changes from casual eatery to thumping beats and dancing. Depending on the night, the music varies from jazz to electronic. Thursday is Ladies' Night, with live DJs belting out reggae, R&B, and hip-hop tunes; on Saturday there's a club atmosphere. Doors open at 5 PM Tuesday through Saturday, the entertainment usually begins after 10 PM, and the party carries on late into the night. $.

SHOPPING

Crysta
787-727-9782
www.crystastore.com
51 Maria Moczo Street, Ocean Park, San Juan

From Brazilian bikinis to everyday clothing, Crysta Fernández's line of clothing is sexy, youthful, and designed to accentuate the female body. In addition to beachwear, Crysta sells dresses, tops, and a line of organic facial and bath products. Open Tuesday through Saturday 10 AM–6 PM, Sunday 10 AM–4 PM. $$$.

Sassy Girl
787-268-6416
2000 Santa Cecilia Avenue, Ocean Park, San Juan

Definitely catering to a young crowd, Sassy Girl sells a little bit of everything—handbags, accessories, lingerie, and bathing suits. Their prices cater to younger budgets as well. Open Monday through Saturday 10 AM–5 PM. $–$$.

The Tackle Box
787-726-1662; 787-409-2701
105 Doncella Street, Ocean Park, San Juan

Near the Punta Las Marías crest, the Tackle Box is a valuable fisherman's resource. The store has everything you need for inshore or offshore fishing, including rods, lines, lures, bait, and some tools. Open Monday through Saturday 9 AM–5 PM. $–$$$.

Velauno
1-866-PR-VELA-1; 787-728-8716
www.velauno.com
2430 Loíza Street, Punta Las Marías, San Juan

Velauno is the second largest, full-service headquarters for windsurfing in the United States. You can buy windsurfing, surfboarding, and kite-boarding equipment and accessories here, or rent equipment on a daily, three-day, weekly, or two-week basis. (Note to kite boarders: Velauno sells, but doesn't rent, kites.) The staff are helpful and happily give their opinions on the best surfing spots on the island. Velauno also has the most experienced instructors in the Caribbean and great beginner packages for those who want to learn. It's also one of the few local places that has in-house repair services for sails, kites, and other components of your surfing equipment. Open Monday through Friday 10 AM–7 PM, Saturday 11 AM–7 PM. $–$$$.

FOOD PURVEYORS, LIQUOR & CIGARS

Kasalta
787-727-7340
www.kasalta.com
1966 McLeary Street, Ocean Park, San Juan

Kasalta sells cakes and prepared foods, and has an impressive collection of wines. They're a great option for large groups and parties, as they sell *pasteles* (a kind of turnover filled with meat), mini sandwiches, and other finger foods by the tray. Open daily 6 AM–10 PM. $–$$$.

GOOD TO KNOW ABOUT . . .

Eros Food Market
787-722-3631
1357 Ashford Avenue, Ocean Park, San Juan

A small but well-stocked market with fruits, vegetables, meats, and other basic groceries. Open daily 7:30 AM–10 PM.

Ocean Park Coin Laundry

787-726-5955
1950 Avenue McCleary, Ocean Park, San Juan

As you're probably staying in smaller inns, it's good to know of a place where you can do your laundry or drop it off. Open daily 6 AM–9 PM.

Shell Gas Station

787-728-8914
Doncella Street, Punta Las Marías, San Juan

This gas station is open 24 hours a day.

ISLA VERDE—THE RESORT STRIP

Isla Verde—literally "Green Island"—is not all that green, but it is a paradise for tourists looking to live the highlife in the sun. Technically part of Carolina, not San Juan, this strip of sand and hotels has annexed itself to the city's tourist district. There are upsides and disadvantages to staying in Isla Verde. On a positive note, visitors have a choice of lodging, from budget to elite. With the Ritz, the Water & Beach Club, El San Juan Hotel & Casino, and the InterContinental all claiming prime real estate along the beach, Isla Verde is a trendy address for tourists. Some of the casinos are beautifully decorated. And, of course, the 2-mile-long swathe of sandy beach and calm waters is within a stone's throw of most hotels. Isla Verde is also conveniently close to Luis Muñoz Marín International Airport.

Isla Verde Beach and resorts

The tradeoffs: Isla Verde is removed from the action in Old San Juan and, if traffic is heavy, a cab ride can easily stretch beyond half an hour. The back and forth from the old city to your hotel can get expensive, whether you're in a taxi (one-way trips run $15-20) or a rental car (you'll pay for parking everywhere). The main Isla Verde Avenue is wide and easy to walk along, but it doesn't make for an interesting stroll. There are some good restaurants, but not a whole lot of shopping, along the road.

A car or scooter rental is advisable if you're staying in Isla Verde but want to tour San Juan. If you've explored the old city, the big hotels in Isla Verde provide plenty of entertainment options. Nightclubs, restaurants, and boutique shopping are available within their air-conditioned walls. The nightlife is especially varied. Stately casinos, hotel lobbies, cool clubs, hip lounges, lively bars, special events at a resort . . . there's usually a party *somewhere* in this part of town. As such, people of all ages and from all walks of life congregate in Isla Verde during the weekend, whether to lose thousands or pick up a cheap slice of pizza at dawn.

LODGING

Borinquen Beach Inn
1-866-728-8400; 787-728-8400
www.borinquenbeachinn.com
5451 Isla Verde Avenue, Isla Verde, Carolina 00979

It's ironic that this section of the book, with all the five-star hotels to come, should kick off with one of the most budget-friendly places to stay on the island. You can't miss the squat, one-floor, bright blue Borinquen Beach Inn. The rooms are very basic, but they all have air-conditioning, cable TV, and private bathroom, and are practically within spitting distance of the beach. $.

The Coqui Inn
1-800-677-8860; 787-726-4330
www.coqui-inn.com
36 Calle Uno, Villamar, Isla Verde, Carolina 00979

Pop quiz: In Isla Verde, can you get a room with kitchenette, private bath, and coffee, tea, and donuts in the morning for under a $100—in high season? The answer is yes, if you book a room at the Coqui Inn. The inn is the combination of two small hotels—

Green Isle Inn and Casa Mathiesen Guest House—that have identical facilities. The new inn is under new management who place an emphasis on service. The rooms are basic, but if you're on a budget, it's a great option. There's a walkway to the beach, and you even get free parking, which is rare in this part of town. $.

Courtyard by Marriott Isla Verde Beach Resort
1-800-791-2553; 787-791-0404
www.sjcourtyard.com
7012 Boca de Cangrejos Avenue, Isla Verde, Carolina 00979

Anchoring the western edge of the Isla Verde strip, the Courtyard by Marriott is one of the best bets for travelers who want it all at a reasonable price. The 24-hour casino is among the better ones, with 400 slot machines and over 14,000 square feet of gaming space. The fitness center is one of the better ones, with room to breathe, run, and lift. And the pool is one of the better ones, with a swim-up bar and a separate area for kids (actually, there's a lot here for kids; the emphasis on service for the whole family is a nice touch). The rooms are spacious, all of them with a work area. One of the newest additions to the hotel is Sirena, their beachfront restaurant serving Caribbean fusion cuisine. $$–$$$.

Embassy Suites Hotel & Casino

787-791-0505
http://embassysuites.hilton.com
8000 Tartak Street, Isla Verde, Carolina 00979

Out of all your lodging options, Embassy Suites is probably the farthest from beautiful Isla Verde Beach (it's still less than two blocks away, however), but there are still plenty of reasons to recommend it. First on this list is the fantastic free-form pool designed to emulate a natural lagoon (with a waterfall). The hotel's atrium is a tropical gem, with a lush garden and waterfall-fed pool. At press time, the 299 suites had just been renovated, offering a clean, new look. Like all Embassy Suites, this hotel comes with a hearty complimentary breakfast and a two-room suite with microwave oven, coffeemaker, and fridge. There's plenty of meeting space for the business traveler, and it's just minutes from the main airport in Carolina. A nice touch for families: The kids' game room is next to the casino. $$–$$$$.

ESJ Towers

787-791-5151
www.esjtowers.com
6165 Isla Verde Avenue, Isla Verde, Carolina 00907

Tourists who regularly visit San Juan love ESJ Towers: They're steps away from one of the nicest casinos on the island but don't have to pay the extra fees charged by casino hotels; they share a beach with a five-star resort hotel but don't have to pay a resort fee; and they get all the amenities of a hotel while enjoying the feel of owning—for a few days—their very own beachfront condo. ESJ offers daily maid service, a pool, and a gym.

The studios have a fully equipped kitchenette, and the one-, two- and three-bedroom suites have a full kitchen, and a washer and dryer. $$–$$$$.

The InterContinental San Juan Resort & Casino

1-888-424-6835; 787-791-6100
www.intercontinental.com/sanjuan
5961 Isla Verde Avenue, Isla Verde, Carolina 00979

The InterContinental is a premier destination in Isla Verde. Directly on the beach, the huge hotel caters equally to the corporate world and the upscale tourist. Although it's right on the ocean, its best asset might well be the spectacular, amorphous pool surrounded by palm trees and resembling a natural lagoon. You can bathe under a free-flowing waterfall under a rocky shelf and have lunch poolside. With its six restaurants, amenities (fitness center, casino, spa, 24-hour room service, boardwalk along the beach) and 400-plus rooms, the InterContinental is almost a self-contained community. The only thing it doesn't offer is great shopping. For business travelers, the hotel provides over 18,000 square feet of meeting space, including two ballrooms. $$$–$$$$.

El San Juan Hotel & Casino

1-866-317-8935; 787-791-1000
www.elsanjuanhotel.com
6063 Isla Verde Avenue, Isla Verde, Carolina 00979

El San Juan Hotel & Casino has long been known for old-world charm and luxury. Just look at its magnificent lobby, a throwback to old-fashioned elegance. But it's out with the old and in with the new these days. At press time, the hotel was undergoing a multimillion-dollar renovation, beginning with the tower rooms and pool, and extending to the rest of the hotel. The new look takes the hotel from tried-and-tropical to white-and-with-it. The revamped rooms are iPod-ready. Minimally yet elegantly furnished, they boast white flat-screen TVs. You'll leave your room often, but you might not be so ready to leave the hotel. The many restaurants (with **La Piccola Fontana** leading the way; see "Dining"), lounges, nightclubs, a shopping arcade, and a lively casino make this one of the most visited hotels on the island. $$$–$$$$.

Hotel Villa del Sol
www.villadelsolpr.com
787-791-2600
Calle Rosa #4, Isla Verde, Carolina 00979

There are cheaper places to stay in Isla Verde, and there are far more expensive ones. But few places offer such good value for the money. Villa del Sol is an affordable hotel set in a modern Spanish villa splashed with the yellow, orange, and white hues of the tropics. The exterior is quaint, with balconies and terra-cotta tiles, a small pool, and lush gardens. The rooms are simply furnished but well maintained, and the hotel is just minutes from Isla Verde Beach. $–$$.

The Ritz-Carlton, San Juan Hotel, Spa & Casino
1-888-451-9868; 787-253-1700
www.ritzcarlton.com/hotels/san_juan
6961 Avenue of the Governors, Isla Verde, Carolina 00979

The grand Ritz-Carlton sits on the corner of Isla Verde Avenue and Avenue of the Governors, apart from the main strip but very much a part of the resort scene. The accolades have piled up for this hotel, which has been open less than a decade: Not least of these has been its nomination among the World's Best Hotels (four times) by *Condé Nast Traveler's* Gold List; it also landed on the "World's Best" list

three times in *Travel & Leisure* Magazine. Ironically, as nice as the rooms are, they may be its least attractive feature. That's not to say they're bad: With marble bathrooms, fully stocked minibars, LCD-screen TVs, and all the little extras the Ritz throws in (those signature plush terry robes, slippers, fresh flowers), you won't lack for anything. But the hotel offers so much more than the quality of its accommodations: direct access to Isla Verde Beach, with airy cabanas on the sand; a fantastic, throwback-style casino; a "who's who" of elite New York City restaurants complementing the Ritz's own fine dining options; a beautiful pool lined with palm trees and

San Juan Water & Beach Club Hotel

adorned with the Ritz's iconic stone lion fountains; and one of the best spas in San Juan. There's ample meeting space, a business center, and high-speed Internet access for the business traveler. If there's a fault, I'd have to say it was the service, which wasn't up to my expectations. $$$$.

The San Juan Water & Beach Club Hotel
1-888-265-6699; 787-728-3666
www.waterbeachclubhotel.com
Two Tartak Street, Isla Verde, Carolina
00979

Think Ocean Drive in Miami Beach; think indigo blue and billowing white; think sexy and hip and popular with the stars. Put it all together, and you have the Water & Beach Club, the hotel that's getting all the raves these days. The hype is understandable; this boutique hotel is set away from the bustle of Isla Verde Avenue, at the end of a cul-de-sac that provides a sense of privileged seclusion. Loads of special touches raise the Water & Beach Club a notch above the ordinary. Want water? You're across the street from the beach; the restaurant and even the funky open-roof elevators have waterfalls in them; the pool on the terrace is at eye level with the ocean. And every room has floor-to-ceiling windows with a view of the ocean. Want beach? You can get a massage right on the sand, your own beach chair, and a beach attendant. Want modern? The rooms are all about modern furniture and economy of space, and come with iHome radio and alarm clocks for your iPod. Want more? Each room has—a "Desires" bulletin board where you can request amenities and services (this is in addition to a prearrival "Desires" service the hotel offers to make sure your particular needs and cravings are satisfied); suites are equipped with tripod-mounted telescopes for stargazing; and the hotel's restaurant and rooftop lounge are among the trendiest in the city. $$–$$$$.

DINING

Ceviche House
787-726-0919
79 Isla Verde Avenue, Isla Verde, Carolina

For a fresh, lemony tingle in your palate, head to Ceviche House and taste true Peruvian cooking, and seafood so fresh it's still contemplating returning to the sea. This unassuming little restaurant on the main strip of Isla Verde is known for its citrus-infused ceviches, a total respite from the rich, dense flavors of Puerto Rico. You can choose your favorite seafood or go with the ceviche misto, which includes conch, shrimp, octopus, squid, and fish, with a pumpkin mash and plantain *tostones* on the side. If the tart zing and chewy texture isn't to your taste, try any of the seafood dishes, such as the halibut or snapper, which are available grilled, in a garlic sauce, or breaded. You'll certainly be feeling macho if you can polish off the *pescado a lo macho* (fish "macho-style"), which is a large filet of halibut completely inundated by a kitchen-sink combination of mussels, shrimp, conch, octopus, and peppers. The decor is pleasant and quaint, and if you get the best seat in the house, you can peak in the open window and watch chef-owner Daniel Sorogastúa in his element. Open Tuesday through Saturday noon–10 PM, Sunday noon–9 PM. $$.

Pescado a lo Macho (fish "macho-style") at Ceviche House

Lupi's

787-253-2198
6369 Isla Verde Avenue, Isla Verde, Carolina

At a few restaurants in Isla Verde, the atmosphere is relaxed, the crowd young, and the bar hopping late into the night. Lupi's is one such place. Owned by Eduardo Figueroa, a former ballplayer with the New York Yankees, Lupi's is a boisterous and fun place to hang out. There are two locations, one in Old San Juan and the other in Isla Verde, which features live music each night. It's far more Cancún than criollo, and you can leave your jacket behind. Specialties include a range of powerful margaritas to go with Tex-Mex classics (the best item on the menu is the Puerto Rican fajitas made with sliced, boneless pork chops in barbecue sauce), burgers, and finger foods. Open Sunday through Thursday 11 AM–10 PM, Friday and Saturday until 2 AM. $–$$.

Mares

787-253-1700
www.ritzcarlton.com/hotels/san_juan
At the Ritz-Carlton, San Juan Hotel, Spa & Casino, 6961 Avenue of the Governors, Isla Verde, Carolina

With New York City's BLT Steak moving in at press time, Mares (formerly the Caribbean Grill) has wisely elected to transition its menu to a seafood-based selection. There are many reasons to like this restaurant. It has the quality of a Ritz establishment, but it's not as pricey as you'd expect; and it has a casual elegance that manages not to be stuffy. The food carries the same dressed-down and yet sophisticated theme, and the menu gives you the freedom of choice: Chef Simon Porter lets you select your fish or shellfish (including grouper, black cod, mahimahi, tuna, and lobster) and pair it with a creative, international menu of sauces, ranging from a jerk rémoulade to a guava, mango, and citrus vinaigrette to a Thai green curry. In case

this smacks of buffet night at your local diner, don't worry: The food is of the freshest and highest quality. Any doubts should be dispelled as soon as you sample the warm, in-house-baked oatmeal bread. There are, of course, standard entrées along with terrific salads. Among the best dishes is the tomato-based Mediterranean seafood stew made with mussels, squid, fish, clams, and a hulking tail of Caribbean lobster. And if you're staying at the Ritz on a Friday night, the seafood buffet is a good reason not to leave the hotel. Open daily 6:30 AM–11 PM. $$$.

La Piccola Fontana

787-791-0966
www.piccolafontana.com
At El San Juan Hotel & Casino, 6063 Isla Verde Avenue, Isla Verde, Carolina

Set in the heart of Puerto Rico's resort strip, La Piccola Fontana takes you away from the Caribbean and into northern Italy. (Dining under the serene gaze of statues, cherubs, and white marble busts at a four-diamond restaurant usually is a transporting experience.) The food is excellent, from the fantastic risottos (try the lobster and champagne combination) to the grilled fresh fish of the day to the homemade pasta specials that aren't too dressed up but prepared just right (like my favorite dish, linguine with fresh clams in a white pinot grigio sauce). La Piccola Fontana is an elegant traditional Italian restaurant with an atmosphere and a clientele to match the service, the menu, and the prices. Given the restaurant's quality, however, the three-course set menus for $35 and the wide range of moderately priced wines are bargains. Open daily 6–11 PM. $$$.

Platos Restaurant

787-791-7474
At Coral By The Sea Hotel, Two Rosa Street, Isla Verde, Carolina

Snacks on the Beach

If you want to experience Puerto Rico at its greasiest, crispiest best, get in a car or taxi and head out to **Piñones.** Just east of Balneario de Carolina in Isla Verde along Route 187, this stretch of road is dotted with seaside shacks and small restaurants serving *alcapurrias* (a fried snack made with plantain and stuffed with meat or seafood), *bacalaítos, pasteles, empanadillas,* and other finger foods. Because they're steps from the beach, you can spend the day snacking and swimming and sunning yourself. Surfers, families, young and old people—you'll find a mix of everybody here, out to enjoy the day and relish the calories.

Soleil Beach Club

787-253-1033
www.soleilbeachclub.com
5900 Route 187, Piñones, Carolina

Soleil Beach Club is not your typical eatery in Piñones. The restaurant calls itself *un sitio diferente* (a different place). By that, Soleil means the combination of the laid-back charm and atmosphere of island life with the gourmet food of the big city. It's hard to argue the point: From appetizers like the *pinchos piñoneros* (fresh fish skewers in a sweet and sour mango sauce) to entrées like *chillo frito* (whole fried red snapper) marinated in spices or halibut filet in an Asian beurre blanc sauce with a side of yucca *mofongo*, the seafood-heavy menu is excellent and far more sophisticated than the typical fare on menus in these parts. You can relax afterward in the adjacent bar and lounge or take a walk on the beach. Then come back and try the bananas Foster with homemade caramel, served in a martini glass. One of the best things about Soleil Beach Club is that you don't need a car to get here. From many of San Juan's hotels, Soleil offers free shuttle transportation to and from the restaurant. Open Sunday through Thursday 11 AM–11 PM, Friday and Saturday 11 AM–1 AM. $$.

Beach at Piñones

Less than two years old at press time, Platos was already gaining recognition for its contemporary Puerto Rican cuisine. The menu is a tour of local favorites, with special touches that gives them a creative twist: the *churrasco a la parrilla* (skirt steak) with a pumpkin risotto is a popular choice, as is the must-try *chillo al horno con salsa de mangó y piña* (oven-roasted red snapper served with a mango and pineapple sauce). Another bold touch (for a typically Puerto Rican restaurant) is their choice of vegetarian dishes, headlined by a grilled portabella mushroom napoleon. Their lunch specials are fantastic deals, offering traditional classics like *asopao, bistec encebollado* (a thin steak served with onions), and pork chops for under $10. Open Sunday through Thursday 11 AM–midnight, Friday and Saturday until 2 AM. $–$$.

Ruth's Chris Steakhouse
787-253-1717
At the InterContinental San Juan Resort & Casino, 5961 Isla Verde Avenue, Isla Verde, Carolina

I've tried to steer clear of mentioning restaurants you can find on the U.S. mainland because . . . well, you can find them on the mainland. With Ruth's Chris, I made an exception, for a few reasons: One, it's the only Ruth's Chris franchise in the Caribbean. Plus, for anyone who has eaten at Ruth's Chris, I'm happy to report that the Isla Verde location applies the same rigorous standards (such as daily quality inspections) that the steakhouse is famous for. It's the place to go for the best corn-fed, aged USDA Prime beef (try the mammoth 41-ounce porterhouse T-bone), and the roasted garlic mashed potatoes and creamed spinach are stellar staples. Steak lovers everywhere will be happy to know they can worship at this altar when they're in Puerto Rico, and for a special night out or a power dinner, it's tough to beat. Open

Sunday through Thursday 6–10 PM, and Friday and Saturday 6–11 PM, for dinner.

Shogun
787-982-5555
35 Isla Verde Avenue, Isla Verde, Carolina

Here's a general tip about dining in Japanese restaurants: You're in good hands when the owner-chef is Japanese. Enter Yosuke "Oscar" Nitta's Shogun, the only Japanese-owned Teppan Yaki grill and sushi bar on the island. Shogun is a two-level restaurant with all the usual trappings of Japanese decor: a full sushi menu with creative rolls, a large choice of Teppan Yaki dishes, and regular favorites like tempura, teriyaki, and *gyoza* or *shumai* (fried or steamed dumplings). Open Monday through Wednesday 11:30 AM–2:30 PM for lunch and 5–11 PM for dinner; open Thursday through Saturday 5 PM–1 AM, and Sunday 4–10 PM, for dinner. $$–$$$$.

Tangerine
787-728-3666
www.waterbeachclubhotel.com
At the San Juan Water & Beach Club Hotel, Two Tartak Street, Isla Verde, Carolina

The Water & Beach Club's restaurant is as sexy as the hotel. Located in the lobby, it continues the hotel's theme brilliantly: It has the requisite (for the Water Club) fountain, and the magnified images of people swimming around and above the bar is just trippy. The dishes are almost scandalous in taste and name: To get you in the mood, try the "Lamb My Rack" of Australian lamb served with a tamarind mint sauce, the "Take My Skirt Off" skirt steak, or the cheeky "It Is Soft Now . . . but Can It Get Harder for Me?" soft-shell crab tempura with a wasabi mash. Tangerine was recognized by *Condé Nast Traveler* as one of the 75 most intriguing new restaurants in the world. The only knock: the stiff parking fees you'll fork over if you drive here. Open daily 7–11 AM for breakfast and 6:30–11 PM for dinner. After 11, the restaurant transforms into Liquid—a lounge (see page 167). $$–$$$.

ATTRACTIONS, PARKS & RECREATION

Casinos

By and large, Isla Verde's casinos are fancier than the ones you'll find in Condado. With El San Juan Hotel & Casino and the Ritz-Carlton leading the way, the gaming spaces along the resort strip can be sumptuous and elegant, and can draw a mixed crowd of gamblers and revelers. Here' a neighborhood directory:

Courtyard by Marriott Isla Verde Beach Resort
787-791-0404
7012 Boca de Cangrejos Avenue

Embassy Suites Hotel & Casino
787-791-0505
8000 Tartak Street

Intercontinental San Juan Resort & Casino
787-791-6100
5961 Isla Verde Avenue

El San Juan Hotel & Casino
787-791-1000
6063 Isla Verde Avenue

The Ritz-Carlton San Juan Hotel, Spa & Casino
787-253-1700
6961 Avenue of the Governors

Beaches

Carolina Beach
787-752-0703
Boca de Cangrejos Avenue, Isla Verde, Carolina

Every tourist knows Isla Verde Beach; every local knows Carolina Beach. Perhaps this is because Carolina Beach is located just after the hotel strip ends. Or maybe because this is another *balneario* (public beach), with ample (paid) parking, picnic tables, and other facilities. In fact, along with El Escambrón, Carolina beach is the only one on the main island to earn Blue Flag status for its services and quality of water. You'll often find families here, making a day of it with their picnic lunches in tow. Another advantage: sweeping views of the Isla Verde strip. However, I find the sand on other beaches much finer and whiter. Open daily 8 AM–6 PM. $.

Isla Verde Beach

Isla Verde Beach

This isn't a public beach, so there are no hours, fees, public parking spaces, or lifeguards. What you will find on Isla Verde Beach, fronted by hotels and condominiums, is a wide crescent with ample, smooth sands, turquoise waters, and plenty of people at play on land and in the water. Despite the casinos, restaurants, and resorts, it's still the star of the neighborhood; and it gets many nods for "Best Beach in San Juan." At press time, plans were underway to make it even nicer with the addition of a boardwalk.

Other Recreation

Ocean Sports
787-268-2329
www.osdivers.com
77 Isla Verde Avenue, Isla Verde, Carolina

Ocean Sports offers a variety of dives from its two stores in Isla Verde. Training is provided for novices, and diving excursions include a night trip, dives from the shore, and dives from a boat. The longer excursions (to Culebra, Mona, and Desecheo islands, for example) include a light lunch. You can also charter a boat. Open Monday through Friday 10 AM–7 PM, Saturday 9 AM–6 PM. $$$–$$$$.

San Juan Waterfun

787-643-4510
www.waterfun-pr.com
On Isla Verde Beach, behind El San Juan Hotel & Casino

This unassuming stand on the sand is the place to go to indulge in water sports. San Juan Waterfun rents kayaks, banana boats (which are pulled by speedboats), Jet Skis, and Hobie catamarans (with captain). They also offer parasailing. Open daily (weather permitting) 10 AM–5 PM. $$–$$$$.

CULTURE

Casa Escuté

787-752-0703
Plaza Recreo de Carolina

Not quite on the Isla Verde circuit, I mention Casa Escuté only because it's so quirky. There's a reason that the municipality of Carolina, which encompasses the main airport and Isla Verde, was once known as La Tierra de Gigantes (The Land of the Giants). It was once home to the almost-8-foot-tall Don Felipe Birriel González. The Casa Escuté museum pays homage to the Giant of Carolina, and also features exhibits of Puerto Rican visual and folk arts. Open Monday through Friday 8 AM–4:30 PM, Saturday and Sunday by appointment only. $.

NIGHTLIFE

Brava

787-641-3500
www.bravapr.com
At El San Juan Hotel & Casino, 6063 Isla Verde Avenue, Isla Verde, Carolina

Welcome to party central for the young and the young at heart in Isla Verde. Brava, which used to be Babylon, has two floors of space to mingle and shake what you've got. The lower level is the main dance floor, and it can get crammed with people. The second floor is the more relaxed lounge area, dominated by the long bar and the VIP room. The music ranges from house and *raggaetón* to electronica. Dress in your flashiest best and get in line for the hottest club in town. Open Thursday through Saturday 10 PM–3 AM. $$.

Liquid

787-728-3666
At the San Juan Water & Beach Club Hotel, Two Tartak Street, Isla Verde, Carolina

After 11 PM, Tangerine, the Water & Beach Club's restaurant, becomes the bar and lounge called Liquid. It has a different atmosphere from the hotel's other lounge, **Wet** (is the water theme clear enough?), which is a somewhat chilled-out rooftop location (see page 169). Liquid has a great bar and, even better, a large lounge area. Don't bother asking when it closes; it closes when you leave. $$.

Oyster Bar & Grill

787-726-2161

6000 Isla Verde Avenue, Isla Verde, Carolina

Mardi Gras comes to San Juan via the Oyster Bar. The restaurant opens at 11 AM every day, but since the kitchen stays open until 3 AM, what's the hurry? Better to go at night and enjoy a boisterous departure from more chic establishments. And while you wait for your plateful of oysters, you can try an Oyster Shot, a snifter full of a raw oyster, Absolut Citron, Tabasco and cocktail sauces, horseradish, and pepper . . . it packs quite a punch. Other popular drinks include the everything-but-the-kitchen-sink New Orleans Iced Tea and the very tropical Cajun Coolerator. Doors stay open, ostensibly, until 5 AM. $$.

Shots Sports Bar & Grill

787-253-1443

At Isla Verde Mall, Isla Verde Avenue, Carolina

Shots is a lot more than a sports bar. Practically every night, it's doing something to keep patrons in their seat or get them out of it. You could come here three nights out of the week and hear three different live bands (with a decent stage for the band, and ample dancing room). Thursday night is devoted to salsa, with free lessons for customers from 7 to 9 PM. On Friday, the bass gets turned up with live *reggaetón*. On Saturday, Shots sticks with rock, and on Sunday they play more hip-hop. Open daily from 4 PM until . . . late. $–$$.

Wet, a lounge at San Juan Water & Beach Club Hotel

The Upper Level Lounge

787-253-1700

At the Ritz-Carlton, San Juan Hotel, Spa & Casino, 6961 Avenue of the Governors, Isla Verde, Carolina

This lounge, newly renovated at press time, sits atop the casino and offers a completely different vibe. It's much more spacious than a typical lounge, with clusters of sofas and chairs, tables for two and four, and a long, communal table. On some nights, you might catch a game on the big screen, which is somewhat incongruous with the Upper Level's dimly lit, late-night ambience. More often than not, you'll have a live DJ spinning the latest tunes. Doors open daily at 7 PM. $$.

Wet

787-728-3666

At the San Juan Water & Beach Club Hotel, Two Tartak Street, Isla Verde, Carolina

Wet is one of the best ways to enjoy San Juan at night. The Water & Beach Club's open-air rooftop lounge is among the most sought-after nighttime destinations in the city. Wet has stylish Asian-accented decor, a mellow ambience, excellent drinks, and above-average sushi served from 6:30 to 11 at night. If you're lucky enough to grab a spot, then relax on a sofa, sip a *mojito*, and enjoy San Juan's moonlit panorama. Wet keeps things interesting with several weekly activities: The schedule includes, at press time, movie night on Monday, Latin beats on Wednesday, and live DJs during the weekends. Open 11 PM until everyone leaves. $$.

SHOPPING

Algo d'Aqui

787-791-4105

5757 Isla Verde Avenue, Isla Verde, Carolina

There's no place like this tiny gift shop in Isla Verde, where you can get arts, crafts, and photographs, all by local artists. The store also carries candles and soaps with Puerto Rican scents and accents, coffee, and a cute "beach in a bag" (sand and shells in a canvas bag) souvenir. Open Monday through Saturday 11 AM–7 PM. $–$$$.

La Galería

787-791-1000

At El San Juan Hotel & Casino, 6063 Isla Verde Avenue, Isla Verde, Carolina

Considering the somewhat anemic boutique shopping in Isla Verde, your best bets to find the finer things in life are in the lobbies of the hotel resorts. The premier hotel shopping destination is La Galería (the Gallery) at El San Juan Hotel & Casino. Twelve establishments constitute this arcade, which has a distinct air of Vegas to it (note the trees in the middle of the hallway and the fountains). Among the boutiques, you'll find a mix of high-end jewelry stores like **Bared & Sons, Hellenis, Joseph Manchini,** and **Reinhold**

Jewelers; fine chocolates at the **Candy Shoppe**; and curios at **A Touch of Europe**. La Galería is open daily 10 AM–9 PM. $–$$$$.

Ocean Sports
787-268-2329
77 Isla Verde Avenue, Isla Verde, Carolina

Ocean Sports has three branches, two of them in Isla Verde, but this location is their flagship store. In addition to stocking everything the diver needs, they offer training and dive tours from shore or boat to many popular dive sites. Open Monday through Friday 10 AM–7 PM, Saturday 9 AM–6 PM. $$–$$$$.

GOOD TO KNOW ABOUT . . .

Cybernet Café
787-728-4195
5960 Isla Verde Avenue, Isla Verde, Carolina

This tiny little store has done its best to cool things up, with funky lighting, a coffee bar and, of course, a few computers where you can go online, check your e-mail, and print out anything you need. Open Monday through Saturday 9 AM–10:30 PM, Sunday 10:30 AM–10 PM.

Pueblo Supermarket
787-791-6633
Los Gobernadores Avenue, Isla Verde, Carolina

This well-known, local supermarket chain carries Puerto Rican brands in addition to the ones you'll be familiar with. This branch is open 24 hours a day.

Shell Select
787-268-6006
Carr 183, Km 2.4, Isla Verde Avenue, Isla Verde, Carolina

Open 24 hours, seven days a week.

Walgreens
787-982-0222
5984 Isla Verde Avenue, Isla Verde, Carolina

Your friendly local drugstore and pharmacy is open 24 hours a day.

WEEKLY & ANNUAL EVENTS

Club Gallístico de Puerto Rico
787-791-1557
6600 Isla Verde Avenue, Isla Verde, Carolina

Don't say I didn't warn you: *This venue is not for everyone.* If you want to see something truly different, and you aren't about to join PETA, you might want to check out a bout of cock-fighting. This is an ancient sport on the island, one that has polarized Puerto Ricans. Some, especially in the interior, uphold it as a time-honored tradition that the "West" doesn't understand. Others denounce it as cruel and immoral. You can judge for yourself. Every Saturday, the Club Gallístico hosts a series of cockfighting events. It's cheap to get in, but the betting is animated and serious. Open 2–9 PM. $.

Puerto Rico Salsa Congress
Final week of July
787-470-8888
www.puertoricosalsacongress.com
At El San Juan Hotel & Casino, 6063 Isla Verde Avenue, Isla Verde, Carolina

The annual Salsa Congress is a fantastic celebration of one of the world's great seductive and social dance forms. In 2007, the Salsa Congress marked its 11th year. Featuring scores of live bands, workshops, and events, this congress is for the serious *salsaficionado.* One of the main events of the congress is the World Salsa Open, the first global salsa competition in the world, which celebrated its sixth year. $$$$.

6

Metropolitan San Juan

Mix It Up with the Locals

The neighborhoods of Santurce, Río Piedras, Hato Rey, and Puerto Nuevo complete the urban sprawl that is Greater San Juan. Hotels are relatively scarce, and the sounds of English dwindle the farther inland you venture. But the tourism industry is catching up—and catching on to—the entertainment, culture, and recreational activities that suburban Sanjuaneros have long cherished. There's good reason for this; from restaurants that set the standard for *comida* criolla to botanical wonders to shopping palaces, Old San Juan has some competition in "New" San Juan.

SANTURCE—OFF THE BEATEN PATH

Santurce reminds me of Brooklyn. Before that statement has you flipping the page, let me clarify. Like my old neighborhood, Santurce is a longtime residential community—with a mix of a young, bohemian crowd and a blue-collar working class—that has only recently begun to encroach into hip and cool status, vulturing tourists from established trendy destinations on the island. It's the neighborhood with a romantic, Everyman-charm, which many people consider the real heart of the city.

There are a few reasons for the growing shift toward tourism. On the whole, Puerto Rico is making a concerted effort to expand its "tourist zone" to include as many locations as possible. Another factor is that this district, along with the others covered in this chapter, offers a distinct departure from the forts and beaches that everyone associates with Puerto Rico. Finally, Santurce has done plenty on its own to merit attention. Shops, restaurants, and attractions have cropped up over time. Two bastions of fine art—the Museo de Arte de Puerto Rico and the Museo de Arte Contemporáneo—along with Centro de Bellas Artes Luis A. Ferré (Luis A. Ferré Performing Arts Center), reinforce Santurce's artistic heritage and have made it a cultural focal point. And the marketplace at Plaza del Mercado (Market Square) gives tourists a look at the "real" local life.

Among Santurce's delights are its *fondas,* the name given to small, no-frills eateries that have faithfully served their neighborhoods and are an integral part of the community. At *fondas* you'll rub shoulders with Sanjuaneros, point and smile if you don't speak Spanish, and feast on down-home Puerto Rican cooking. There are many to choose from, and a few—like the revered La Casita Blanca—have histories as rich as their food.

Where does Santurce end and Condado begin? That is a matter of some debate. Some people, including business owners in the neighborhood, tell me that Condado is

Pool and gardens at Museo del Arte de Puerto Rico

technically part of Santurce. Even if that's true, most people segregate the two; Loíza Street seems to be a popular line of demarcation. Certainly, once you're beyond Baldorioty de Castro Avenue, you're in Santurce proper. Of course, leaving the more heavily trafficked tourist zones behind also means that, after dark, visitors must be more aware and alert. It's not crime infested, but Santurce is not the safest area in Puerto Rico. But that's the trade-off every time you step off the beaten path.

LODGING

Best Western Hotel Pierre

787-721-1200
www.bestwestern.com
105 Calle de Diego, Santurce, San Juan 00925

There are few lodging options in Santurce, primarily because neighboring Condado and Isla Verde have so much to offer. Tourists who want to stay away from these areas are best served by booking a room at the Best Western. The hotel is centrally located in the neighborhood, it's next to Baldorioty de Castro Avenue—a main thoroughfare to the old city—and it's a short walk to either the beach or the Museo de Arte de Puerto. The rooms are spacious and clean, and come with complimentary breakfast. In addition, there's a pool, a fitness center, and the usual reliable amenities and service of a Best Western. $$.

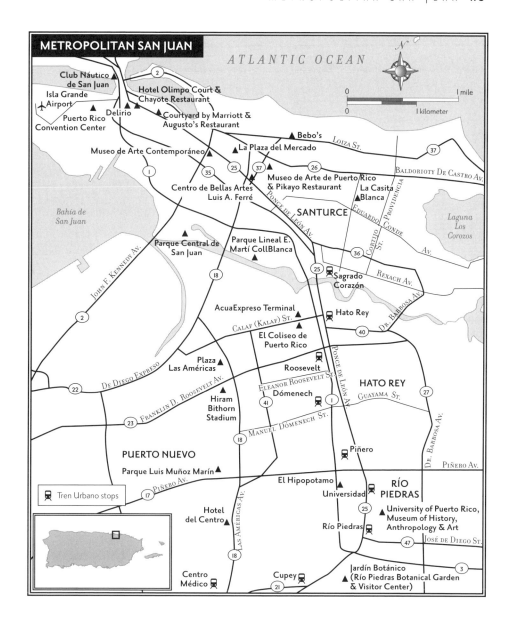

Mic-figure map:

METROPOLITAN SAN JUAN

ATLANTIC OCEAN

Club Náutico de San Juan
Isla Grande Airport
Puerto Rico Convention Center
Delirio
Hotel Olimpo Court & Chayote Restaurant
Courtyard by Marriott & Augusto's Restaurant
Bebo's
Museo de Arte Contemporáneo
La Plaza del Mercado
LOIZA ST.
BALDORIOTY DE CASTRO AV.
Centro de Bellas Artes Luis A. Ferré
Museo de Arte de Puerto Rico & Pikayo Restaurant
La Casita Blanca
SANTURCE
PONCE DE LEÓN AV.
EDUARDO CONDE
PROVIDENCIA
CORTIJO ST.
Bahía de San Juan
Laguna Los Corozos
Parque Central de San Juan
Parque Lineal E. Martí CollBlanca
JOHN F. KENNEDY AV.
Sagrado Corazón
REXACH AV.
DR. BARBOSA AV.
AcuaExpreso Terminal
CALAF (KALAF) ST.
Hato Rey
El Coliseo de Puerto Rico
DE DIEGO EXPRESO
Plaza Las Américas
Roosevelt
HATO REY
Hiram Bithorn Stadium
FRANKLIN D. ROOSEVELT AV.
ELEANOR ROOSEVELT ST.
Dómenech
GUAYAMA ST.
PONCE DE LEÓN AV.
MANUEL DÓMENECH ST.
DR. BARBOSA AV.
PUERTO NUEVO
Piñero
Parque Luis Muñoz Marín
PIÑERO AV.
El Hipopotamo
RÍO PIEDRAS
Universidad
PIÑERO AV.

🚇 Tren Urbano stops

Hotel del Centro
LAS AMÉRICAS AV.
Río Piedras
University of Puerto Rico, Museum of History, Anthropology & Art
JOSÉ DE DIEGO ST.
Centro Médico
Cupey
Jardín Botánico (Río Piedras Botanical Garden & Visitor Center)

DINING

Bebo's Café

787-726-1008

1600 Loíza Street, Santurce, San Juan

Bebo's typifies Santurce: laid back, off the beaten path, and yet always busy. It's an extremely popular Puerto Rican restaurant with Dominican accents where you get the standard fare (rice 'n' beans, skirt steaks, plantain-heavy entrées) at very affordable prices. The biggest knock on the restaurant is the sometimes excruciatingly slow service, but the regulars are used to it and take it in stride. (You'll also be hard-pressed to find English speakers among the staff.) If you have a full agenda and want a quick lunch or dinner, avoid this place; otherwise, come in, eat well, relax, and pay little. Open daily 7 AM–midnight. $–$$.

La Casita Blanca

787-726-5501
351 Tapia Street, Santurce, San Juan
www.casitablancapr.com

A restaurant owner in San Juan, knowing I was writing a guidebook, asked me to name my favorite restaurants on the island. After reflecting, I gave him a few names. As soon as I said "La Casita Blanca," he clapped his hands and said, "Yes! I'm so glad you went there." That's the reaction this place produces in Puerto Rico. La Casita Blanca is hallowed culinary ground. Set in a quiet corner of Santurce, the rustic restaurant has a storied history. Before it became La Casita Blanca, another restaurant—El Cafetín De Doña Chacón—operated at this location, which has been feeding the community since 1922. Today, La Casita Blanca carries the torch for pure *cocina del barrio* (cuisine of the neighborhood). The regulars here, who are a loud, fun lot, include artists, politicians, families . . . the gamut of Puerto Rican society. And the food . . . the food! The menu is scribbled every day on a chalkboard, no more than 10 to 12

La Casita Blanca

dishes, with popular favorites such as *arroz con pollo* (rice with chicken), *patitos de cerdo* (pigs' feet), and *pastelón de carne* (a delicious local take on lasagna, made with mashed plantain instead of potato). On Sunday, great pots of food line the bar, and you can go at them with gusto. Even though it's out of the way, tourists do frequent La Casita Blanca; Rachel Ray made a stop here recently, and so should you. Open Monday through Wednesday 11 AM–4 PM, Thursday 11 AM–6 PM, Friday and Saturday 11 AM–9 PM, and Sunday noon–4 PM. $$.

La Casona

787-727-2717
www.lacasonapr.com
609 Jorge Street, Santurce, San Juan

From La Casita to La Casona, the change could not be more dramatic. Both are dining institutions, but La Casona celebrates the traditions of Spain. Set in an old Spanish villa, La Casona is all about elegance. Stained-glass windows, warm, intimate lighting, live music on weekends, and separate rooms that break up the crowd make this restaurant ideal for a romantic date, a special family gathering, or a power business dinner. The Spanish-based menu has international twists thrown in, and the food is artistically placed on the plate. While the fresh fish and seafood dishes are excellent, the rosemary-infused veal chop and rack of lamb bring nostalgic smiles to diners' faces. And then they remember the bill. Open Monday through Friday noon–3 PM and 6–11:30 PM, Saturday 6–11:30 PM. $$$–$$$$.

Pikayo

787-721-6194
www.pikayo.com
In the Museo de Arte de Puerto Rico, 299 De Diego Avenue, Santurce, San Juan

I could be the latest in a long line to write a stellar review of Pikayo. I could tell you about its breathtaking setting in the museum of art and its clean, modern decor, which evoke the natural elements of Puerto Rico: the draped white of ocean breeze and sea foam, the blend of dark wood of the forest and lighter wood of the sand, and the gorgeous cloud-white and crystal-rain lamps. I could describe the constantly changing menu that starts off in Puerto Rico but navigates the globe. Or I could wax eloquent about Chef Wilo Benet's take on classics like the *empanadilla*, which is made with truffles and cheese and served with a truffle *mojito*, or his *bistec encebollado*, made with caramelized onions. But I'd rather you save up some money and head out to one of the most celebrated restaurants around. Open Tuesday through Friday noon–3 PM for lunch, and Monday through Saturday 6–11 PM for dinner. $$$–$$$$.

La Plaza del Mercado

At Dos Hermanos and Capitol streets, Santurce, San Juan

Remember what I said about trying out a *fonda*? Well, you'll find plenty in and around the Plaza del Mercado, which is also called La Placita, along with some larger restaurants all specializing in local fare. Among the most frequented are **El Popular** (787-722-4653), the oldest one in the market; **El Pescador** (787-721-0995), a tiny place with plastic chairs and delicious fried and grilled fish; **El Coco de Luis** (787-721-7595), a great place for fried finger foods; and **Café de la Plaza** (787-721-1526), which stays open until 1 AM and has great *churrasco* steaks and *mofongos*. $–$$.

La Tasca de Yiyo

787-728-5009
1753 Loíza Street, Santurce, San Juan

A popular spot with the locals for Puerto Rican and Cuban food, La Tasca de Yiyo has a loyal following and a menu with all the classics, including *chuletas can can* (fried pork chops) and a variety of *mofongos*, and *vaca frita* (literally "fried cow"). There are daily specials, which are almost all under $10, in addition to the à la carte selections. Open Monday through Thursday noon–10 PM, Friday and Saturday noon–11 PM, and Sunday noon–6 PM. $–$$.

ATTRACTIONS, PARKS & RECREATION

Parque Central de San Juan

787-722-1646
Roberto H. Todd Avenue and Cerra Street, Santurce, San Juan

On the edge of a mangrove forest, this 35-acre park has a vast network of jogging and cycling trails, tennis courts, soccer fields, and playgrounds for children. Open Monday through Thursday 6 AM–10 PM, Friday 6 AM–9 PM, and weekends 6 AM–7 PM. $ for parking.

La Placita

At Dos Hermanos and Capitol streets, Santurce, San Juan

The Santurce marketplace is a local institution and a place that, day or night, captures the past and the present of Puerto Rico. It is still actively engaged in its time-honored custom: Beginning at 5 every morning, Sanjuaneros armed with shopping bags descend here to buy everything from fresh fruit and vegetables to *santos* and *caretas*. Good, cheap, local restaurants and bars run a lively trade from morning till night. From Thursday until Sunday, the marketplace transforms into an open-air party after the vendors pack up their stalls. If you want a truly local experience, come to this weekly gathering place for food, music, and dancing.

CULTURE

Centro de Bellas Artes Luis A. Ferré (Luis A. Ferré Performing Arts Center)
787-724-4747
www.cba.gobierno.pr
Ponce de León Avenue, Santurce, San Juan

For a night of ballet, opera, a concert or a play, check the listings at this beautiful, modern, and spacious performing arts center. Named after a Puerto Rican politician and philanthropist, the center boasts three main concert and theater halls, and is full of expositions of art. One of the most poignant and apt is Annex Burgos's work depicting the Muses—a series of 6-foot bronze sculptures in the Plaza Juan Morel Campos. Each sculpture represents a different art form. The center is free to visit, but performances vary in price.

Museo de Arte Contemporáneo (Museum of Contemporary Art)
787-977-4030
Rafael M. de Labra Historical Building
At the corner of Juan Ponce de León and Roberto H. Todd avenues, Santurce, San Juan

The Museo de Arte Contemporáneo celebrates the best of the modern masters from Puerto Rico, the Caribbean, and Latin America. The permanent collection focuses on all manner of artistic expression—painting, sculpture, photography, video—and features local artists such as Myrna Báez, Domingo García, and Noemí Ruiz. The museum also offers courses throughout the year to promote art on the island. Open Monday through Saturday 10 AM—4 PM, Sunday noon—4 PM. Free.

Museo de Arte de Puerto Rico (Puerto Rico Museum of Art)
787-977-6277
www.mapr.org
299 De Diego Avenue, Santurce, San Juan

The Museo de Arte de Puerto Rico has quickly become one of the island's most beautiful modern landmarks. Actually, the collection of works inside the building is rather small when compared to the massive building that houses them. The permanent collection includes old masters like José Campeche and Francisco Oller, as well as modern artists like Angel Botello, Rafael Trelles, and Noemí Ruiz. The galleries on the second floor host temporary exhibits of works by local artists. The museum has a magnificent great hall dominated at the far end by a spectacular wall of oxidized glass designed to filter the sunlight, as well as a theater, the award-winning **Pikayo** restaurant (known as the best museum restaurant in the world; see "Dining"), and a gift shop. Beneath the lobby level, there's a gallery dedicated to students and families, and a wonderful interactive exhibit where children can learn about various forms of art. The interior is exquisite, but the exterior isn't too shabby either. Circling a pond is a sculpture garden that is definitely worth

Museo de Arte de Puerto Rico

the walk. Open Tuesday, and Thursday through Saturday, 10 AM–5 PM; Wednesday 10 AM–8 PM; and Sunday 11 AM–6 PM. $$.

NIGHTLIFE

El Bar Rubí
787-289-8080
213 Canals Street, Santurce, San Juan

Strictly for the weekend revelers, this is a popular spot to go to once you leave La Placita (if you leave La Placita). From the owner of Pinky's in Ocean Park, El Bar Rubí is known for its powerful cocktails. It's got ample space and draws a lively crowd. The music ranges from local hits to hip-hop and R&B. Open Thursday and Friday 7 PM–3 AM. $.

Krash
787-722-1131
www.krashklubpr.com
1257 Ponce de León Avenue, Santurce, San Juan

Puerto Rico's premier gay club has a new name. "Eros" is now called "Krash," but the lively and often times frisky (you will get touched) club remains ever popular. The two-level club has a large dance floor that gets packed quickly, balconies on the second level for people-watching, a stage for the always entertaining drag show competitions, and decor that screams gay pride. Doors open Wednesday through Saturday at 10 PM, and on Sunday whenever Monday is a holiday. $.

La Placita
At Dos Hermanos and Capitol streets, Santurce, San Juan

From Thursday to Saturday night, La Placita becomes an all-out block party. The bars and restaurants stay open late, and the plaza is full of people milling around, enjoying the night and the company and hopping from one spot to another. There's music pumping from at least one corner, and vendors of all kinds vying for your attention. The only drawback, if you're driving here, is parking. (Of course, chances are, you won't want to drive back either.) Friday is usually the best day to go.

SHOPPING

Harry Robles
787-727-3885
1752 Loíza Street, Santurce, San Juan

Harry Robles is one of the most exclusive and sought-after designers in Puerto Rico. So it says something that he will often be in the store to attend to you personally as you peruse his line of high-end couture. Everything from casual clothing to dresses to wedding gowns is custom-made, and there are two collections each year, in fall and summer. The boutique is open by appointment only. Open Monday through Friday 9 AM–5 PM. $$$$.

Koishma
787-633-3333
www.koishma.com
110 Calle del Parque, Suite G-C, Santurce, San Juan

The athlete's superstore, Koishma carries top brands of clothing, equipment, footwear, supplements, and accessories for runners, swimmers, and cyclists. Open Monday through Friday 10 AM–6 PM, Saturday noon–5 PM. $–$$$.

GOOD TO KNOW ABOUT . . .

Pueblo
787-723-1611
114 De Diego Avenue, Santurce, San Juan

This branch of the local supermarket chain is open 24 hours a day.

Walgreens
787-728-0510
1963 Loíza Street, Santurce, San Juan

This 24-hour branch has drive-thru prescription pickup service.

WEEKLY & ANNUAL EVENTS

Festival Casals de Puerto Rico (Casals Festival)
February–March
787-268-0657; 787-620-4444 (for tickets)
www.festcasalspr.gobierno.pr/index2.html
At Centro de Bellas Artes Luis A. Ferré, Ponce de León Avenue, Santurce, San Juan

This annual homage to Puerto Rico's greatest maestro has become one of the premier classical music events in the Caribbean. The Casals Festival draws musicians and patrons of the arts from all over the world for a series of concerts and performances that stretch over three weeks. The 2007 festival featured pianist Vladimir Feltsman, violinist Julia Fischer, conductor Giancarlo Guerrero, and the Moscow String Quartet. $$–$$$$.

HATO REY—THE GOLDEN MILE AND THE GOLDEN MALL

Unless you have a deep and abiding love for financial institutions, there is little motivation to make the trip out to Hato Rey. Despite some nice examples of modern architecture, the city's cluster of austere-looking buildings cannot rival the skylines of many U.S. downtowns. Of course, if you need take out a second mortgage in order to push your luck at the casino, you might want to check it out: The banking district of Puerto Rico is here, and the strip of Luis Muñoz Rivera Avenue where you'll find the corporate towers is known as "the Golden Mile." Among the financial movers and shakers to call this stretch of road home are Banco Santander, Chase Manhattan Bank, and the Banco Popular headquarters.

Hato Rey is a stop on the Tren Urbano, making it very accessible if you don't have a car. From here, Franklin Delano Roosevelt Avenue is the main thoroughfare for restaurants, bakeries, and shops. Many local restaurants include banquet halls that cater to nearby corporations. There are precious few hotels, clubs, or cultural activities in Hato Rey; it's all about big business.

Actually, I lied. It's not *all* about big business. Hato Rey does offer entertainment centers, stadiums, and parks. **El Coliseo de Puerto Rico** is the main arena for concerts in the city; **Hiram Bithorn Stadium** hosts baseball games during the Puerto Rico Professional Baseball League's winter season; and **Luis Muñoz Marín Park** is among the nicest in San Juan. Although I've left it for last, there is one overriding reason to visit Hato Rey, and it has nothing to do with the Golden Mile. This is the home of **Plaza Las Américas**, the largest mall in the Caribbean. A favorite hangout of Sanjuaneros, it's also a top tourist destination.

DINING

El Bodegón de Gaspar
787-763-0990
282 F. D. Roosevelt Avenue, Hato Rey, San Juan

For 30 years, Chef Gaspar Ballestero has brought Spain to Hato Rey. The menu in this warm, intimate restaurant features old-world classics, including a wide selection of tapas such as serrano ham, chorizo, mushrooms, and figs. *Camarones al champagne* (shrimp cooked in champagne) and, of course, Paella Valenciana (the most common variety, with chicken, chorizo, and seafood) highlight the entrées. There is a dash of *boricua* in Ballestero's cooking, so don't be surprised to find *tostones* and *asopao* on the menu. Trios provide live Puerto Rican music Thursday through Monday. Open daily from noon to midnight. $$.

Metropol 3
787-751-4022
124 F. D. Roosevelt Avenue, Hato Rey, San Juan

For over 40 years, the Metropol name has been synonymous with down-home, basic Puerto Rican cooking. In truth, it might be a bit too basic. The menu is fairly typical, with favorites including *bistec de palomilla* (prime steak filet), *rodaballo a la plancha* (grilled halibut), and *gallinita rellena* (Cornish hen stuffed with rice and beans). The food is tasty but quite plain, and others do it better. Still, the three locations of Metropol—in Hato Rey, on Isla Verde, and in Fajardo—remain popular local spots. Open daily 11:30 AM–11 PM. $–$$.

El Paseo
787-756-6840
244 F. D. Roosevelt Avenue, Hato Rey, San Juan

A favorite of many locals, El Paseo serves Puerto Rican and Cuban fare in a friendly, warm atmosphere. Much of the clientele is comprised of office workers taking their lunch or enjoying a casual dinner after hours. The menu is extensive and includes daily specials, the prices are reasonable, and the portions will satisfy most appetites. The *gallinita relleno de congri* (stuffed Cornish hen with rice and beans) is succulent and very filling. Another classic is the *chuletas can can* (fried pork chops), and the *churrasco* (skirt steak). Open Monday through Thursday 11:30 AM–10 PM, Friday and Saturday until 11 PM. $$.

El Zipperle
787-751-4335
www.elzipperle.com
352 F. D. Roosevelt Avenue, Hato Rey, San Juan

Regulars say the German half of this German-Spanish restaurant has diluted over the years, and even the professional staff will courteously steer you toward the paellas. Still, the schnitzels and breaded veal are available, and El Zipperle certainly looks more Bavarian than Spanish on the outside. Opened in 1950, it's a long-standing stalwart of the business and formal dining scene. My advice: Stick with the paellas (try the *Paella Terrera*, which is all meat and no seafood, for a new twist on the classic version). $$$.

ATTRACTIONS, PARKS & RECREATION

El Coliseo de Puerto Rico
1-877-COLISEO
www.coliseodepuertorico.com
500 Arterial B Street, Hato Rey, San Juan

From the biggest rock concerts to prime sporting bouts, if there's a major event going on in the city, it's probably being held at the coliseum. San Juan's biggest sports and entertainment complex is the largest two-level covered facility on the island, with a seating capacity of 18,000. The box office is open Monday through Friday 10 AM–5 PM. $$–$$$$.

Galaxy Lanes
787-777-5016
At Plaza Las Americas, 525 F. D. Roosevelt Avenue, Hato Rey, San Juan
www.plazalasamericas.com

Galaxy Lanes is a two-level entertainment center in Plaza Las Américas mall with 32 modern-style bowling lanes, a dance area, pool tables, two bars, and a restaurant. Open Monday through Wednesday 8 AM–1 AM, Thursday through Saturday 8 AM–3 AM, and Sunday 10 AM–1 AM. $$.

Hiram Bithorn Stadium
787-294-0001 (for tickets)
Intersection of F. D. Roosevelt Avenue and Route 18, Hato Rey, San Juan

Baseball is popular in Puerto Rico. Hiram Bithorn, the first Puerto Rican to enter major-league baseball, made it to the big leagues with the Cubs in 1942. His legacy lives on today in the Bithorn Stadium, Puerto Rico's largest baseball stadium. From November to January, you can catch a game of the Puerto Rican Professional Baseball League here. The talent, not including the occasional major leaguer spending his off-season here, is not as good as it is in the States; but it's definitely a cheaper ticket . . . and hey, where else can you drink a piña colada while watching a game? $.

Parque Nacional Lineal Enrique Martí Coll
787-763-0568
www.parquesnacionalespr.com/marti_coll_par.asp
50 Prudencio Martinez Avenue, Hato Rey, San Juan

Known to the locals simply as the Paseo Lineal, this park is a favorite of runners, bikers, and bird-watchers. Its 1.5-mile-long elevated trail runs through a mangrove forest, the habitat of the largest concentration of native and migratory birds on the island. Open weekdays 6 AM–9 PM, Saturday and Sunday 6 AM–5 PM. Free.

Parque Nacional Luis Muñoz Marín
787-763-0568
www.parquesnacionalespr.com/munoz_marin_par.asp
Avenida Piñero and Route 18, Hato Rey, San Juan

Across from Plaza Las Américas and behind the Roberto Clemente Coliseum and Hiram Bithorn Stadium, you'll come to one of San Juan's nicest and largest parks. Covering 140 acres, the park has many walking and biking trails, children's playgrounds set amid small lakes, an amphitheater, even golf practice areas. A cable car takes you across the park, giving you fantastic views of the area. Open Wednesday through Sunday 8:30 AM–5 PM. $ for cable car ride.

NIGHTLIFE

Coaches

787-758-3598
www.coachespr.com
137 F. D. Roosevelt Avenue, Hato Rey, San Juan

This well-known bar and restaurant, conveniently located near "the Golden Mile," has a casual and friendly vibe, all kinds of happy hours and special events, a dance floor with live bands from Wednesday to Saturday, and great bar food (including a juicy *churrasco*). The bar's decor is sports-themed, and Sunday and Monday are devoted to sports. With plenty of TVs, including a big screen, you can watch your favorite game. It's good to be a woman at Coaches: On Saturday, you'll get free cosmopolitans after 7 PM, and on Wednesday, you'll get free wine from 5 to 8 PM. The kitchen stays open until 2 AM, the bar . . . longer. $–$$.

Galaxy Lanes

787-777-5016
At Plaza Las Americas, 525 F. D. Roosevelt Avenue, Hato Rey, San Juan
www.plazalasamericas.com

Bowl. Dance. Drink. Eat. Party till late. Galaxy Lanes, the two-level entertainment center in the Plaza Las Americas mall, lets you do it all. The place can comfortably accommodate large numbers in its two bars, a dance floor with live DJ, and a pool hall. Open Monday through Wednesday, and Sunday, until 1 AM; open Thursday through Saturday until 3 AM. $$.

Plaza Las Américas

SHOPPING

Plaza Las Américas
787-767-5202
525 F. D. Roosevelt Avenue, Hato Rey, San Juan
www.plazalasamericas.com

Over 40 places to eat. Thirteen cinemas with English- and Spanish-language versions of the latest blockbusters. Oh, and over 300 stores selling everything from cookies to cars. Plaza Las Américas, the Caribbean's biggest mall and one of the island's top destinations, has the world's largest JCPenney and Sears department stores; the only Macy's in the Caribbean; over 20 jewelry stores; and a mix of popular local brands and the most globally recognized labels. Plus, with its myriad fountains and sculptures, it's more picturesque than most malls. With good reason, they call this place *el centro de todo* ("the center of it all"). Open Monday through Saturday 9 AM–9 PM, Sunday 11 AM–5 PM. $–$$$$.

FOOD PURVEYORS, LIQUOR & CIGARS

The Swiss Cake
787-759-8222
237 Roosevelt Avenue, Hato Rey, San Juan

Good luck weighing the same when you leave as when you entered. Decadent and delicious fresh cakes, a variety of Swiss rolls, tarts, and pastries of all kinds are available at this store, which many feel is the best bakery and cake shop on the island. For a bit of Puerto Rico, try the *tres leches*. Open daily 8 AM–8:30 PM.

WEEKLY & ANNUAL EVENTS

Heineken Jazz Fest
June
1-866-994-0001; 787-294-0001 (for tickets)
www.prheinekenjazz.com
Tito Puente Amphitheater

One of Puerto Rico's premier musical events, the Heineken Jazz Festival, held annually in the open-air Tito Puente Amphitheater, is a four-day musical party that includes several headliners, and jazz workshops for musicians. $$.

International Orchid Festival
March
787-758-9981
Pedrín Zorrilla Coliseum
Intersection of F. D. Roosevelt Avenue and Route 18, Hato Rey, San Juan

With over 25,000 species, orchids belong to the largest and most varied family of the plant world. At the annual festival of the Puerto Rico Orchid Society, orchid fans and those who love colorful flowers come to enjoy the huge variety of these fascinating plants in all their splendor. There are exhibitions of plants and gardens, seminars, arts and crafts, raffles, lectures, and sales. Show runs from 9 AM to 6 PM each day. $.

RÍO PIEDRAS—CAMPUS CENTER

As you cross Jesus T. Piñero Avenue, you pass over the threshold separating Hato Rey from Río Piedras. The district would have very little to offer visitors but for the University of Puerto Rico. There is a marketplace, which fills up on the weekends but is not worth a second trip if you've seen the one in Santurce (which is closer, and more accessible, to the tourism zones). Río Piedras has a handful of interesting restaurants and shops, but again, nothing that on its own merits the journey from Old San Juan, Condado, or Isla Verde.

So what's so special about the UPR, or "Yupi", as the locals call the university? Founded in 1903, it's the oldest on the island, and the largest, with a student body of over 20,000 on the Río Piedras campus alone. (The total number of students connected to the University of Puerto Rico is about 70,000.) And the Río Piedras campus is just beautiful. Many of the structures are architecturally stunning, evoking a variety of styles and eras. The clock tower that soars above the rest of the buildings, a graceful icon of the university, is a

University of Puerto Rico

beautiful example of the Spanish Renaissance style. The university's museum and botanical gardens are also worth the trip.

One of the most important landmarks in Río Piedras is a place I hope you never have to visit. The massive Centro Médico (Medical Center), strategically located just off the Las Americas Expressway, is a state-of-the-art complex and among the most advanced medical centers in the region. Among its institutions and facilities are the Caribbean Cardiovascular Center, University of Puerto Rico Medical Sciences Campus, Veterans Hospital, and Psychiatric Hospital.

LODGING

Hotel del Centro
787-751-1335
On the fourth floor of the Caribbean Cardiovascular Center, *Centro Médico* complex, Río Piedras, San Juan 00926

With the medical center nearby, it follows that the main hotel in Río Piedras would be situated here and dedicated to serving the health-care industry. It's affordable and clean, and has meeting space and a business center. It's also a lot farther than you'll want to be from the all the sights. This place is perfect for the traveler who needs to be near the university or the medical center. All others should move on. $.

DINING

El Hipopotamo
787-767-2660
880 Muñoz Rivera Avenue, Río Piedras, San Juan

Why the hippopotamus was chosen as the unlikely symbol of this Puerto Rican and Spanish restaurant, deli, and liquor store is a mystery. In every other way, this place is a typical, quaint eatery in the heart of Río Piedras. Ham hocks line the walls, and the menu offers local classics you've seen elsewhere—like *asopao* and *filete de mero* (grouper filet)—and some you probably haven't—like *crema de platano* (cream of plantain), a thick soup similar to cream of potato, and *sesos frescos a la romana* (calf brains fried in egg batter). University professors, students, and locals of every walk of life eat here regularly. Open Sunday through Thursday 7 AM–1 AM, Friday and Saturday until 3 AM. $$.

Tropical
787-761-1415
Las Vistas Shopping Village, Suite 53, Las Cumbras Avenue, Río Piedras, San Juan

Tropical is Caribbean food in all its black-beans-and-rice glory. Tasty, simple Cuban and criollo dishes like grilled halibut, roast chicken, and succulent ribs are to be had here. The restaurant is known for its friendly service and relaxed ambience, and people tend to recognize each other. Open daily 11:45 AM–10:30 PM. $$.

ATTRACTIONS, PARKS & RECREATION

Jardín Botánico (Botanical Garden)

787-767-1710

At the intersection of Route 1 and Route 847, University of Puerto Rico, Río Piedras, San Juan

www.upr.clu.edu/jardin1200.html

The university's botanical garden, spread over a massive 300 acres, is equal parts verdant oasis, learning center, and living laboratory. Visitors will encounter an astounding variety of Puerto Rico's flora organized and displayed in a series of interconnected parks, each picturesque and unique. From the lush aquatic garden with its Japanese wooden bridge to the French-inspired Monet garden, to the incredible orchid garden, the winding trails take you on a rich botanical tour. There's also a herbarium with about 36,000 species of dry plants. Along your walk, you'll see waterfalls, lakes, fountains, sculptures, and some of the 63 species of birds found here. Guided tours are offered daily from 9 AM to 3 PM, but it's just as fun to grab a map and explore on your own. The only flaw about this beautifully maintained retreat is access. Not only is it a bit of a pain to get to, but once you're here, it's not easy to find the Information Center (look for the pink building). Those minor inconveniences shouldn't deter you from enjoying a few hours here. Open daily from 6 AM–6 PM. Free.

Jardín Botánico

Museum of History, Anthropology & Art

CULTURE

The Museum of History, Anthropology & Art
787-763-3939
University of Puerto Rico Río Piedras Campus, Río Piedras, San Juan

This is not the largest or fanciest museum on the island; far from it. But its collection of art and artifacts is central to Puerto Rican culture and history. Since it opened its doors in 1959, the museum has worked to further awareness of the island's archaeological and artistic heritage. Today, its collection of over 30,000 pieces includes perhaps the most famous and well-known painting to emerge from Puerto Rico: Francisco Oller's dark and intense *El Velorio* (The Wake). The archaeological collection of the island's indigenous peoples is the most comprehensive of its kind in the world. And the historical pieces include the famous "Grito de Lares" flag, symbol of Puerto Rican independence. Open daily 9 AM–4 PM, except Wednesday and Thursday until 9 PM. Free.

SHOPPING

Librería La Tertulia
787-765-1148
www.tertulia.com
1002 Ponce de León Avenue, Río Piedras, San Juan

Move over, Barnes & Noble. In this university town, Tertulia is king. This bookstore is the oldest in San Juan, and is much more than a university institution. For almost 40 years, La

Tertulia has been a resource for the promotion of Puerto Rican literature, culture, and history. Its look and feel is very much that of a college bookstore that has hosted hundreds of book readings, conferences, and meetings for the student and literary communities. The bookstore café is a nice place to relax and listen to the buzz of Puerto Rican academic life. $–$$$.

Weekly & Annual Events

Festival de Jazz Borinquen (Borinquen Jazz Festival)
March 30-31
787-473-2273
www.tallersr.com
Grand Theater of the University of Puerto Rico at Río Piedras, San Juan

The brainchild of local composer and saxophonist José "Furito" Ríos, the Borinquen Jazz Festival celebrates its fifth year in 2007, combining jazz concerts with art expositions, local crafts, classes, and conferences. Local and international artists participate. $$$.

Miramar—The Local Life
Located on the southern side of Condado Lagoon, the small residential neighborhood of Miramar is a mix of a busy business district, an upscale sector with beautiful homes, and sketchy areas you'd do well to avoid. San Juan's second airport, Isla Grande, is in Miramar. If you're traveling to Culebra, Vieques, and other parts of Puerto Rico, you'll probably pass through Isla Grande. Miramar's most celebrated landmark (and one of its most beautiful buildings) is the Academia del Perpetuo Socorro, a college–prep school that is second to none in Puerto Rico. And Club Náutico is a large marina that hosts some of the city's biggest sailing and fishing events.

For the everyday tourist, however, it's not a place to spend a lot of time . . . for now. I say that because Miramar's sparkling new convention center is sure to give the city a huge boost as a social and business destination. With a hotel and urban park under development, and some of the biggest events in town already booked, it has already begun to change the face of San Juan.

Having said that, Miramar is far enough east of Old San Juan, south of Condado, and west of Isla Verde to make it inconveniently removed from the sights. But it *is* a place to come for dinner. Miramar has some terrific restaurants, including a newcomer that has quickly become one of my favorites in the city.

Lodging

Courtyard by Marriott
1-800-289-4274; 787-721-7400
www.courtyardpr.com
801 Ponce de León Avenue, Miramar, San Juan 00907

The Courtyard by Marriott, previously known (and well regarded) as the Excelsior Hotel, is in the heart of Miramar's business district and ideal for business travelers. The rooms are nothing special to look at but very comfortable, some with wonderful views of the city and Condado Lagoon. Suites come with a separate work area. The hotel supplies meeting space, a pool, a gym, and one of the best restaurants in the city (and its other restaurant is no slouch). $$–$$$.

Hotel Olimpo Court
787-724-0600
603 Miramar Avenue, Miramar, San Juan 00907

If management doesn't want to pay a lot for your lodgings while you're in town—or if you just want a budget hotel and don't mind a short bus or cab ride—you might want to consider the Olimpo Court. This family-owned and -operated hotel is very affordable. Set in the heart of the business district, it has a friendly staff and well-maintained rooms. Although some rooms have a kitchenette, you're much better off dining at **Chayote**, one of the best dining tickets in town. It's pricey, but if you're staying at Olimpo Court, you've already saved some money. $.

DINING

Augusto's
787-725-7700
At the Courtyard by Marriott, 801 Ponce de León Avenue, Miramar, San Juan

Augusto's would fit perfectly in midtown Manhattan, central London . . . just about anywhere people are happy to pay top dollar for top-quality food. This is a classy place: The waiters are formal and polite, the wine menu extensive, the setting elegant, and the Continental menu is the clear star of the show. While the seafood dishes are fine, I'll stick with the meats at Augusto's. The melt-in-your-mouth Kobe beef ribs and the Colorado lamb duo (a rosemary-crusted lamb loin paired with seared chops) are phenomenal. If you're a chocolate-lover, you'd be masochistic to miss the hot chocolate soufflé. Open Tuesday through Friday noon–3 PM for lunch, Tuesday through Saturday 7 –10:30 PM for dinner. $$$$.

Bistro de Paris
787-721-8925
At the Courtyard by Marriott, 801 Ponce de León Avenue, Miramar, San Juan

Except for the poolside al fresco dining, this Courtyard by Marriott's casual restaurant does an admirable job of emulating an authentic Parisian bistro. The proof, as they say, is in the pudding . . . or in this case, the French onion soup, escargots, and (my favorite), the filet mignon in peppercorn sauce. Thursday night is fondue night. Open daily 7 AM–4 PM for lunch, 6:30–10 PM for dinner. $$.

Chayote
787-722-9385
At the Hotel Olimpo Court, 603 Miramar Avenue, Miramar, San Juan

Putting a *boricua* twist on international
cuisine never tasted so good. *Chayote,* the
name of a locally grown vegetable, takes
you away from Puerto Rico . . . and yet
doesn't. The menu changes often, but the
chef keeps things interesting by throwing
together unusual combinations, such as
the lobster spring roll with guava sauce,
the sea bass filet over yucca-truffle puree,
and red snapper with a tangy passion fruit,
orange, and lemon vinaigrette. Whether
you try a fish, meat, or seafood dish, save
some room for the mango flan. Open
Tuesday through Friday noon–2:30 PM for
lunch, Tuesday through Saturday 7–10:30
PM for dinner. $$$.

Delirio
787-722-0444
762 Ponce de León Avenue, Miramar, San
Juan

The private dining area at Delirio in Miramar

Delirio, the brand-new creation of
celebrity chef Alfredo Ayala (of Chayote
fame), is, in my opinion, one of the top restaurants in Puerto Rico. My proof? One, the
setting—in a gorgeous turn-of-the-20th-century house. Delirio has many personalities,
from the brilliantly red hall to the private room with an open kitchen where the chef per-
sonally cooks for you, to the main hall and bar, to the outdoor garden in the back. Then
there's the food, which doesn't fall into a specific category but does subscribe to a culinary
philosophy: to combine a minimum of ingredients while fully utilizing their flavors. The
result tantalizes with creative dishes you won't find elsewhere on the island, including
duck meatballs with almonds and a passion fruit reduction, followed by main courses such
as a crispy-skinned black grouper filet in a lentil stew. The amply stocked wine cellar
boasts a wide selection of Spanish wines, blends, and varietals. Contemplating the wildly
inventive menu, glamorous decor, and absolutely flawless service, you'd think this was
among the most expensive restaurants in Puerto Rico. And that's the last bit of magic about
Delirio: Although it's well aware of its product, it keeps its prices moderate. Open Monday
through Thursday noon–2:30 PM for lunch, 6–10:30 PM for dinner; Friday noon–2:30 PM
for lunch, 6–11:30 PM for dinner; and Saturday 6–10:30 PM for dinner only. $$–$$$.

ATTRACTIONS, PARKS & RECREATION

Club Náutico de San Juan
787-722-0177
www.nauticodesanjuan.com
482 Fernandez Juncos Avenue, Stop 9.5, Miramar, San Juan

Puerto Rico Convention Center © 2005 Puerto Rico Convention Center

Founded in 1934, Club Náutico is San Juan's premier marina and sailing club. While it's home to several regattas and tournaments, it's not just for the pros. The club offers sailing lessons for adults and children. The sailing program comprises three sessions of three hours each on a 14-foot boat (students must pass a prequalification swim test beforehand) with a certified instructor. $$$$.

Puerto Rico Convention Center
1-800-875-4765; 787-725-2110
www.prconvention.com
100 Convention Boulevard, Miramar, San Juan

Since it opened in November 2005, the Puerto Rico Convention Center has changed the landscape of Miramar. It is an architectural marvel that must be seen to be appreciated. The sweeping rooftop wave is a fine example of the oceanic themes prevalent in the design of the building, which contains 580,000 square feet of space. It's the largest and most technologically advanced structure of its type in the Caribbean. More than $1.3 billion has been invested in transforming the landscape around the convention center, incorporating an urban park and hotel. Much of the work will take place over the next few years, but one element is already in place: the half-moon-shaped reflecting pool with a periodic fountain show synchronized to music and light—similar to the Bellagio in Las Vegas.

WEEKLY & ANNUAL EVENTS

International Billfish Tournament
August–September
787-722-0177

www.sanjuaninternational.com
At Club Náutico, 482 Fernandez Juncos Avenue, Stop 9.5, Miramar, San Juan

The International Billfish Tournament is the oldest consecutively held billfish tournament in the world, and one of the premier game-fishing events. The weeklong competition attracts over 100 participating yachts each year for four days of tag-and-release blue marlin fishing. Tourists aren't permitted during the launch, but entrance to the club is free for activities during the afternoon and evening.

Puerto Rico Art & Wine Fair
October
787-458-5834
www.prarwi.com
At the Puerto Rico Convention Center, 100 Convention Boulevard, Miramar, San Juan

The name tells you all you need to know. This fair welcomes artists, wholesalers, businesses, and visitors for three days of art and wine appreciation. With over 100 exhibitors, there are plenty of free samples (naturally!) and opportunities to discuss wine and art with a wide range of experts in their trade. You can pay just to enter and visit, or you can add a wine tasting to your ticket. $–$$.

7

EL YUNQUE:

The Anvil of the Gods

During a trip to Puerto Rico, I met a Brazilian tourist who told me he'd visited El Yunque and was most unimpressed. I looked at him with a wry smile and said, "You've got the Amazon." And that made me think about what visitors should, and shouldn't, expect from their visit to Puerto Rico's rain forest.

El Yunque National Forest (also called the Caribbean National Forest) is not part of San Juan, but it is such a popular destination for tourists, and such a unique and cherished part of Puerto Rico, that it deserves to be mentioned in detail in this guide. El Yunque is one of a range of mountains that makes up the forest system. Whether wreathed in clouds or framed against a clear blue sky, the mountain rises majestically and then flattens out into the distinct plateau that gives the rain forest its name: El Yunque (The Anvil). The mountain is so aptly named, you can almost picture a tribal god bringing down a giant iron hammer on its surface. In fact, according to Taíno mythology, the rain forest is the home of the benevolent god of creation, Yuquiyú (the myth makes no mention of a hammer). These days, El Yunque National Forest is home to the only tropical rain forest in the U.S. National Forest system, and it's definitely worth the quick day trip from San Juan.

Several topographical and meteorological factors produce the unique environment that allows the rain forest to

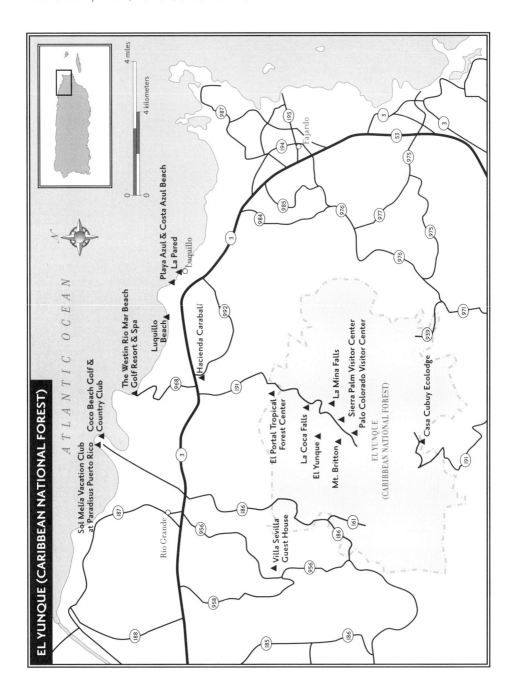

thrive. First, Puerto Rico is a volcanic island, so its soil is very rich. In addition, trade winds from the southeast maintain steady island temperatures that range from 80 to 90°F year-round. Last, the mountains capture moisture created by these atmospheric conditions The result is the perfect environment to sustain a rain forest.

For more information, visit www.fs.fed.us/r8/caribbean.

View of El Yunger Peak

How to Get There

Many hotels and most tour operators offer tours to the rain forest from San Juan. My preference is to rent a car, drive about an hour out of the city, and make a day (or two) out of it. Renting a car gives visitors the freedom of exploring nearby hidden treasures, which include all the fried food you can eat, a Blue Flag beach, and terrific golf courses. From the old city, take Route 3 East and turn onto Route 191, which will take you all the way into the forest. The roads are in great condition, and you won't need four-wheel drive to get there.

Take a Hike, but Don't Forget Your Bathing Suit

El Yunque is truly a unique experience in the Caribbean, and your first stop should be the stark white, impressive-looking El Portal Rain Forest Center, where you'll find area maps and detailed information on the ecology, history, and environment of the rain forest. From here, you can pay for a guided tour or strike out on your own. There are additional visitors centers and lookout towers as you venture deeper into the forest.

After a day (or days) of baking on a beach, a hike under the canopy of forest trees is a welcome respite from the tropical sun. The atmosphere is cool and damp, and some trails run alongside tumbling rivers, while others take you to El Yunque Peak. But the real treats for visitors to El Yunque are the waterfalls—especially the ones that invite you to swim under their cascading torrents. That's why it's essential to wear a bathing suit if you go (or pack one, if you don't mind changing your clothes from behind a bush).

La Coca Falls

El Yunque offers spectacular views of San Juan, the lush valleys of the forest, and the agricultural terrain of the island. What it doesn't give you is much opportunity to see wildlife; this is a gentle forest, not the Amazon. It's surprisingly devoid of visible fauna. (Actually, there are no large mammals native to Puerto Rico; even the Mongooses that you'll find here were imported in the 18th century to help control the rat population on the sugar plantations.) Anyone looking for a safari will be disappointed.

There are 79 types of birds in the rain forest, including the rare green-feathered Puerto Rican parrot, but good luck getting more than a fleeting glance of one. Iguanas and other native lizards abound, as does the irrepressible *coquí* tree frog. Speaking of the *coquí*, these inch-long amphibian wonders, named for the lilting whistling sound they make, can be heard in droves once the urban sounds of San Juan melt away. Spend a night in the suburbs or the countryside, and you'll be serenaded all night long.

El Yunque's trees and flowers are as breathtaking as they are invigorating. The rain forest sustains over 50 species of orchids, as well as giant tree ferns, sierra palms, bamboo thickets, heliconia, ginger, bromeliads, and 225 native tree species, all growing in a wild conflagration of color and natural beauty. Aside from the trails carved into the mountain, El Yunque looks much the way it did when Columbus arrived in the New World. And that's the real draw of this rain forest: its rugged, back-to-the-land beauty—and, of course, the chance to dive under a deliciously cold waterfall.

If you are planning to spend the day at El Yunque, a picnic lunch is highly advisable. For many people, one day is not enough. Villas nestled in the heart of the forest make an extended, total escape possible.

Where the Water Falls

The first major attraction of El Yunque is **La Coca Falls**, which is visible from Route 191. These waters fall 85 feet, and—in a land where there are dry spells—have never dried up. None of the trails let you get closer than the road, but the falls offer a pretty photo opportunity.

Looking at a waterfall is nice, but it's nothing compared to peeling off your clothes and diving underneath one—to experience this, head straight to **La Mina Falls.** A 45-minute hike from the Palma de Sierra Visitors Center, La Mina lets you wade right up to the falls and feel its foamy curtain of water engulf you. It's a popular place, and you may have to wait your turn before taking a dip. If you're willing to explore a little, you'll find other pools and cascades a few feet from the main site. Be careful where you venture, however, as some pools are quite deep and isolated. After your dip, you can sunbathe on the rocky banks of the river until you're ready to resume your hike.

After almost 10 km along Route 191, you'll find **Juan Diego Creek.** Continue and you'll get to the beautiful **Juan Diego Falls.** Close to the Palo Colorado Visitor Center is the **Baño de Oro** (Pool of Gold), an artificially constructed pool that was designed to be a children's pool (swimming is no longer allowed). Finally, follow the Angelito Trail to its end and you get to **Baño de Las Damas**, a natural pond in a lush setting.

La Mina Falls

Where the Trails Lead

El Yunque offers 12 well-marked forest trails that vary in difficulty level and cover 24 miles. You can take the family for a pleasant walk amid El Yunque's verdant foliage, or you can pick out the expert paths that will test your hiking skills. Here's a sample (all trails can be accessed from www.fs.fed.us/r8/caribbean/recreation/recreation_hiking.shtml):

The **Big Tree Trail** is moderate in difficulty, asphalt-paved, and leads you to La Mina Falls. There are picnic areas along the way, and the trail has ample signs describing wildlife and foliage.

The **La Mina Trail** is the most traveled path in the rain forest, even though it is more challenging than Big Tree. You might want to rest at one of the stone picnic shelters. The trail follows the Mina River down to the falls.

The **Caimitillo Trail** is your best bet if time is limited. Its short, (about 0.2 mile), well marked, and relatively easy. The trail ends at Baño Grande.

The **Baño de Oro Trail** is a small, somewhat challenging route to the Baño de Oro. It's only 0.3 mile long, making it a good choice for people who are here for only a short while.

The **El Yunque Trail** is difficult, very steep in places, and not always paved. The hike can take between 2 and 2.5 hours each way, and will guide you to the rain-forest peak almost 3,500 feet above sea level. Along the way, you'll encounter streams, panoramic vistas and, at the end, the moss-covered trees of Dwarf Forest. Hikers who make the journey all the way to the peak are rewarded with a stone tower, which they can climb to reach an observation deck.

The **Mt. Britton Trail** starts off easy but gets harder the higher up you get. You'll cross two active streams and a service road (closed to the public) before you arrive at Mount Britton's peak and the stone, circular Mount Britton Tower. From here you can see the bright blue ribbon of the Atlantic Ocean and the Caribbean Sea.

A forest stream in El Yungue

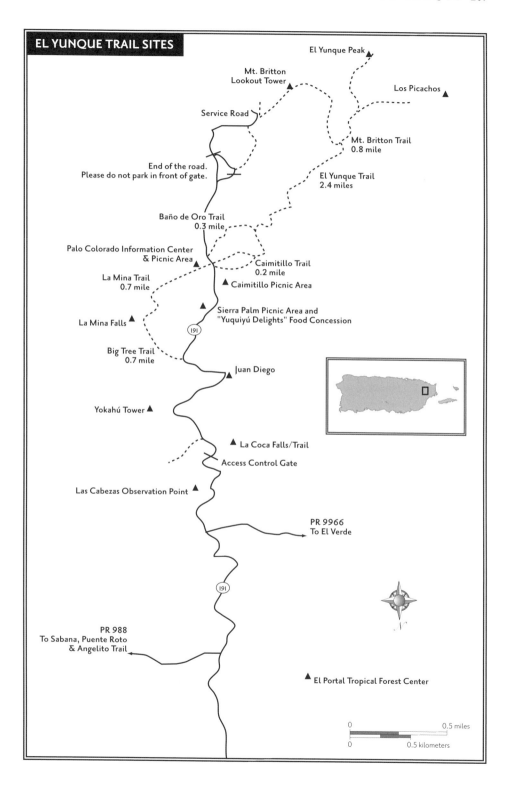

EL YUNQUE TRAIL SITES

El Yunque Peak ▲

Mt. Britton
Lookout Tower ▲

Los Picachos ▲

Service Road

Mt. Britton Trail
0.8 mile

End of the road.
Please do not park in front of gate.

El Yunque Trail
2.4 miles

Baño de Oro Trail
0.3 mile

Palo Colorado Information Center
& Picnic Area ▲

Caimitillo Trail
0.2 mile

La Mina Trail
0.7 mile

▲ Caimitillo Picnic Area

La Mina Falls ▲

▲ Sierra Palm Picnic Area and
"Yuquiyú Delights" Food Concession

(191)

Big Tree Trail
0.7 mile

▲ Juan Diego

Yokahú Tower ▲

▲ La Coca Falls/Trail

Access Control Gate

Las Cabezas Observation Point ▲

PR 9966
To El Verde

(191)

PR 988
To Sabana, Puente Roto
& Angelito Trail

▲ El Portal Tropical Forest Center

0   0.5 miles

0   0.5 kilometers

LODGING

Camping in El Yunque
787-888-1880
www.fs.fed.us/r8/caribbean
El Yunque National Forest
Permits issued at the Catalina Service
Center and Palo Colorado Visitor Center,
El Yunque Rain Forest, Río Grande 00745

Camping in El Yunque isn't an orderly
experience. It can get wet. Really wet. And
muddy. Really muddy. Especially during
hurricane season from June to November.
There are no designated camping areas or
developed fields where you can pitch your
tent. Open fires aren't permitted, and nei-
ther is washing in the streams and rivers.
Car camping beyond La Coca Falls is pro-
hibited. That said, the intrepid camper can
look for a suitable place near any of the
trails and roads that aren't closed. Camping
in El Yunque is not for the novice, but the
seasoned camper will experience a true in-
the-rough experience without having to
worry about any danger from local wildlife.
Permits are free.

Casa Cubuy Ecolodge
787-874-6221
www.casacubuy.com
P.O. Box 721, Río Blanco 00744 (e-mail or
call for driving directions)

The lime green walls of Casa Cubuy frame it
beautifully against the darker hues of the
rain forest. Located on the less-trafficked
south side of El Yunque, this charming bed
& breakfast is a lovely retreat from the city
life. There are no air conditioners in the
rooms, but the balmy temperature this high
up in the mountains makes them obsolete.
At night, the song of the *coquí* and the mur-
mur of waterfalls lull you to sleep. Your
room includes breakfast, and you can get a
snack lunch and dinner on the premises.
There's also a fairly well-stocked honor bar

where you can microwave a lasagna, have a
Coke, and finish it all off with ice cream.
Perhaps the best feature of all is the natural
Jacuzzi, pool, and waterfall of the Cubuy and
the Sabana rivers, just a short walk away.
There's a two-night minimum stay. $$.

Río Grande Plantation Eco Resort
1-877-78-HOTEL; 787-887-2779
www.riograndeplantation.com
Road No. 956, Guzmán Abajo, Km 4,
Hm 2, Río Grande 00745

How would you like to stay on the grounds
of a converted 200-acre sugar plantation?
The Río Grande Plantation Eco Resort, a
massive facility overgrown with the dense
foliage of the rain forest, offers villas over-
looking the river. (Junior suites and single
rooms are available as well.) The resort
seems to have found a special niche:
Catering to corporations and groups, it
offers a perfect off-site retreat where com-
panies can host team-building exercises or
hold meetings and conferences. Amenities
include a large pool, a restaurant that
serves snacks and refreshments, and meal
plans that include breakfast, lunch, and
dinner. $$–$$$.

Villa Sevilla
787-887-5889
www.villasevilla.net
Bo. Guzman Abajo
Carr 956, Km 7.9
Camino Rivera, Río Grande 00745

I'd happily stay at Villa Sevilla every time I
feel like visiting El Yunque. This unique
oasis is not a hotel and not a private home,
but the best of both. You can rent your own
apartment, cottage, or chalet, with the
spectacular Bella Vista Chalet being the
best of the (all good) bunch. Wally and
Marina are gracious and charming hosts,
and they're happy to leave you alone to
enjoy your peace and quiet but equally

The Bella Vista chalet at Villa Sevilla

ready to offer their services. Villa Sevilla is ideal for a romantic retreat, a family vacation, or just a get-away-from-it-all experience. The lodgings are well furnished and kept immaculately clean (honestly, I don't know how they do it). The pool at the foot of the villa resembles a natural lagoon, and the balcony (with hammock) offers incredible views of the forest, San Juan, and the ocean. Authors and artists will fall in love with this place, as will your kids. Wally will gladly take them to feed the chickens in the morning, or to pick a wonderful variety of fruit, and they can explore the area in total safety. A short (but not easy) hike away is Cubuy River, with natural pools so isolated that you could swim in the nude if you chose. A new addition is a private chef, Fransisco Collazo, who prepares excellent catered meals for guests. There are minimum-night stays, depending on which lodging option you choose. If your stay is less than four nights, sister operation **Pablo's Place** offers a well-appointed one-bedroom apartment nearby. $$–$$$.

Westin Río Mar Beach Golf Resort & Spa
1-888-627-8556
www.westinriomar.com
6000 Río Mar Boulevard, Río Grande
00745

If you want the Jekyll-and-Hyde experience of roughing it in the rain forest and then getting pampered in a luxury hotel, check in at the Westin Río Mar once you leave El Yunque. This is not a lodging option if you want to continue your communion with the forest; the hotel is perched on the coast several miles from the forest, but I mention it here because it's the resort that's closest to the mountains. It also happens to be Puerto Rico's most comprehensive beach-front resort. With plush rooms, championship golf courses, tennis courts, a fitness center, a pristine beach, lovely pools, a renowned spa, a casino, and eight restaurants, the Westin is 500 acres of tropical opulence. $$$$.

DINING

Note: With the exception of the **Yuquiyú Delights** food concession areas in the **El Portal Rain Forest Center** and the Sierra Palm Picnic Area, there aren't any dining options in El Yunque. The ones listed below are located nearby, in Río Grande. Also near the rain forest are the restaurants listed in "Luquillo" (see the next section).

Las Brisas del Verde
787-887-0958
Route 3, Km 25.0, Río Grande

On the way to El Yunque, you'll pass numerous shacks and roadside eateries selling everything from pizza to roast pig. You'll be surprised at how good some of these are, and Las Brisas del Verde is one of the best places near the rain forest to veer off the road. Little more than a shack, this green-and-white building often has a bunch of people milling around it, waiting for fresh-off-the-grill barbecued meats, rice and beans, and *maduros* or *tostones*. Open weekdays and Sunday 9 AM–midnight, Friday and Saturday 9 AM–2 AM. $–$$.

Don Pepe's Mexican and Puerto Rican Cuisine
787-888-7373
Route 3, Km 29.0, in Palmer, Río Grande

Don Pepe's offers solid Mexican fare as well as traditional *boricua* dishes (their *mofongo* is quite good). True to many Mexican restaurants, the portions are massive; after a hike, this may be just what you need. It's hearty, cheap food, with cheap drinks to boot and a very friendly staff. Open Sunday through Thursday 11 AM–11 PM, Friday 11 AM–midnight, and Saturday 4 PM–midnight. $$.

Palio
1-888-627-8556
www.westinriomar.com
6000 Río Mar Boulevard, Río Grande

Of all the restaurants at the Westin, Palio is the most acclaimed. The decor is formal and classy, and the menu strictly Italian (no criollo twists) and extensive, offering a variety of appetizers, salads, pizzas, pastas, and *secondi* meat dishes. If you love pasta à la vodka, try the fettuccine made in this style, with sautéed Caribbean lobster meat. Open Sunday through Thursday 5:30–10:30 PM, and Friday and Saturday 6–11 PM, for dinner. $$$–$$$$.

ATTRACTIONS, PARKS & RECREATION

El Portal Rain Forest Center
787-888-1810
El Yunque National Forest

As you stroll along the elevated walkway past the El Portalito entrance to El Portal Rain Forest Center, you can't help but be struck by the clean and elegant beauty of the place. Located 60 feet aboveground, this complex houses a theater where you can watch a short film about the rain forest (in English or Spanish); three exhibits designed to educate tourists about the importance of the forest and the continuous efforts to preserve it; and a book and gift shop. Open daily 9 AM–4:30 PM. $.

SHOPPING

Coquí International
787-887-0770
www.coquiinternational.com
Calle Principal #18, Bo Palmer, Río Grande

Just off the exit from Route 3 to El Yunque, Coquí International is a unique gift shop. They are known for their wonderful handmade soaps (with selections like "Puerto Rico Rain" and "Peppermint with Oatmeal") but also carry candles, bath products, arts and crafts, and other souvenirs. Open Monday through Saturday 10 AM–6:00 PM, Sunday noon–6 PM. $–$$$.

FOOD PURVEYORS, LIQUOR & CIGARS

Palmer Bakery
787-888-4049
Nine Principal, Bo Palmer, Río Grande

On the road to El Yunque, in the town of Palmer, you'll find this bakery just across from the post office. It's a good place to buy sandwiches and pastries for your picnic lunch in El Yunque. Open daily 5 AM–10 PM. $.

Panadería Don Nico
787-809-2737
Route 3, Km 20.5, Cienaga Baja

Don Nico is famed for its *quesitos.* You can also buy sandwiches (try the Cubano, a ham and cheese sandwich on flat, toasted bread) and pastries here. Open daily 5:30 AM–10:30 PM. $.

GOOD TO KNOW ABOUT . . .

Amigo Supermarket
787-888-5200
Río Grande State Commercial Center, Route 3, Km 28.0, Río Grande

Amigo is a large local grocery store (owned by the Wal-Mart chain). They also carry some organic foods. Open Monday through Friday 7 AM–10 PM, Sunday 11 AM–5 PM.

Walgreens
787-256-2121
Commercial Center NE, Route 3, Canóvanas

This branch is open daily 7 AM–10 PM.

WEEKLY & ANNUAL EVENTS

Carnaval del Ciudad del Yunque
End of June, beginning of July
787-887-2370

Río Grande hosts the Carnaval Ciudad del Yunque (Carnival of the City of El Yunque), which celebrated its 20th year in 2006, with five evenings of revelry, including parades, *vejigantes,* music, and food. One highlight is a parade of queens, with a coronation of the year's Río Grande Queen. Free.

Palm trees at Luquillo Beach

LUQUILLO, LAND OF THE KIOSKS

For most people visiting San Juan, traveling for 45 minutes to the municipality of Luquillo isn't on their top 10 list of things to do. But Puerto Ricans love to visit this place for two reasons: the idyllic sands of Luquillo Beach and the rustic charm of the Luquillo kiosks. To get to either one, you won't even have to veer far off Route 3.

Balneario de Luquillo is one of the premier beaches in Puerto Rico, a solid mile of fabulous, finely groomed sand nestled against a backdrop of neat columns of palm trees. This beach offers snorkeling, kayaking, and the standard aquatic amenities, as well as camping facilities. One thing used to make Luquillo Beach truly special: Mar Sin Barreras (Sea without Borders). This used to be the island's only stretch of beach dedicated to serving the needs of those with special needs. It was wheelchair accessible, and a trained staff was on hand to assist the elderly and disabled. Specially designed equipment allowed those with disabilities to enjoy the water in Puerto Rico. Unfortunately, Mar Sin Barreras has been inactive for a few years. It is still advertised in brochures but has yet to reopen.

As you approach the *balneario,* you'll see a long, unbroken line of about 75 roadside kiosks, all independently named and run. Please . . . if they're open, stop the car and get out. These eateries are legendary in Puerto Rico, home to all manner of fried seafood, croquettes, *pinchos* (skewers), and fritters. Some are full-service restaurants, and most people have a favorite. You can also get fresh coconut juice, drinks, and other snacks. It's tempting, but impossible, to sample every stall's products, and many of them sell the same stuff. But it's a kitschy, if artery-clogging, diversion that allows you to believe for just a second, while nibbling away at something that you don't quite recognize, that you're a full-blooded Puerto Rican.

LODGING

Hotel Yunque Mar
787-889-5555
www.yunquemar.com
Calle 1 #6, Fortuna Playa, Luquillo 00773

To be honest, there is little reason to spend the night in Luquillo, unless you have completely fallen in love with Luquillo Beach and have decided to be as close to it as possible. If that's the case, then this is a cheap, friendly hotel close to the *balneario*. Its location right on the water offers stunning views. The rooms are basic, but all come with cable TV, air-conditioning, and a private balcony. If you can, try to book a room with an ocean view for gorgeous sunrise and sunset views. The nice-sized pool is delicious on a hot day. You might notice the art hanging in the hotel; it's all the work of local artists. $–$$$.

DINING

The Brass Cactus
787-889-5735
www.thebrasscactus.com
Condominio Complejo Turistico, Luquillo

The closest thing to a saloon in these parts, the Brass Cactus is well known to locals and tourists. (Actually, there are two locations, the other in Canóvanas on the way back from El Yunque to San Juan.) Serving large portions of Tex-Mex, Southwestern, and American classics, this is a boisterous and fun place with funky decor, great drinks, and friendly service. As for the food, you can't go wrong with their *Churrasco Veracruz* Steak (served with a two-pepper sauce), Brass Cactus Burger (an 8-ounce burger topped with two cheeses, green peppers, sautéed onions, and bacon), and Cajun Mahi Wrap (in a toasted flour tortilla). Open Sunday through Thursday 11 AM–midnight, Friday and Saturday 11 AM–2 AM. $–$$.

The Kiosks
Route 3, Luquillo

The kiosks are a must-try if you're visiting Luquillo for the first time. After all, the long lines of cars and motorcycles can't be a bad omen. However, it's hard to pick from the long row of similar-looking, numbered shacks. Probably the most popular one is #2 (**La Parrilla**), which is known for its yucca rings (as opposed to onion rings), steaks, and grilled mahimahi; kiosk #46 for its excellent crab *alcapurrias,* and #57 for its *chapín* (a local fish) tacos. Don't be afraid to kiosk-hop. In general, they're open Sunday through Thursday until midnight, Friday and Saturday until around 2 AM.

Lolita's
787-889-5770
Route 3, Km 41.8, Luquillo

Widely considered the best Mexican restaurant in the area (some say in all of Puerto Rico), Lolita's serves up the full menu of burritos, enchiladas, fajitas, chimichangas, and other typical fare. If you love nachos, you have to try the Ultra Nachos, which are covered with refried beans, guacamole, sour cream, cheese, and chicken or beef. Open Sunday through Thursday 11 AM–10 PM, Friday and Saturday 11 AM–midnight. The lunch specials are a bargain. $–$$.

Sandy's Seafood
787-889-5765
276 Fernandez García Street, Luquillo

Sandy's is known for its large portions of simple but delectable Puerto Rican seafood. Surprisingly for such a no-frills place, Sandy's has a devoted following that stretches all the way to San Juan and beyond. This is one of the cheapest places to try one of several excellent Caribbean lobster dishes. Open daily from 11 AM until the kitchen closes (usually between 9 and 11 PM, depending on how busy they are). $–$$.

Attractions, Parks & Recreation

Balneario de Luquillo
787-889-5871
Route 3, Km 35.4, Luquillo

The Luquillo Beach complex includes snack shops, souvenirs, showers, changing rooms, and picnic areas with barbecue grills. You can also camp in the area. Available for rent are beach chairs, umbrellas, and kayaks. Open daily 8:30 AM–5:30 PM. $.

Luquillo Beach

Hacienda Carabalí
787-889-5820
Route 992, Km 3.0, Luquillo

The ranch at Hacienda Carabalí offers a great experience for horseback riding enthusiasts. Riders are matched, based on experience, to a lovely Paso Fino horse, a breed so called for its elegant gait. A trail guide will then lead you either on a one-hour ride around the ranch or a two-hour trip to the foothills of the rain forest. Hacienda Carabali also rents out ATVs and mountain bikes. $$–$$$.

Playa Azul and Playa La Pared
Route 193, Km 1.1, Luquillo

These adjacent public beaches are just east of Luquillo Beach. Playa Azul (Blue Beach) is a local favorite for snorkelers, while Playa La Pared ("The Wall" Beach) attracts surfers.

Nightlife

The Brass Cactus
787-889-5735
www.thebrasscactus.com
Condominio Complejo Turistico off Route 3, Luquillo

Things get going early at the Brass Cactus, with daily Happy Hours from 4 to 6 PM. Friday night is karaoke night from 10 PM to 2 AM, and women get to drink free for the first hour.

The Kiosks
Route 3, Luquillo

As the sun goes down, the action picks up in the kiosks, especially from Thursday to Sunday. Locals come from miles around to enjoy the festive, sometimes raucous, atmosphere. Some kiosks will draw your attention with live music, others with their ambience, and still others by virtue of being near the entrance. In general, they're open Sunday through Thursday until midnight, Friday and Saturday until around 2 AM.

SHOPPING

La Selva Surf Shop
787-889-6205
250 Fernández García, Luquillo

In addition to surfboard and bodyboard sales and rentals, La Selva sells swimwear, clothing, and accessories for the beach. Surfing lessons are available for beginners. Open daily 9 AM–5 PM. $–$$$.

GOOD TO KNOW ABOUT . . .

Amigo Supermarket
787-889-1077
Calle 2 Urb. Brisas del Mar, Brisas del Mar Commercial Center, Luquillo

Large local grocery store (owned by the Wal-Mart chain). Open Monday through Friday 7 AM–10 PM, Sunday 11 AM–5 PM.

Esso Gas Station
787-889-7624; 787-889-0088
Route 3, Km 36.2, Brisas del Mar, Luquillo

Open 24 hours a day, seven days a week.

Shell Station
787-889-0500; 787-889-0526
Route 3, Km 3.20, Bo Pitahaya, Luquillo

Open 24 hours a day, seven days a week.

WEEKLY & ANNUAL EVENTS

Festival de Los Platos Típicos
November
787-889-2851
Plaza de Recreo, Luquillo

This annual festival features local dishes and coconut beverages, live music, and exhibits. Artists and craftspeople also participate. Free.

8

VIEQUES

Breathtaking Beaches, Part 1

INTRODUCTION TO THE ISLANDS

When traveling to a tropical island in the Caribbean, you're typically not thinking about leaving it to visit *another* island. But Vieques and Culebra are different enough—and special enough—to merit the trip. These islands are more than the flawless beaches they're famous for. When you visit them, you get the sense that you're taking one more step away from the world you know, even if that world is San Juan.

That's why the islands are popular destinations with Puerto Ricans as well as tourists. Everybody who visits Vieques and Culebra can't help but slow down and get in sync with the islands' leisurely pace. Things may not be as efficient as they are on the mainland—any mainland. Things may not be as convenient. But you're not visiting an island for convenience. You're on Vieques or Culebra to get away from busy city life; to enjoy the multihued blue of the water, the silky golden sands, and the vivid green of the dense, encroaching foliage. Rather than bar-hop, you'll beach-hop, looking for that stretch of sand that you can claim for yourself, just for one day.

When you step off the ferry or when your Cessna lands, do yourself a favor: Throw your watch in your suitcase and forget about it; you're on island time.

Located just 7 miles off the east coast of Puerto Rico, Vieques is a world away from the "Big Island"—at least, its capital city of San Juan. Isla Nena (Baby Girl Island), as Vieques is affectionately called, is "Fantasy Island" with a few unusual twists; it's both rustic and refined. Distinct from the big island, Vieques has its own history and culture, and an intensely proud heritage. And there are ample reasons why people keep coming, by the thousands, to this tropical jungle jewel: to relax and unwind, to bask and bathe, and to glow in the night.

HOW TO GET THERE AND WHEN TO GO THERE

Like mainland Puerto Rico, because of its moderate climate Vieques is a year-round destination. Unlike San Juan, which goes through a tourism drought in the low season, Vieques simply changes shifts; in summer, it's usually the residents of mainland Puerto Rico who take their holidays on the island. In winter, people from all over the world travel to Vieques to enjoy the combination of dense forests and secluded beaches.

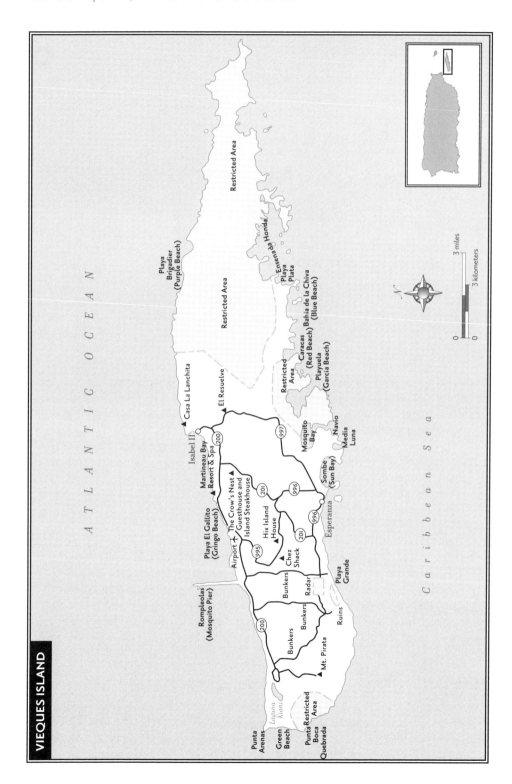

VIEQUES ISLAND

ATLANTIC OCEAN

Caribbean Sea

Restricted Area

Restricted Area

Restricted Area

Playa Brigadier (Purple Beach)

Ensenada Honda

Playa Plata

Caracas (Red Beach)

Bahia de la Chiva (Blue Beach)

Playuela (Garcia Beach)

Navio

Media Luna

Mosquito Bay

Casa La Lanchita

El Resuelve

Isabel II

Martineau Bay Resort & Spa

The Crow's Nest Guesthouse and Island Steakhouse

Playa El Gallito (Gringo Beach)

Airport

Hix Island House

Chez Shack

Sombe (Sun Bay)

Esperanza

Playa Grande

Rompieolas (Mosquito Pier)

Bunkers

Radar

Bunkers

Bunkers

Ruins

Mt. Pirata

Laguna Kiani

Punta Arenas

Green Beach

Punta Quebrada

Restricted Boca Area

200

200

995

997

996

201

996

201

N

3 miles

3 kilometers

0

0

You can get to Vieques via high-speed catamaran, ferry, or airplane. Your budget will most likely determine which of these options will appeal to you, but if you don't mind spending a little bit more, I highly recommend flying. Even longtime residents of Vieques opt to fly to Fajardo when visiting the big island rather than depend on the time-consuming and inconsistent ferry service. Flying saves time and hassle, and you'll be treated to complimentary, spectacular aerial views of the island. The only catch is your luggage: You can't carry too much with you (some airlines cap the weight limit at 25 pounds) without paying extra. Several local and regional airlines make stops at Vieques, but all use small planes, the largest of which is a 42-passenger ATR Turboprop.

Signpost in Isabel II

By Sea

Puerto Rico Maritime Authority

787-863-0705

The cheapest and most popular way to reach the islands is with the passenger ferry service from the east-coast town of Fajardo. There are four trips daily during the week, and three trips daily on weekends and holidays. It's not the most efficient service, but it's adequate and will get you to Vieques for next to nothing. A cargo ferry travels to the island several times a day during the week only, for those who want to take their car. However, bringing a car to Vieques is highly inadvisable, for two reasons: Even with a prior reservation (and you must have one), the service is spotty, and passengers run the danger of getting bumped off. Second, you'll need a Jeep, not a sedan, to explore Vieques properly. $.

Island Hi-Speed Ferry

1-877-899-3993
www.islandhispeedferry.com/puertorico
AquaExpreso Ferry Terminal, Pier 2, Old San Juan 00901

You don't have to travel to Fajardo to take a ferry to Vieques. This new high-speed catamaran service can take you from Old San Juan to Vieques in about three hours (stopping at Culebra first). The ferry runs only during peak tourist season, from December to late April; but even then, service is spotty. Amenities include cushioned seats, air-conditioning, and a snack bar. Unless you have a fear of small planes, I recommend flying, which is about the same price as the ferry but much quicker. $$$.

By Air

Air America
787-276-5669
www.airamericacaribbean.com

Traveling in a group? Money not an issue? Out on one incredible date? Maybe you'd like to charter a plane to Vieques. If so, check out Air America's services. $$$$.

Air Flamenco
787-741-8811
www.airflamenco.net

Flights are available from Isla Grande Airport in Miramar and from Fajardo. Prices are standard unless there are no other passengers scheduled for the date you want to fly. $$–$$$.

Cape Air
1-800-352-0714; 508-771-6944

Flies from Luis Muñoz Marín Airport to Vieques and gives you Continental OnePass frequent-flyer miles.

Isla Nena
1-877-812-5144; 787-863-4447
www.islanena.8m.com

A charter plane company with on-demand, daily service to and from Vieques and points throughout the Caribbean. Flights depart from Luis Muñoz Marín International Airport in Carolina and Diego Jeménez Torres Airport in Fajardo. $$$.

Vieques Air Link
1-888-901-9247; 787-741-8331
www.viequesairlink.com

Flights are available to and from Isla Grande Airport in Miramar and Luis Muñoz Marín International Airport in Carolina, as well as from Fajardo, among other locations. Prices are standard unless there are no other passengers scheduled for the date you want to fly. $$–$$$.

Getting Around

Extreme Scooter Rental & Watersports
787-741-8141; 787-435-9345

Scooters can be a fun way to explore the island. Sea-Doos can be an even more fun way to explore off the island. $$–$$$.

Maritza's Car Rental

787-741-7108
www.islavieques.com/smaritzas.html

A reputable agency with a fleet of Jeeps to help you brave Vieques's rugged trails. $$$.

Martineau Car Rentals

787-741-0087
www.martineaucarrental.com

Get your hands on a Jeep, a PT Cruiser, Honda Element, or a Suzuki hatchback at this agency. $$$.

Vieques Car Rental

787-741-1037
www.viequescarrental.com

A good bet for a sturdy Jeep and excellent service. $$$.

A TURBULENT HISTORY

The history of this small island is a tale of global power struggles and David-vs.-Goliath confrontations. When the Spanish first settled Puerto Rico, they ignored the small islands around it, believing them to have little value, and the Taíno who lived here on Vieques were consequently left alone. But Spain was not the only empire with a presence in the Caribbean. The French were the first Europeans to settle on the island, in the 1520s, and they had a pivotal role in shaping modern Vieques. The British, seeking as many footholds as they could find in these waters, displaced the French in 1666, only to be displaced in turn by the Spanish, who rushed in to protect their interests.

The British did not give up easily. In the 1700s, they tried repeatedly to claim Vieques,

Western Vieques

Military bunkers at the Navy Ammunition Facility

and were repeatedly (and violently) kicked out by the Spanish. The island remained in a state of anarchy, with a volatile mix of native Taíno, pirates, and colonies of opposing empires all vying for control. Finally, in 1811, a Frenchman named Roselló landed in Vieques under orders of the Spanish governor of Puerto Rico to restore order. He failed. In 1823, he was replaced by another Frenchman, Teófilo Le Guillou, who succeeded. Le Guillou also established a sugar industry to complement the sugar boom that was taking place on main island of Puerto Rico at this time.

To secure their hold over Vieques, the Spanish built a small fort in 1845—the last fort they would build. It never saw active duty but was used by the Spanish, and later by the Americans, as a jail. The United States had its own plans for the island—and it was under their rule that the fight for Vieques took on a new dimension, and renewed political importance.

Vieques is often praised for its "unspoiled" beauty, but many people fail to realize the reasons it was left undeveloped—reasons which, to this day, cause a rift among its people. In 1939, the U. S. Navy purchased 27,000 acres of land on the island. Over the next two decades, the navy came to occupy three-quarters of all privately held land, as well as large tracts of unoccupied land they called "buffer zones." The area was divided according to strategic purpose: The eastern side was used as a bombing range (weapons tested here include artillery shells, napalm, and Agent Orange), while the western portion served as an ammunition dump.

The U.S. Navy's long occupation of much of Vieques can be summed up in two ways. On one hand, it would prove extremely damaging to the island and its people. The navy dispossessed thousands of Viequenses, replacing farmlands with tenements and resettlement camps. They used the western part of the island, which had the most fertile land and once

Key Events: The U.S. Navy in Vieques

A few singular events highlight the longstanding conflict between the local residents of Vieques and the U.S. Navy.

1940s The navy begins to build a long seawall in an attempt to link Vieques with the Roosevelt Roads Naval Base in Ceiba on the main island, creating the largest U.S. naval facility in the Atlantic. The construction project brought short-lived prosperity to the island before it ground to a halt in 1943.

1978 In February, the navy invited 20 NATO members to Vieques to participate in maneuvers. During the 28 days of those maneuvers, the navy declared that no Viequense fishing boats would be allowed to leave port. The Vieques Fishermen's Association reacted. On the first morning of a planned landing on Blue Beach, naval warships squared off against local fishing boats. The fishermen managed to neutralize each amphibious landing craft before it could deploy a single marine onto the shore.

1997 On May 11, the beach at Sun Bay was crowded as families gathered to celebrate Mother's Day. Suddenly, four Dutch and Belgian warships arrived to participate in naval exercises with the U.S. Navy. Viequense fishermen responded immediately. They approached the ships, asking them to leave, but were dispersed. They returned, armed with bottles of paint and rocks. Having learned that the naval ships' numbers would have to be repainted as quickly as possible, the fishermen cleverly hurled the paint at the hulls, where the ships' numbers were written. After an exchange of rocks, bottles, and other debris, the warships abandoned their maneuvers.

1999–2000 On April 19, 1999, a 500-pound bomb missed its intended target and landed near an observation post, killing David Sanes, a local man working as a security guard. This event sparked a civil disobedience protest in which island residents set up camps within the bombing range, preventing further bombings. On May 4, 2000, everyone present at the camps was arrested, including nuns and religious leaders who were praying in the chapel built by the protesters.

2000 On January 1, President Clinton instructed the navy to return all 8,000 acres of the Naval Ammunition Facility (NAF) to the government of Puerto Rico. Congress then modified this directive, giving back 4,000 acres to the municipality of Vieques; 3,100 acres were transferred to the U.S. Fish and Wildlife Service, and 700 acres to the Puerto Rico Department of Natural Resources; 200 acres were kept by the U.S. Navy.

2003 On May 1, the U.S. Fish and Wildlife Service formally took over the eastern lands of the navy for management as a wildlife preserve.

supported sugar plantations, for ammunition storage. As such, the island's agricultural output was greatly diminished. On the eastern side, the bombings left ecological scars and radioactive zones that are still restricted areas. Some of the best beaches on Vieques are on the eastern side of the island and remain closed to the public. The navy also prevented commercial airplanes from using the airport, which stifled the tourist industry. Last, naval warships routinely cut apart fishing traps laid by local fishermen, severely hampering the island's fishing industry, which had been a mainstay of the local economy.

On the other hand, the navy's occupation resulted in one major, albeit unintended, benefit: the absolute preservation of a breathtaking tropical island. Think about it, for 60 years, as hotels, resorts, fast-food chains, and related services that support a growing tourist industry descended on San Juan, there was no large-scale development on Vieques and no urbanization of the island's pristine acres of beachfront land. In remaining isolated, Vieques remained pure, untamed, and undiscovered.

All of that is changing now. Although Vieques remains undeveloped when compared to San Juan and St. Thomas, resorts, boutique hotels, lovely inns, and fine restaurants are popping up on the island. Its two main towns—Isabel II, the larger and more commercial, and Esperanza, little more than a charming seaside village—are still tiny and quaint, but Vieques has never been more accessible and hospitable as a tourist destination than it is today. The island is being rediscovered, by tourists from around Puerto Rico, the United States, and the rest of the world. And what they have found keeps them coming back for more.

To Bask or Not to Bask: The Beaches and Beyond

The siren call of the beaches of Vieques is understandably strong and seductive, and goes beyond the startling beauty of their sands and waters. Whatever your aquatic interest, there is a beach for you on Vieques. If you want isolation, you'll find it. If you want to be in the midst of a crowd, you'll know where to go. And with some of these beaches, part of the fun is the journey over bumpy dirt roads and through mangrove forests that seem, in places, too difficult to pass through even in your sturdy Jeep. (A note about these roads: If you see a branch in your way, stop the car and pick it up; the thorny acacia branches guarantee a flat tire.)

If basking on the beach isn't on your itinerary, Vieques offers many other diversions. There is a small boardwalk that leads into a mangrove forest, where you might see birds, iguanas, turtles, and other native wildlife. There are the eerie grasslands on the western side of the island, where the naval magazines lie hidden. There are the two towns, each with a different personality. Visitors can go hiking, observe nature, ride horses, and tour historic sites.

Yet all of these activities fall a distant second for the majority of tourists, who want nothing more than to explore the island and find *their* beach. There's nothing quite like driving around, following dirt trails until you see a yellow marker that tells you you've found another beach. And guess what: On this small island, you have over 20 to choose from (and that's simply staggering when you think of all the beaches you *can't* get to because they are still in a restricted area). You can swim in the Caribbean Sea if you're on the south side of the island, or in the Atlantic Ocean if you're on the northern coast. Here's a brief introduction to some of Vieques's best beaches. The names in parenthesis following each beach are the original *boricua* names.

Sun Bay

Sun Bay (which the locals pronounce "Sombe") is the most commercial of Vieques's beaches. With a large public parking area (which may charge a nominal fee if a parking attendant is present), it's the only beach on the island with full public facilities. These include bathrooms, outdoor showers, public telephones, camping, water fountains, and

The western end of Sun Bay Beach

garbage bins—all rarities at most Vieques beaches. Because of this, and also because of Sun Bay's easy access by car and by foot (it's a short walk from Esperanza), it gets much of the tourist traffic. Many locals shy away from Sun Bay, though there's nothing wrong with this beautiful bowl-shaped strand fringed by coconut palms. The waters are generally calm, with the two *cayos* on the western side providing some protection from the waves and winds. Its mile-long stretch of sand ranks Sun Bay among the island's larger beaches.

Media Luna (Half Moon)
As much as you might like Sun Bay, you're doing yourself a great disservice if you don't follow the road past Sun Bay and then bear to the left. Take this manageable road all the way to the end, to a perfect half-moon-shaped stretch of sand. Media Luna has far fewer facilities than its bigger neighbor, but it compensates for this with calm, shallow waters protected by buoys, which make it perfect for kids.

Navío
The last beach accessible from the Sun Bay gate, Navío is the hardest to get to but rewards visitors with two different treats. The trade winds provide great surfing and bodyboarding, and in summer it's probably the best beach in Vieques for surfers. In calmer conditions, you can have fun reaching Navío's secret hideout: Just wade along the left side of the beach, hugging the rocks, and then turn inland around the point and you'll find a natural cave with a saltwater pool. The more daring can scramble along the cliffs to the rocky promontory and jump into the water. Navío is also a great spot for snorkeling.

Media Luna (Half Moon) Beach

Red Beach (Caracas)

Only open since 2003, when the U.S. Navy returned it to the municipality, Red Beach has quickly become a favorite with many Sanjuaneros and Viequenses I talked to. It's a big beach with near-white sands, perfectly clear water that's ideal for snorkeling, and farther out, nice waves for surfers and boarders. If you get here early, you'll be able to secure a covered cabana.

Blue Beach (Manuelquí)

The next time you watch a dramatic movie scene in which U.S. Marines storm a beach, think about this: There's a good chance that the footage was shot at Blue Beach. This is a very long beach, with calm waters lapping against sloping sands, and several parking areas and "entrances" giving you a choice of places to lay down your beach blanket. It's great for snorkeling, especially along the sandbar to the small *cayo*. Blue Beach is a favorite for groups, families, locals, and tourists . . . it's got a bit of everything.

Garcia Beach (Playuela)

Small and secluded, Garcia Beach is often overlooked as people rush by to reach bigger and more famous Red Beach, which is next door. But this is a picturesque little spot that you can call your own if you're lucky, and the tiny island that's almost smack in the middle of the water about 600 feet out is a good snorkeling destination.

Colors of War, Colors of Sand

During their war-simulation exercises, U.S. Marines were informed only that they would deploy from their ships and conduct an age-old wartime activity: a beach landing. As the ships reached Vieques's deserted shoreline, reconnaissance teams disembarked and planted colored flags at different points along the coast. These flags indicated to the teams which area of the beach they would assault: red, green, blue, purple, and so on. To this day, most tourists know some of Vieques's best beaches by these colors: Red Beach, Green Beach, Blue Beach, and Purple Beach. The locals hope that, over time, this reminder of the U.S. Navy's occupation of the island will fade, and the original names of the beaches (which are posted on signs) will be the only ones they retain.

Silver Beach (Playa Plata)

Continue east past Blue Beach and you'll get to this often empty retreat. The sands aren't as wide as on some of the other beaches, but Silver Beach is quite long and the snorkeling is unparalleled, thanks to reefs about a hundred feet offshore. This is the last of the main beaches as you head east on the Caribbean side of the island.

Secret Beach

Okay, so this beach isn't listed on the tourist map. That doesn't matter; it's not so secret these days. Still, Secret Beach is a lovely, small beach with excellent snorkeling and—sometimes—topless sunbathers. How to get to Secret Beach: Drive past Garcia Gate (which leads to Garcia, Red, Blue, and Silver beaches) and continue until you see two garbage barrels. Take a right onto the road at the barrels, and then take the first right.

Rocky Point at the eastern end of Blue Beach

Green Beach

On the western side of the island, past the metal bridges and the mangrove lagoon, you'll come to one of the most remote beaches on Vieques. This is a thin beach, but it's long and the coconut palms are lovely. The tip of this beach, Punta Arenas, is the closest point to the main island. The sandflies, which can be extremely unfriendly in the late afternoon, are the only drawback at Green Beach.

Playa Grande

West of Esperanza, this beach lives up to its name (*grande* means "big"). It might not be as picturesque as some of the others, but Playa Grande has lovely views of Mount Pirata inland, and the *cayos* off Esperanza. It's remote and often deserted.

Black Sand Beach

Less visited than Secret Beach, Black Sand Beach is for those who crave something truly different. As the name implies, the volcanic sand, which stretches west for roughly a half mile, is indeed jet black. It's made up of magnetite, which, also as its name implies, will cling to a magnet (bring one). It's a very cool place, but it's a pain to get to, taking you along dried-up riverbeds, through barbed wire fences, and past bugs and beasts (such as there are).

Gringo Beach (Playa El Gallito)

Between the airport and Martineau Bay, Gringo Beach is immediately off the main road, making it very accessible. Perhaps for this reason, I find it rather exposed. It can be rocky in places, but its calm waters and nearby reefs makes it popular with people who like to swim and snorkel.

Playa Esperanza

Definitely not the prettiest or most private beach, Playa Esperanza is immediately in front of the boardwalk in Esperanza. That makes it the closest beach to lunch and drinks. It's also close to Cayo Afuera, and if you're a good swimmer, you can reach this little islet to hike, snorkel, watch turtles (in season), or just get even farther away from it all.

Playa Cofí

The beach closest to Isabel II, this one is unique for its approach, its history, and for its . . . well, trash. To get to Playa Cofí, you'll have to walk down a small cliff (there's a natural footpath). The beach is named after the Puerto Rican pirate Roberto Cofresí, who—depending on whom you ask—was a good-for-nothing criminal or a noble Robin Hood type. Finally, this is a great beach for collecting sea glass; essentially, the glass is from a former landfill and has been smoothed and polished by the waves over the years to its current, oddly beautiful, multicolored shapes.

ISLAND LIFE

From the ferry, Isabel II is the first stop on Vieques, and it has a different vibe from the quainter and quieter Esperanza. The main government and cultural buildings are in Isabel II, which is the artistic as well as the historic focal point on the island. (It's also the only place to get gas for your car.) You'll get more of a taste for Viequense life in Isabel II than in

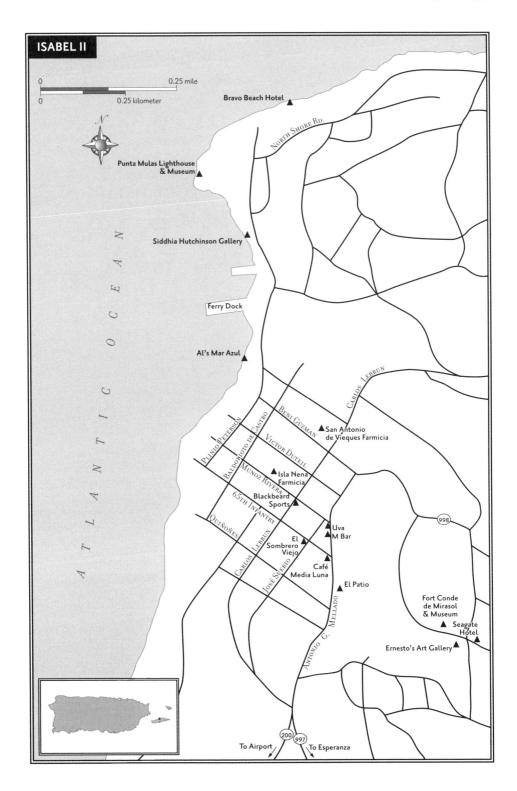

ISABEL II

0 _____ 0.25 mile
0 _____ 0.25 kilometer

N

ATLANTIC OCEAN

Bravo Beach Hotel ▲

NORTH SHORE RD.

Punta Mulas Lighthouse
& Museum ▲

Siddhia Hutchinson Gallery ▲

Ferry Dock

Al's Mar Azul ▲

CARLOS LEBRUN

PLINIO PETERSON

BALDORIOTO DE CASTRO

BENI GUZMAN

VICTOR DUTEIL

▲ San Antonio
de Vieques Farmicia

MUÑOZ RIVERA

▲ Isla Nena
Farmicia

65TH INFANTRY

Blackbeard
Sports ▲

QUIÑONES

CARLOS LEBRUN

JOSÉ SERRIO

Uva ▲
M Bar ▲

El ▲
Sombrero
Viejo

Café ▲
Media Luna

El Patio ▲

998

Fort Conde
de Mirasol
& Museum

▲ Seagate
Hotel

Ernesto's Art Gallery ▲

ANTONIO G. MELLADO

200 997

To Airport ← → To Esperanza

Church at the main plaza in Isabel II

Esperanza, which—thanks to its beaches, concentration of hotels, and expat community—caters more to tourists. Don't be surprised to see a local man riding a horse into Isabel II. The town square is a perfect example of island life, Vieques-style: It's picturesque but a little run-down (although the plaza is currently undergoing a renovation) and very laid back. Hotels in Isabel II tend to be budget accommodations, and there are precious few signs of the degree of wealth present in San Juan.

Esperanza marches to a different beat. It is the quintessential tropical island town, complete with beachfront boardwalk, cluster of restaurants, guesthouses, souvenir shops, and other tourist-friendly businesses. Its casual hangouts and its proximity to ever-popular Sun Bay Beach ensure that Esperanza stays busy; and if you get the impression that the town grew out of the tourist business, you wouldn't be far wrong. Just like the clientele, the majority of the business owners in Esperanza aren't Puerto Rican.

The two towns offer plenty of eateries, from *panaderías* (bakeries) that serve cheap and delicious sandwiches to contemporary bistros offering gourmet fusion food. When the sun goes down, both Isabel II and Esperanza offer options for nightlife; and while these are relatively few, there are fun places to go. You have a choice of San Juan–style bars, hotel bars, and dive bars. You can check out the Vieques version of a casino (poker night at a great local hangout) or take a walk along the boardwalk or the beach. (Whatever you do at night, don't forget to look up: The stars shine bright and beautiful over Vieques.) But the action is not all localized in Esperanza and Isabel II, and it doesn't take long to explore the rest of Vieques and discover places to eat, hang out, and mingle.

Incidentally, you can explore the island using *públicos* (you can even jot down a driver's name and make arrangements, much like a private taxi service), but I strongly recommend

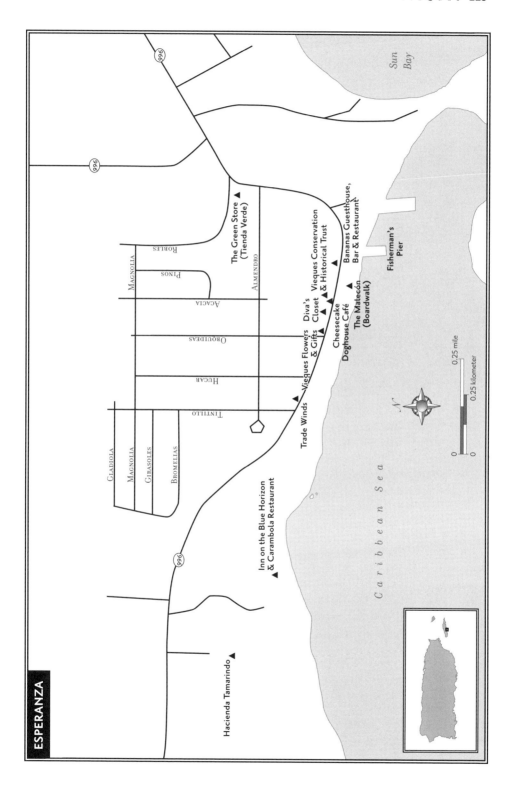

ESPERANZA

Sun Bay

Caribbean Sea

The Green Store (Tienda Verde)

Vieques Conservation & Historical Trust

Bananas Guesthouse, Bar & Restaurant

Fisherman's Pier

Diva's Closet

Cheesecake

Doghouse Café

The Malecón (Boardwalk)

Vieques Flowers & Gifts

Trade Winds

Inn on the Blue Horizon & Carambola Restaurant

Hacienda Tamarindo

ROBLES

MAGNOLIA

PINOS

ALMENDRO

ACACIA

ORQUIDEAS

HUCAR

TINTILLO

GLADIOLA

MAGNOLIA

GIRASOLES

BROMELIAS

996

N

0   0.25 mile

0   0.25 kilometer

The malecón *(boardwalk) and the town of Esperanza*

calling ahead (and I mean a good three to four weeks ahead) for a rental. And although you can rent a car, I would advise getting a Jeep. These are expensive, but traveling by Jeep is the best way to strike out on a bumpy, muddy trail that looks like it might be heading somewhere interesting. I rented mine from Allen Thompson's Vieques Car Rental (see page 215), and I was grateful for my sturdy white Jeep as I passed a worried-looking couple coping with a bad patch of road in their PT Cruiser. Scooters can also be a fun option, but be aware that the island's poorly lit roads and somewhat reckless local drivers can be hazardous to your health.

Apart from rampaging motorists, the island is quite safe, and you won't have any problems traveling to even the most remote corners. The crime most often reported is petty theft (no one will steal your car, for example; there's nowhere to take it). When parking at a beach, visitors are cautioned to leave nothing in the car but to leave the windows rolled down and the doors unlocked, because someone might come along and rifle through, looking for something valuable. Assaults and muggings are relatively rare—by and large, your personal safety is not at stake, but it's best to leave jewelry and cash in your room.

A Glow-in-the-Dark Dream

Even if you're spending just one night in Vieques, you simply cannot leave the island without visiting its glowing star: the bioluminescent bay, or biobay. No matter what you read about it (including my description), words don't do the biobay justice. The ethereal beauty of the place has to be witnessed firsthand, and this is the place to do it. There are three biobays in Puerto Rico, and the popular consensus is that none match the watery brilliance of Vieques's Mosquito Bay. But before we get into that, you might be asking yourself just what is a biobay.

In essence, it's a unique and fragile ecosystem that can exist only under certain conditions. There is bioluminescence all over the world, but very few places can classify as a "biobay." It all starts with a tiny single-cell organism called a dinoflagellate (*pyrodinium bahamense,* if you want to get technical). When these microscopic creatures get agitated (for example, when they're being attacked or when a human body wades by), they release energy in the form of light. In layperson's terms, they glow. And when they glow, so does anything that's moving in the water. Like fish, which dart beneath the surface like tiny comets trailing stars. Like the oars of a canoe, which dip in the water and come away dripping neon green. And like people, who suddenly start to shimmer with an almost alien beauty.

So why is Mosquito Bay more luminescent than any other biobay? Part of the answer is geography and density. Mosquito Bay has a very narrow opening to the sea. As such, it is sheltered from the brunt of the sea's winds and tides. Its dinoflagellates are protected from being dragged out to sea, which enables them to thrive—to the tune of over 700,000 organisms per gallon of water. No other biobay can boast a heavier concentration.

Another factor that contributes to the bay's bioluminescence is the island's ecology. The mangroves that line the bay provide essential nutrients for our little glowing friends, and the weather is just right year-round. Last, it is humankind, for once, that has helped the dinoflagellates. While other biobays have suffered due to motorboats polluting the water, Mosquito Bay has been preserved and protected for the jewel that it is. You can get here only by kayak or electric boat.

And get here you must. This is a breathtaking experience. And in case you're wondering, this interaction between human and dinoflagellate is not harmful to either party. Nor are you in danger of being preyed on; there are no sharks or other dangerous creatures in the biobay. So go ahead: Take a tour, and take a dip. Make a "glow-angel" in the water. Wave your hands around and watch the magic.

Destination Biobay

We were in luck: It was raining. Our guide, Nestor Guishard of Vieques Tours (see "Tours" on page 238), explained how this would make the experience all the more worthwhile, and he was right. We had been kayaking in Mosquito Bay for about 15 minutes, with five kayaks in the tour group, going with the wind (the return trip wouldn't be so easy) and hugging the mangroves to let paddlers with a different tour pass us. The night sky was dotted with stars, and there was very little moonlight. Perfect. As we made our way deeper into the bay, I began to see the bioluminescence. Raindrops glittered green on the water. Around us, streaking, iridescent fish swam past. We quickened our pace.

When we reached the rendezvous point, out in the center of the bay, we tied our kayaks together. Nestor explained the what, how, and why of Mosquito Bay, the best bioluminescent bay on earth. He described the dinoflagellates, how they live and thrive, and how they remain protected from the ravages of nature and human beings. And then, it was time to meet them. We dove, slipped, or fell off our kayaks and into the temperate waters, and the effects were immediate. We were glowing green, splashing around with delight and wonder, oblivious of anything but the electric silhouettes of our bodies. Everyone was in awe, and I, for one, grinned broadly all the way back to the shore.

LODGING

Bananas Guesthouse
787-741-8700
www.bananasguesthouse.com
142 Flamboyán Street, P.O. Box 1300,
Esperanza, Vieques 00765

Located behind Bananas restaurant, this family-friendly guesthouse is beach living for the budget minded. The rooms are among the most basic accommodations you'll find, with no TV or phones. They are kept clean, but with a minimum of decor to liven them up. In the same vein, the guesthouse offers little in the way of hotel amenities, but it does have a great restaurant and bar, and a small patio at the back. It's ideally located across from the *malecón* (boardwalk), and just steps from the beach and the shops and restaurants of Esperanza. It's also near Sun Bay. $.

Bravo Beach Hotel
787-741-1128
www.bravobeachhotel.com
One North Shore Road, Vieques 00765

Removed from the bustle of Isabel II, Bravo Beach is a little bit of South Beach in Vieques. Stylish and sophisticated, it's the only boutique hotel of its kind on the island. The rooms have a cool, clean, and predominantly white look patterned after the rest of the hotel, from the white mosquito-net-draped beds to the white, minimally adorned walls. Modern touches include ergonomic chairs and iPod docking stations. The wooden furniture and beds were designed by local artist Ernesto Peña, whose workshop is in Isabel II. Oceanfront rooms come with a private terrace that offer commanding views of the Atlantic; for more opulence, guests can rent one of two larger suites or the grand *casona*, a two-bedroom, two-bathroom villa separate from the main hotel building. The hotel's small but lovely pool is eye-level with the ocean and steps away from your room. $$–$$$$.

Casa La Lanchita
1-800-774-4717; 787-741-8449
www.viequeslalanchita.com
374 North Shore Road, Vieques 00765

La Lanchita is well known and well loved for its prices, its views, and the hospitality of its owners, Doug and Marikay McHaul. This three-story guesthouse faces the ocean and has a distinctly fun and family-oriented feel—from the funky pool with the dolphin fountains and the fake shark's head to the casual atmosphere. The eight suites are spacious, and all come fully furnished with kitchens and separate living and dining areas. Each one has a private balcony facing the ocean, which is about 30 feet away. The four-night minimum stay completes the feeling of being in a home away from home. $–$$.

Crow's Nest Inn
1-877-CROWSNEST; 787-741-0033
www.crowsnestvieques.com
www.crowsnestrealty.com
Route 201, Km 1.1, P.O. Box 1521, Vieques 00765

One of the best values for the money on the island, the Crow's Nest Inn offers decent rooms, solid dining options, a nice pool, and wonderful green views at bargain prices. The rooms are designed for comfort: Most come with a kitchenette or full kitchen, and all have a microwave toaster-oven and coffeemaker. The furniture is nothing fancy, but it's comfortable and well maintained. The Crow's Nest is removed from the beach but surrounded by tropical flowers and the island's lush, verdant landscape. The staff are very friendly, and the hotel is casual and pleasant. For guests seeking something grander (like a two-bedroom villa), **Crow's Nest Realty** is in the same building. $–$$.

The Enchanted Garden Inn
787-741-2805
HC-01, Box 9509, Vieques 00765

What do a pink house, an astounding variety of fruit and vegetable trees, and aerobic spin classes have in common? Easy: They can all be found at the Enchanted Garden Inn. The inn offers flexible accommodations —from a private studio separate from the main house to the entire main villa—to suit your needs and desires. The main house has four bedrooms upstairs, which can be rented out together or broken into two- and three-bedroom apartments. The separate studio is for single travelers or couples. Whatever you rent, you'll have a kitchen, an air conditioner, and a satellite TV. For a fee, you can sign up for one of owner Violet's spin classes during peak season. Café Violeta, also on the compound but separate from the lodgings, serves breakfasts made with ingredients taken from the inn's garden, which includes 14 varieties of mango, pineapple, papaya, sour sop, and guava, just to name a few. $–$$$.

Hacienda Tamarindo
787-741-8525; 787-741-0420
www.haciendatamarindo.com
Route 996, Km 4.5, P.O. Box 1569, Vieques 00765

"Wayfarers Accommodated" is the slogan at Hacienda Tamarindo, but it's not quite accurate. Truth is, everyone and anyone is accommodated here, and hospitality rules. Owners Burr and Linda Vail are your friendly hosts, and they take a great deal of deserved pride in their beautiful hotel. An old tamarind tree rises through the center of Hacienda Tamarindo, giving it its name, but the personality of the place comes entirely from its owners. The hotel is small, with only 16 rooms, and each room is unique. All are furnished in a tropical theme, and you can see the meticulous care and thought that went into their design (if you can, try to get one with a balcony facing the sea). There are a few common areas, including a pool and an indoor, air-conditioned study/library that I love and which has the added convenience of free Internet access. If you're lucky you'll catch Burr in the atrium, giving a guide to Vieques. He highlights good places to eat, which beaches to visit, and other useful tidbits. Hacienda Tamarindo also serves the best complimentary breakfast of any hotel on the island, and they'll pack a box lunch— along with one of the beach chairs in your room—to take on your day trip to the beach. The warmth and comfort of this place are hard to forget. $$–$$$.

Hector's By The Sea
787-741-1178
www.hectorsbythesea.com
HC-02, Box 14008, Vieques 00765

Hector's offers something a little different. With just three *casitas* (little houses) available, this is an intimate and private escape for tourists rather than a standard hotel or inn. The casitas come with air-conditioned rooms; a microwave, refrigerator, and coffeemaker; and a private deck stocked with a hammock. With views of the Caribbean stretching before you, you might want to do nothing but swing in the breeze in total privacy. If you're more energetic, you can wander down to the beach, take a dip in the pool, or head west about a mile until you get to Esperanza. $$.

Hix Island House
787-741-2302
www.hixislandhouse.com
HC-02, Box 14902, Vieques 00765

Square. Circle. Triangle. These are the most basic, and most solid, shapes in geometry. They are also the shapes of the three buildings that make up Hix Island House, an architectural blend of clean lines, simplicity, and unity with nature. Ayn Rand would

Round Building at Hix Island House

have been proud to stay here. When John Hix designed the Triangular House (the first of the three), it was his home. Over time, he expanded it to what is now, in my opinion, the coolest hotel in Puerto Rico. There are no air conditioners, no window panes (a mosquito net will protect you from the bugs at night), and no elevators at Hix. The walls and floors are bare concrete. The houses of Hix rise from the ground almost like natural formations, and the hotel aims to maintain harmony with its environment. But its respect for nature doesn't come at your expense. The accommodations are roomy and comfortable. A fresh loaf of nut-bread and a bowl of fruit are waiting for you in your room. Each room has a kitchen, and a few rooms have private porches. The pool, which resembles a grotto carved from rock, is among the best in Vieques. Prices are dictated by size and view. You'll be supremely comfortable at Hix, as long as

you're okay with an experience that brings you closer to nature. If you prefer the look and feel of a standard resort hotel, managers Michael and Diane will be happy to point you in the right direction. $$$.

Inn on the Blue Horizon

1-877-741-3318; 787-741-3318
www.innonthebluehorizon.com
Route 996, Km 4.2, P.O. Box 1556, Vieques 00765

Blue horizon, indeed. Built on a bluff overlooking the Caribbean Sea, this beautiful and picturesque hotel enchants guests with its intimate charm. But there's a lot more to the inn than the view, and there's good reason why this is one of the most popular and acclaimed lodging options on the island. The hotel is actually a cluster of small houses built on what was once a sugar plantation. From the main reception area, well-

Inn on the Blue Horizon's pool and ocean view

groomed trails lead to villas that each house two guest rooms and provide a sense of privacy that's rare in a hotel. The rooms are beautifully decorated in a tropical theme, with antique four-poster beds, dark wood furniture, and all the modern amenities you need. In and around the main house is where all the action is. There's a pleasant, casual open-air atrium where you can lounge about and enjoy the view, a fine restaurant with formal indoor dining as well as outdoor seating, and one of Vieques's best bars. The hotel has tennis courts and a small gym. At press time, renovations included an upgrade of the rooftop terrace. Last, there's the *pièce de résistance:* a fabulous pool designed to appear as though it was naturally carved out of the rock, with amazing views of the ocean. As nice as it is by day, the pool is magical at night; changing colored lights along the pool's bottom mirror the stars above. This inn is one of those places you hate to leave. $$–$$$$.

Martineau Bay Resort & Spa
787-741-4100
www.martineaubayresort.com
State Road 200, Km 3.2, Vieques 00765

If you want to enjoy the rustic beauty of Vieques while not immersing yourself in it, then the Martineau Bay is for you. As soon as you drive through the gate, you leave the natural landscape behind and enter a world of manicured lawns, tennis courts, and immaculate villas. This is the only resort hotel on Vieques, and you'll pay for the exclusivity; but the Martineau Bay is perfect for those who want to get away from it all yet not *really* get away from it all. You'll have a pretty room, private stretch of beach (the hotel is right on the ocean), fitness center, 5,000-square-foot spa facility, and your choice of in-hotel restaurants. $$$–$$$$.

Rainbow Realty
787-741-4312; 787-741-5068
http://enchanted-isle.com/rainbow

278 Flamboyán Street, Esperanza, Vieques 00765

If you don't want to stay in a hotel, there are plenty of private homes available for rent, typically on a weekly basis. For travelers interested in this option, Rainbow Realty in Esperanza is worth a call. Lin Weatherby and Gustavo Marin offer vacation rentals, from one-bedroom suites to family accommodations in Vieques. $$–$$$$.

Sea Gate Guest House

787-741-4661
www.seagatehotel.com
P.O. Box 747, Isabel II, Vieques 00765

Perched at the top of a hill overlooking Isabel II, the Sea Gate is a great retreat for budget travelers. This is one of those "come on in and make yourself at home" kind of places. Once you arrive at Sea Gate (getting here is a bit tricky, but it's right near the fort), you'll have to push open the gate, seek out someone who will attend to you, and acquaint yourself with the welcoming committee. This can include dogs, cats, and chickens, so it's helpful if you like animals. The path from the gate leads to the main guesthouse, where each room is clean, well kept, and simply furnished. Sea Gate offers anything from a single room to a large apartment. Some rooms have kitchens, and all have a porch; second-floor rooms boast a great view. No air-conditioning is provided and, really, none is needed. A complimentary breakfast is brought to your room each morning. Sea Gate has its own rustic, family charm, and you can't beat the price. $.

The Trade Winds

787-741-8666
www.enchanted-isle.com/tradewinds
On the *malecón*, P.O. Box 1012, Esperanza, Vieques 00765

Another hotel for the backpacking and budget-minded crowds, Trade Winds is a place to drop off your stuff and go enjoy the island. The 10 rooms are small, some with a funky arrangement of beds. All have private baths, some have balconies, and some have air-conditioning (although with the sea breeze the AC is a waste). Like Bananas (see page 228), the guesthouse's biggest draws are its cheap rooms, the attached restaurant, and its location across from the boardwalk and near all that Esperanza has to offer. Another advantage of the guesthouse is that it's kid-friendly, which is uncommon in Vieques's hotels. $.

Vieques Vacation Rentals

www.vieques-island.com/rentals

For travelers interested in renting a place for a minimum of a week rather than booking a hotel room, Vieques Vacation Rentals is a useful portal with several properties ranging from single apartments to deluxe villas. $$–$$$$.

DINING

Bananas

787-741-8700
www.bananasguesthouse.com
142 Flamboyán Street, Esperanza, Vieques

The sign above the bar proclaims Bananas to be a "gin-u-wine sleazy waterfront dive." Well, it's a good one, and it was one of the first tourist destinations to set up shop in Vieques. Now, Bananas is an institution; almost everybody who comes to the island will stop by to sample a delicious, freshly grilled half-pound burger (no frozen patties here; this is the real deal) or fish sandwich with fries or homemade chips. The menu is limited and simple, in keeping with the bar tradition; and the drinks flow till late at night, also in keeping with bar tradition. The restaurant is ideally located on the *malecón*, just in front of the ocean. At night, the second floor serves as another dining area and bar, with a beautiful mangrove mural painted by local artist Ernesto Peña. Things get really hopping on Friday night during high season, with a DJ and dancing on the upper deck. Open daily 11 AM—10 PM, with the bar staying open later on weekends. $.

BBH

787-741-1128
www.bravobeachhotel.com
At the Bravo Beach Hotel, One North Shore Road, Vieques

BBH marches to a different beat than the other restaurants in Vieques. Dinner is a tasty exploration of ingredient-driven tapas-sized dishes that can range from fancy finger foods (like the trio of dips with root vegetables) to delicious mini entrées (try the chipotle barbecued pork and the pan-roasted duck breast with a mango rice salad). The menu changes constantly as the chef plays with different flavors and local ingredients, but the walk-in wine gallery is sure to complement your favorite dish. BBH is also considered by some to have the best lunch in town. You can dine on light fare like fresh salads, curried pumpkin soup, and wraps (go with the jerk-marinated mahi wrap), or try a quesadilla or gourmet pizza. The poolside setting with a view of the ocean almost trumps the menu. Open Thursday through Sunday 11 AM—3 PM for lunch and 6—10 PM for dinner. $$.

Café Media Luna

787-741-2594
351 Antonio G. Mellado Street, Isabel II, Vieques

Of the many Sanjuaneros I spoke to before I first came to Vieques, most told me not to miss Café Media Luna. Small wonder: This is, in my opinion, frontrunner for best restaurant in Vieques. The setting is beautiful, a yellow and blue two-story villa on a quiet corner of town (admittedly, the view's not the best). The menu is an interesting mix of Indian and Caribbean tastes, with a few other Asian influences thrown in. The open kitchen allows you to see the chef mix together uncommon combinations and make them work. The two levels are quite different, with the ground floor done up in a more relaxed, loungelike style, and the second floor serving as the main dining room (couples and hot dates, try to get a table by the balcony). The menu changes daily, so you can always expect fresh ingredients and inventive flare. With its mood music, casual elegance, soft lighting, and surprising menu, Media Luna is one of the few places that can make you feel like you're not in Vieques. Open for dinner Wednesday through Sunday 6:30—10 PM. $$.

Café Violeta

787-741-2805; 787-741-7890
HC-01, Box 9509, Vieques

Adjacent to the Enchanted Garden Inn is Café Violeta, a breakfast-only restaurant that offers traditional, hearty morning meals. The menu ranges from a basic Continental breakfast to three-egg omelets, breakfast burritos, and belgian waffles. A worthy stop on the way to the beach, or you can take your meal to go. Open daily 8 AM—noon, except Wednesday. $-$$.

Carambola

787-741-3318
www.innonthebluehorizon.com
At the Inn on the Blue Horizon, Route 996, Km 4.2, Vieques

Chef Xandra reigns at Carambola, one of the most elegant restaurants on the island. Located in the beautiful Inn on the Blue Horizon, Carambola offers a varied but sophisticated menu. In the mix are criollo favorites like seafood *mofongo*, Continental classics like minted, grilled lamb chops, and international touches like coconut

Carambola Restaurant at Inn on the Blue Horizon

curry chicken. The menu changes often to accommodate the hotel guests, but one standard is what many call the best calamari on the island. Also worthy of your fork is the mixed salad, tossed with tropical fruits in a blueberry vinaigrette. For breakfast, dive into the blueberry or Grand Marnier banana pancakes, try the local *pan de agua* french toast, or feast on the Vieques eggs benedict (served with *churrasco* steak and *amarillos*). For scenery, decor, and quality of food, you can't beat it. Open Thursday through Sunday 6–9 PM. $$–$$$.

The Cheesecake Doghouse Café

787-741-0341
On the *malecón*, Esperanza, Vieques

Quite possibly the friendliest place in town, you'll feel like one of the crowd in no time at the Cheesecake Doghouse (at press time, they were considering dropping *Cheesecake* from the name). Serving simple fare on an outdoor porch, the café is a classic beach-front hangout. Grab a quick burger, an order of fajitas, or a "Michigan," which is a hot dog with meat sauce, and a very reasonably priced beer, and mingle with the regulars. Or, come here for breakfast and test your arteries with the Doghouse Breakfast Sandwich, which is made with eggs, cheese, bacon, sausage, and ham, on fresh local bread (*pan de agua*). On Sunday, the Doghouse shakes things up with guest chefs doing their own thing. Open Monday through Wednesday 8 AM–2 PM, Friday and Saturday 6 AM–whenever, and Sunday 8 AM–1 PM. $.

Chez Shack

787-741-2175
Route 995 north of Esperanza, Vieques

You can't call a place that serves fine food a dive, can you? This shack along Route 995, in the middle of the forest, is known for fine dining in a purposefully bare ambience. Its decor is colorful and bright, but proudly stripped of any finery. The food, thankfully, does not get the same treatment. Chez Shack is at its liveliest on Monday night, which is Grill Night. While a live band plays reggae music, you can choose your barbe-cued meat and then help yourself to a pic-nic-style salad bar. It's a fun night to visit Chez Shack, but call ahead and make reser-vations. Even though it's pricey, and I found better dining options, it remains extremely popular. Open Thursday through Monday 6:30–10 PM for dinner. $$–$$$.

Island Steakhouse

787-741-0011
At the Crow's Nest Inn, Route 201, Km 1.1, Vieques

One of the better dining options in Vieques, Island Steakhouse captures the essence of the tropics while serving deli-cious fare for the meat lover. The open-air dining area is on the second floor of a separate building from the rest of the Crow's Nest Inn, and it has a pleasant, warm vibe. As the name implies, the restaurant is known for its certified Black Angus steaks, and it has a reputation for the best *churrasco* (skirt steak) in town. Tuesday nights are the best time to go: Start with happy hour from 5 to 7 PM (you get a ripped section of a playing card when you get there; at 7, if the rest of your card is drawn from the pile, your drinks are free). Then proceed to an all-you-can-eat barbecue fest that's a godsend if you're famished after a day of diving or snorkeling. To wash down your meal, Island Steakhouse has a decent choice of wines and cocktails, including the signature "Caribbean Cosmopolitan": a "manly" version of the classic drink with white cranberry juice to remove the pink color, and rum instead of vodka. Open Friday through Tuesday 6–10 PM for dinner. $$–$$$$.

El Patio
787-741-6381
340 Antonio G. Mellado Street, Isabel II, Vieques

A popular spot for local food in a casual (even for Vieques!) setting, El Patio is recommended by many hotels for down-home cooking and terrific breakfasts. There's nothing out of the ordinary on the menu, which changes daily and can be found on a small blackboard, but dishes like the *bistec encebollado* and fresh seafood are always good budget bets. Open Monday through Friday 7 AM–5:30 PM, Saturday 9 AM–4 PM. $–$$.

El Resuelve
787-741-1427
Route 997, Barrio Destino, Vieques

You can't get more *boricua* than this Puerto Rican eatery on Route 997, between Isabel II and Esperanza. The place is little more than a shack with a couple of outdoor tables, *raggaetón* and salsa blaring from the boom box, and a steady clientele of regulars. Whatever is on the menu that day (or whatever they have left) is simple, hearty, and tasty. Open Wednesday 9 AM–6 PM, Thursday through Saturday 9 AM–9 PM, and Sunday 9 AM–7 PM. $.

Richard's Café
787-741-5242
36 Antonio G. Mellado Street, Isabel II, Vieques

Many locals recommend this unassuming redbrick home of tasty, authentic local fare. The fresh fish dishes are prepared in typical criollo fashion, and the paella is among the best you'll find on Vieques. Open daily 11 AM–11 PM. $$.

Trade Winds
787-741-8666
On the *malecón* in Esperanza, Vieques

It's open for breakfast, lunch, and dinner, and you'll want to make one stop at Trade Winds while you're on the island. Its combination of seaside ambience, with open-air dining in a nautical setting, views of the water and the boardwalk, and excellent food make it an island favorite. The *churrasco* steak, Caribbean lobster (they serve up more lobster than anybody else on the island), and coconut curried shrimp are all tasty choices, but my preference at Trade Winds is the fresh catch of the day, which you can have grilled in a pineapple salsa or gristmill-corn-encrusted, pan-seared, and topped with almond butter (my favorite). For breakfast, try the South Side Omelet, made with corned beef hash and cheddar cheese, or the filling *huevos rancheros*. Open daily 8 AM–2 PM for breakfast and lunch, and 6–9:30 PM for dinner. $$.

Uva
787-741-2050
www.uvarest.com
359 Antonio G. Mellado Street, Isabel II, Vieques

Uva is one of Vieques's standard bearers for fine dining. Dim lighting, an intimate dining room with modern decor, and an inventive menu of Asian and Caribbean fusion food draw a well-dressed crowd out for a nice night out. The menu changes often, blending traditional tropical ingredients with more exotic flavors. Examples include the king salmon with a Chinese spice glaze well balanced with a coconut cream sauce, and the grilled lamb and ostrich loin. Whatever you order, there will be a wine to go with it—the restaurant stocks over 80 wines from around the world. Or, you can sample something from the excellent martini menu. Open daily, except Tuesday, 7–10 PM for dinner. $$–$$$.

ATTRACTIONS, PARKS & RECREATION

Kiani Lagoon
On the northwestern section of the island, if you keep driving along Route 200 you'll cross a metal bridge and come to Kiani Lagoon. This is a small, wooden boardwalk through the mangrove reserve that you can access at any time (it's a good idea to wear bug spray when you go). The boardwalk lets you get close to the dense tangle of the mangroves' roots and branches, and you might catch a glimpse of local wildlife—mostly turtles, lizards, and a variety of birds. This excursion isn't spectacular, but if you're in an exploratory mood or want a change from the beach, it won't take long to check out Kiani Lagoon.

Mosquito Pier
This mile-long, weird finger of constructed seawall off the island's northern shore was initially the beginning of a massive land bridge that the U.S. Navy embarked upon in the 1940s to connect Vieques to the big island. The plan was to create a massive naval base from which to command the defense of the Caribbean. When the tide of World War II turned, the idea was abandoned. What you see today is all that's left: a very long pier with great spots for fishing, beaches, and a cool phenomenon that has earned Mosquito Pier the nickname *rompeolas* (wave breakers)—toward the east, you'll see choppy waves and strong winds, but turn around to the west, and all is calm. The breakwater also offers great views of the big island.

The Naval Ammunition Facility (NAF)
Most of the "attractions and parks" of Vieques aren't your typical fare, and the naval magazines are a great example. The NAF is a bizarre, jarring, and eerie reminder of what once took place on this island of pristine natural beauty. My jaw drops every time I see them: hundreds of bunkers used to store ammunition, cut into the hills of western Vieques, and camouflaged beneath earth and grass and surrounding foliage. Drive along the unmarked military road that stretches from north to south, and you'll soon come upon them. Some of the older ones, built during World War II, are so densely camouflaged that they can be mistaken for pleasant, rolling hillocks. A few are unlocked, and you can go in and test the echoing acoustics. Close by, you'll also find the Relocatable Over the Horizon Radar (ROTHR), a huge facility that remains under guard today. A visit to these military structures is a surreal trip through a landscape that belongs in another time, and another place, far from the glittering sands and serene beauty of Vieques.

Punta Mulas Lighthouse

Punta Mulas Lighthouse

87-741-0060
Northeast of the ferry dock in Isabel II, Vieques 00765

This picturesque landmark has overlooked the Isabel II harbor for over a century. At press time it the lighthouse museum was closed for renovations, but the exhibits typically focus on the maritime history of the island.

Ruins of the Playa Grande Sugar Plantation

There is no phone number and no physical address for this site. I'm not even sure it belongs in the "Attractions" section; it's actually a haunting monument to the harmful consequences of the U.S. Navy's long occupation of the island. Playa Grande was one of five large estates that dominated agricultural production on the island in the late 1800s and early 1900s. The sugar industry in Vieques has a tragic and impoverished history, the familiar tale of a very wealthy minority dominating a near-slave, impoverished workforce. When the navy arrived on the island during the 1930s, they expropriated the Playa Grande estate, along with much of Vieques's land. The owners and workers were forced to leave, and the area was left in a derelict state. Today, the ruins of the plantation still stand. You have to really hunt for them. . . or get lost in just the right way. Hidden in the southwestern corner of the island, just west of the Relocatable Over The Horizon Radar (ROTHR), is one small building that's representative of the ruins.

TOURS

Abe's Snorkeling

787-741-2134; 787-436-2686

Abe's gives visitors a few different options for enjoying the water. An all-in-one, six-hour excursion includes kayaking through mangroves, snorkeling, enjoying a secluded beach, eating a dinner by a bonfire as the sun sets and, finally, exploring the bioluminescent bay at night. You can also book separate trips, including a kayak/snorkeling adventure and a snorkeling-for-beginners trip. $$–$$$.

Black Beard Sports

787-741-1892
www.blackbeardsports.com
100 Muñoz Rivera Street, Vieques

With two certified dive masters, Black Beard is a full dive center, offering dive excursions to Isla Real, Angel Reef, and other prime dive spots. The company also provides surf- and shore-fishing trips. $$$.

Island Adventures

787-741-0720; 787-741-2544
www.biobay.com

Vieques's stunning bioluminescent bay is accessible in two ways: kayaking, which involves two-person teams paddling out to the bay; and Island Adventures' ride on an electric boat, which is a great option for those who cannot (or prefer not) to exert themselves. The boat doesn't harm the fragile ecosystem you're visiting, which makes the trip that much better. To maximize your experience, the boat doesn't sail during the three days of the full moon, when the brightness of the moonlight dims the bioluminescence of the bay. $$.

La Dulce Vida

info@bikevieques.com
www.bikevieques.com

Vieques's only mountain-bike tour combines a fun romp through along muddy trails and beaches and an interpretive guide to the island's natural wonders. Designed by owner Karl Alexander for pros or newcomers, the tour provides state-of-the-art biking equipment and a unique way to see, enjoy, and learn about the island. $$$.

Kiani Tours

787-556-6003
www.kianitours.com
9 AM–noon and 2–5 PM, by appointment

A cultural and historic tour of the island provided by Letty Pérez, a knowledgeable guide and certified licensed excursionist. $$.

MARAUDER Sailing Charters

787-435-4858

If you want a luxury cruise experience in Vieques, check out the *Marauder*. The all-day sailing trip aboard this beautiful white yacht runs from 10 AM to 3 PM and includes two snorkel stops at coral reefs (with gear and instruction provided), lunch cooked on board, and an open bar. There's a sunset cruise as well (no snorkeling). $$$–$$$$.

Nan-Sea Charters

787-741-2390
www.nanseacharters.com

Divers and snorkelers have a few options when they set sail in Nan-Sea's 28-foot boat. Snorkeling trips to Blue Tang Reef and Cayo Real give you full access to Vieques's coral reefs, while half-day trips for certified divers take you to places accessible only by boat. There are also shore dives, certification classes, and dives for noncertified divers. $$–$$$$.

Vieques Sailing

787-508-7245

Half-day, all-day, and sunset cruises let you enjoy the waters and keys of the island. You can sail to the southern point of the Bermuda Triangle, snorkel reefs off Mosquito Pier, and reach areas that are inaccessible from the land. There's an open bar, lunch is served on the all-day trip, and snorkeling gear is included on the half-day and full-day excursions. $$$.

Vieques Tours

787-447-4104; 939-630-1267
www.vieques-tours.com

Vieques Tours specializes in ecotours that entertain and enlighten people about the environment. In addition to excursions to the bioluminescent bay, they offer kayak trips and rentals, snorkeling trips, and historical tours of the island. Nestor Guishard is a knowledgeable, friendly local guide, and a Viequense genuinely committed to preserving and protecting the island's ecology. $$.

The Liberator's Pit Stop

Simón Bolívar is one of the most revered figures in Latin America today. "The Great Liberator," as he was called, was a driving force for independence for the Spanish colonies as well as an ardent opponent of slavery. Bolívar traveled far and wide in the Americas as he sought to rid the land of the yoke of empire, but he never set foot in Puerto Rico—except for one brief a stop in Vieques. In 1816, following a battle that he lost in Venezuela, Bolívar escaped with two ships, seeking the safety of Dutch-owned St. Thomas, but his ship ran aground off the coast of Vieques. The Spanish, who approached to investigate, were quickly subdued and agreed to give Bolívar safe passage to St. Thomas. He then went ashore to gather provisions before continuing his journey. His only pit stop on Puerto Rican soil is commemorated today by a bust in Isabel II's main plaza.

CULTURE

Ernesto Peña Art Gallery & Fine Woodworking

787-741-1922
358 Barriada Fuerte, Vieques

Ernesto is one of the true personalities of Vieques. A political activist, artist, woodworker, wine lover, and general student of things common and esoteric, he's one of those people who can talk about anything. He can also work magic with wood and paint, and a visit to his gallery will show you some of his original art. You can also find Ernesto's pieces in many hotels and restaurants around Vieques. The gallery hours are somewhat erratic, so you might want to call ahead and make an appointment, or drop by after you've visited the fort just across the road. Open daily 8:30 AM–5 PM. $$$$.

Fuerte Conde de Mirasol

787-741-1717
www.icp.gobierno.pr/myp/museos/m8.htm
471 Magnolia, Vieques

The largest cultural edifice on Vieques, the tiny Fort Count Mirasol has nothing on the sprawling castles in Old San Juan, but it is a striking landmark in Isabel II. Perched on a hill overlooking the Atlantic, the fort is typical of Spanish neoclassical architecture. Built between 1845 and 1855 by Vieques's governor, it was designed to repel colonization efforts

Fuerte Conde de Mirasol

by the British and Danish. It was never tested in battle, however, and remains the last military fort ever built by the Spanish empire. After doing time as a barracks and a jail, the fort is now a museum with exhibits showcasing the arts, archaeology, and history of the island. Some of the artifacts on display are over 2,000 years old, and there is an interesting video and photography exhibit of the naval occupation of Vieques. Open Wednesday through Sunday 8:30 AM–4 PM. $.

The Puerto Ferro Man
Off Route 997, just past Sun Bay, Vieques

Call it "the Stonehenge of Vieques." This odd, almost alien landmark is a haphazard collection of massive boulders that looks as if it fell from the sky. This is also the site of an archaeological dig in 1990 that unearthed a 4,000-year-old skeleton. You can't see evidence of the dig anymore, but the place has a surreal feel to it. There's no entrance, and there are no posted hours or phone numbers to call. Just stop by and see if this strange place stirs anything inside you.

Siddhia Hutchinson Fine Art Design Studio & Gallery
787-741-8780
www.siddhiahutchinson.com
15A Calle 3, Vieques

There's a dearth of facilities for artists in Vieques, but Siddhia makes up for it with a beautiful gallery in Isabel II. Her work includes sculpture, paintings, and ceramics, and among her pieces are attractive collections of dinnerware and home accessories. Siddhia showcases the work of other local artists as well. Everything on display has ties to the natural

Siddhia Hutchinson Fine Art Design Studio & Gallery

and cultural beauty of the island, and since her merchandise ranges from postcards and printed napkins to elaborate works of art, there's something for every budget. Open daily 9 AM–3 PM. $–$$$$.

Vieques Conservation and Historical Trust
787-741-8850
www.vcht.com
138 Flamboyán Street, Vieques

Viequenses are environmentally aware, but both locals and tourists understand that conservation of the island's natural resources is paramount to its survival and identity. The Vieques Conservation and Historical Trust, which was principally created to help protect the bioluminescent bay, has become a force for the preservation of the ecology as well as the archaeological heritage of the island. Today, the trust has numerous programs that specifically focus on helping children understand and protect the environment. A visit to the trust's small museum is an interesting and educational experience. On display are artifacts from colonial and Taíno times, an interesting collection of the various classifications of seashells found on Vieques's beaches, and a unique, hands-on marine-life exhibit that lets kids can gather around two shallow pools and learn about starfish and other local sea creatures. The gift shop has an excellent collection of books specific to Vieques's wildlife and culture. Open Tuesday through Sunday 11 AM–4 PM. Donations welcome.

NIGHTLIFE

Al's Mar Azul

787-741-3400

Plinio Peterson Street, on the waterfront near the pier in Isabel II, Vieuqes

Come for the spectacular sunsets on the water, stay for the daily happy hour from 5 to 7 PM, and relax with new friends. Val and Al make Al's Mar Azul a laid-back, fun local hangout. Saturday night is Karaoke Night. Open daily (closed Tuesday during low season) 11 AM–1 AM, until 2 on the weekends.

Bananas

787-741-8700

www.bananasguesthouse.com

142 Flamboyán Street, Esperanza, Vieques

For a night out on the town, many people simply go Bananas. On weekends, the bar stays open until late, and during high season there's a DJ every Friday night. The upstairs bar and dance floor is great place to wile away the night with a rum punch, or a piña or parcha colada. Open weekends until 1:30 AM. $.

Blue Moon Bar & Grill

787-741-3318

www.innonthebluehorizon.com

Route 996, Km 4.2, Vieques

A great circular bar with friendly bartenders, large screens on which to watch your favorite game, and a lovely open-air setting at the Inn on the Blue Horizon make Blue Moon Bar a well-loved hangout at night. Monday is Movie Night, Tuesday and Wednesday are Tapas Nights at the bar, and Saturday is Mexican Night. The bar stays open until 11 PM and sometimes later. $–$$.

M Bar

787-741-4000

359 Antonio G. Mellado Street, Isabel II, Vieques

Recently relocated near Uva in Isabel II, M Bar has sophisticated Puerto Rican food and a swank, almost gloomy look. They serve up classics like *mofongos, chillo,* and *churrasco,* and it's a good place for the pretty people to wear a little more fabric than their bathing suits and throw back a cocktail or two. Open Tuesday through Saturday 7–10 PM. $$–$$$.

Poker Night at the Cheesecake Doghouse Café

787-741-0341

On the *malecón,* Esperanza, Vieques

You can hang out until late at the Doghouse on weekends, but the real action is on Tuesday night, when the island's take on the San Juan casinos. Tuesday night is Hold 'Em Poker Night at the Cheesecake Doghouse, and while it's open to anybody, it's one of the hottest tickets in town. So, come early, get a (very cheap) beer or glass of wine, and settle in for a fun night. It's a great way to meet and mingle with a friendly bunch of Viequenses (no Spanish required). Tuesday night at 8 PM. $$ for poker, $ for everything else.

Woodworker's Cheese and Wine Bar
787-741-1922
358 Barriada Fuerte, Vieques

Enjoy a night of art and wine and cheese in Ernesto Peña's studio, part of which has been converted to host this unique gathering space. A novelty in Vieques, the wine and cheese bar is a bit of sophistication in the tropics. In addition to cheese, you might find some local culinary specialties. Open Wednesday through Sunday until midnight. $$–$$$$.

SHOPPING

Black Beard Sports
787-741-1892
www.blackbeardsports.com
101 Muñoz Rivera Street, Vieques 00765

One-stop shopping for outdoors types, Black Beard carries a full range of diving gear and equipment, bikes, snorkeling gear, tents and camping equipment, clothing, even army gear. Centrally located in Isabel II, it's your source for good-quality supplies. You can also rent bikes, and scuba and snorkeling gear, and there's a business center in the corner where you can access the Internet and print documents. Open Monday through Saturday 10 AM–5 PM, Sunday 10 AM–2 PM. $–$$$$.

Caribbean Walk
787-741-7770
353 Antonio G. Mellado Street, Isabel II, Vieques

This small shop—Vieques's first crafts boutique and one of few souvenir shops in Isabel II—features the work of local artisans. There's a selection of paintings, carvings, candles, and sea glass, as well as a large stock of shell jewelry. Open Monday through Saturday 10 AM–4 PM. $–$$$.

Diva's Closet
787-741-7595
134 Flamboyán Street, Esperanza, Vieques

As the name implies, this store carries primarily women's clothing but also has a limited men's line. Their fabrics and designs are ideal for the tropics, but they'd look good any-where. Diva's also stocks swimsuits, beach accessories, and their own line of body lotions and bath products. Open daily 10 AM–5 PM. $–$$.

Kim's Cabin
787-741-3145
136 Flamboyán Street, Esperanza, Vieques

You won't find Gucci and Ferragamo on Vieques, but if you're looking for upscale beach-wear, head to Kim's Cabin. Here you'll find light summer clothing for the whole family (with very nice Vieques T-shirt designs), footwear for the beach, and some beautiful hand-carved sterling silver jewelry set with fossils, minerals, and gemstones. They also have a room of nonlocal arts and crafts. Open daily 9:30 AM–5 PM, sometimes 6. $–$$$$.

Vieques Flowers and Gifts Too!!
1-800-746-4197; 787-741-4197
134 Flamboyán Street, Esperanza, Vieques

The "Gifts Too!!" part of the name is appropriate: There's something for everyone with a tourist's needs at this place. The nifty collection includes snacks, beach accessories, a selection of *vejigante* masks from an artist in Ponce, decorative wind chimes and, of course, local and exotic flowers. Open daily 10 AM–4 PM. $–$$$.

FOOD PURVEYORS, LIQUOR & CIGARS

Panadería La Viequense
787-741-8213
352 Antonio G. Mellado Street, P.O. Box 370, Vieques 00765

Come early on the weekends, because the lines get long at this popular bakery and deli. People flock here for local pastries like *pan de mallorca* and *quesitos,* donuts, baked goods, and a tremendous variety of delicious sandwiches with creative names and plenty of filling (the Viequense Sandwich is a monster with pork, turkey, ham, pepperoni, and *pepinillo* stuffed into it). You can eat in at one of the cafeteria-style tables or take your food to the beach. $.

Roy's Coffee Shop
787-741-0685
355 Antonio G. Mellado Street, Isabel II, Vieques

The Vieques equivalent of Starbucks, Roy's is a welcome pit stop during the day. Step into the pink building, order something to drink at the bar, and relax on a sofa. Or you can check your e-mail while slurping a wide range of hot and cold coffees. On a hot day, cool down with a "Frozen Roy," which comes in a variety of rich flavors. There's also a small menu of light lunch items and a few pastries at the bar. Open daily 8 AM–4 PM. $.

El Sombrero Viejo
787-741-2416
65th Infantry Road, Vieques

A cute name (it means "the Old Hat"); a large selection of wine, beer, and liquors; and a simple philosophy of "a gourmet dinner without wine is just another fast-food take-out" pretty much sums up this local bar and liquor store. Open daily, as they proclaim, from around midday to around midnight. $–$$.

Vieques Fruit Market

787-741-1697
On Route 997 heading out of Isabel II, Vieques

The expansively named Vieques Fruit Market is nothing more than a trailer where you can get locally grown fruit, juices, and other snacks. The best thing they have is fresh coconut milk—they slice open the coconut with a machete and serve it up with a straw. On a hot day, it's heaven. Open Monday through Saturday 7 AM–6 PM, Sunday 8 AM–2 PM. $.

Vieques Health & Gourmet Market

787-741-4744
Route 200, Km 1.8, Vieques

Not quite a grocery store, this small market just outside Isabel II stocks an unusual assortment of organic foods and produce, quick-prepare light meals, energy foods, and specialty items. An extremely popular choice among locals is the homemade bread that gets delivered once a week to the store. Open Monday through Friday 10 AM–3 PM and 5:30–7 PM, Saturday 10 AM–6 PM. $–$$.

GOOD TO KNOW ABOUT . . .

Colmado El Molino

787-741-0015
342 Antonio J. Mellado Street, Isabel II, Vieques

This well-stocked grocery store in Isabel II sells food and household items. Open Monday through Saturday 7 AM–11 PM, Sunday 10 AM–11 PM.

Colmado Mambo

787-741-8080
Route 997, Barrio Destino, Vieques

Located between the main towns in the Barrio Destino area, this grocery store also sells snacks, sundries, beer, phone cards, and more. Open daily 7 AM–10:30 PM, later on weekends.

Farmacia San Antonio

787-741-8397
52 Benítez Guzmán Avenue, Isabel II, Vieques

This local pharmacy has prescription medicines and basic health and beauty products. Medical plans are accepted. Open Monday through Saturday 8:30 AM–6 PM.

The Green Store

787-741-8711
Intersection of Route 996 and Robles Street, Vieques

Located in Esperanza, this store is the most convenient place on the island to buy wine for your beach picnic. You can also get fresh bread and all your basic groceries. Open daily 9 AM–9 PM.

WEEKLY & ANNUAL EVENTS

Fiestas de Pueblo (Town Fair)
Second or third week of July
787-741-0800; 787-741-0290
Island-wide (the 2006 fair was held on the western end of the island)

The Vieques Town Fair is an annual carnival. The whole island gets into it, with music, dance, and children's events in full swing. This is the unofficial time to partake of Vieques moonshine, or *bili*, which is made of *quenepa*, a local fruit, white rum, cinnamon, and sugar. Free.

Cultural Festival
April (usually after Easter)
787-741-1717
At the Fuerte Conde de Mirasol, Vieques

The annual Cultural Festival in Vieques celebrated its 30th anniversary in 2007. This event takes place in the historic fort in Isabel II and features three days and nights of exhibitions by local artisans, and folkloric musicians and dancers. There are also activities for children.

Paso Fino Competition
Mother's Day and Father's Day
787-741-0800
Club Equestre, Barrio Santa María, Vieques

A Mother's Day and Father's Day tradition, families come out to see this competition of Paso Fino horses, whose delicate, high-stepping gait ensures a bump-free ride. Free.

Christmas and New Year's Eve
Late December–early January
787-741-0290
Throughout the island

The island holds numerous Christmas and New Year's Eve events, including a lighting of the Christmas lights, a gift-giving day for children, and troubadour festivals. Throughout the season, there are activities for the public, music, and arts and crafts.

9

Culebra

Breathtaking Beaches, Part 2

Take everything I said about how different Vieques is from San Juan, and double it. Maybe triple it. Now you're talking about Culebra (which, incidentally, means "snake" in Spanish —supposedly, this name refers to the shape of the island, but I don't see it). To newcomers, Culebra will feel like a cross between a quiet, sleepy fishing village and an end-of-the-earth paradise. Things like schedules and street addresses aren't all that important here. Culebra is where people go to escape the modern world . . . although these days, so many people are doing the same thing that the modern world may soon be turning its attention this way. So far, the resort hotels haven't brought their spas and landscapers here. McDonald's and Burger King are still a ferry ride away. Culebra is the very definition of a rustic waterfront town, and the locals fervently hope it stays that way.

How to Get There and When to Go There

Like Vieques, Culebra is a year-round destination that cycles between foreign and local tourists. Summer season on the island is one big beach party for Puerto Ricans. There's little downtime before the tourists from other parts begin popping up. And the modes of transportation to and from the island are the same: high-speed catamaran, ferry, or airplane.

By Sea

Puerto Rico Maritime Authority
787-863-0705

The ferry service from the east-coast town of Fajardo on the big island runs three times a day to Culebra. Make sure you call for the schedule: Cancellations, interruptions, and schedule changes are always possible. The cargo ferry goes to the island during the week only, but, I don't recommend it for the same reasons detailed in the chapter on Vieques. Although you don't need a Jeep to explore Culebra, the hassle of dragging your car to the island isn't really worth it. $.

Island Hi-Speed Ferry
1-877-899-3993

www.islandhispeedferry.com/puertorico
AquaExpreso Ferry Terminal, Pier 2, Old San Juan 00901

The high-speed catamaran service makes the trip from Old San Juan to Culebra in roughly 1 hour, 45 minutes. The ferry runs during only peak tourist season, from December to late April; but even then, service is spotty. Amenities include cushioned seats, air-conditioning, and a snack bar. I recommend taking a plane rather than the ferry. $$$.

By Air

Air America
787-276-5669
www.airamericacaribbean.com

Charter your own plane to Culebra, as well as other points in the Caribbean. $$$$.

Air Flamenco
787-741-1818; 787-742-1040
www.airflamenco.net

787.724.1818 - reservations

Flights are available from Isla Grande Airport in Miramar and from Fajardo. Prices are standard unless there are no other passengers scheduled for the date you want to fly. $$–$$$.

Isla Nena
1-877-812-5144; 787-863-4447
www.islanena.8m.com

$38 Vieques to Culebra 45 minute flights

This charter-plane company offers on-demand, daily service to and from Culebra and points throughout the Caribbean. Flights depart from Luis Muñoz Marín International Airport in Carolina and Diego Jeménez Torres Airport in Fajardo. $$$.

Vieques Air Link
1-888-901-9247; 787-741-8331
www.viequesairlink.com

Flights are available to and from the Isla Grande Airport in Miramar and Luis Muñoz Marín International Airport in Carolina as well as Diego Jeménez Torres Airport in Fajardo, among other locations. Prices are standard unless there are no other passengers scheduled for the date you want to fly. $$–$$$.

GETTING AROUND

Carlos Jeep Rental
787-742-3514
www.carlosjeeprental.com

Carlos offers daily, weekly, and monthly rentals of a continuously updated fleet of Jeeps, compact cars, and Dodge Caravans. They're expensive but nice. Plus, Carlos gets bonus points for being right in the airport and having a very cool logo. $$$.

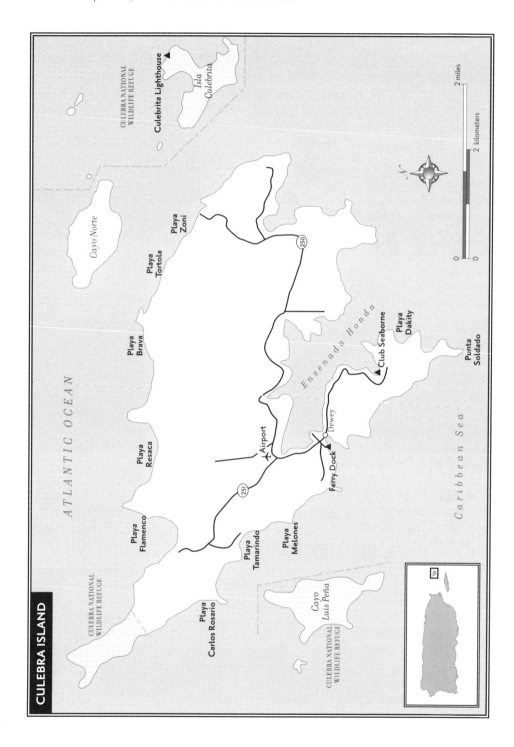

CULEBRA ISLAND

ATLANTIC OCEAN

Caribbean Sea

Ensenada Honda

Cayo Norte

CULEBRA NATIONAL
WILDLIFE REFUGE

Culebrita Lighthouse

Isla
Culebrita

Playa
Zoni

Playa
Tortola

Playa
Brava

Playa
Resaca

Playa
Flamenco

Playa
Carlos Rosario

Playa
Tamarindo

Playa
Melones

Cayo
Luis Peña

CULEBRA NATIONAL
WILDLIFE REFUGE

Airport

Dewey

Ferry Dock

Club Seaborne

Playa
Dakity

Punta
Soldado

CULEBRA NATIONAL
WILDLIFE REFUGE

250

251

2 miles

2 kilometers

0

0

N

Dick & Cathie's Rentals
787-742-0062

If you want a different rental experience, call Dick and book yourself one of his "things." These are old-fashioned, beat-up but serviceable Volkswagen buggies. Roaring around in these clunking classics (don't even think about an automatic transmission) that will get you pretty much anywhere can be either a wonderfully fun romp or a total nightmare, depending on your sense of adventure. This place is cheaper than the flashier rental agencies. Dick and Cathie also rent bikes and have a laundry service. $$.

Jerry's Jeeps
787-742-0587

Jerry's is a reliable service with a solid fleet of over 30 vehicles. In addition to complimentary pickup and delivery, Jerry provides a great introduction and orientation to the island. $$$.

JM Rentals, Inc.
787-742-0521
www.scooterspr.com

A scooter won't be able to negotiate all of Culebra's terrain, but it will get you to most places you need to go, like many of the beaches.

Thrifty
787-742-0521
www.thrifty.com

The only big name you'll find in Culebra, Thrifty is conveniently located right across from the airport. $$$.

RUSTIC, REMOTE & RESPLENDENT: THE UNPOLISHED JEWEL OF THE CARIBBEAN

When people talk about how much they love Culebra, they're certainly not referring to the town, the anemic nightlife, or the cultural attractions of the island. The combination of nature and the stuck-in-time serenity of the place is what make it special. Recent efforts by one developer to transform prime land into a luxury resort were met with stiff resistance and protests by the townspeople. Everywhere, you'll see graffiti, posters, and signs urging you to help preserve the natural beauty of the island and maintain the status quo. To be a Culebrense means you have to help protect your island, says one such sign. The people here aren't interested in prosperity at the expense of changing the wild beauty of their home.

And it's a fascinating home, with a unique history. Culebra is only 17 miles east of Puerto Rico, 12 miles west of St. Thomas, and 9 miles north of Vieques. Yet for decades, this was an almost totally ignored island. As few as 15 years ago, there were just two ferry trips a day to and from the main island (and these were not the large boats you see today): a morning and an evening trip that were mainly for the benefit of Culebra residents needing to get to Fajardo and beyond. The present-day caravan of *públicos*, assortment of guest-houses, and variety of restaurants are relatively new phenomena. Older residents remember a very different life on the island. Even with all the recent change, Culebra is in many ways a land lost in time.

Why such isolation? There are a few reasons. One, of course, is the U.S. military, which used the island as a firing range and for naval exercises from the early 1900s to the 1970s. Another is the island's geography. There are fantastic beaches on Culebra, but also quite a few that are strips of rough rock and bone coral with surf too rough to risk swimming in. The entire area of Culebra, including the nearby islets, comprise a mere 7,000 acres, and much of this land is hilly, with dense vegetation and little to welcome humanity. It wasn't colonized until the 1880s, and before U.S. forces arrived, only around 500 people lived on the island. Even today, there are just over 2,000 residents on Culebra.

It was Jim Galasso, longtime Culebrense and real estate agent, who revealed to me the two main reasons for Culebra's seclusion: zoning and turtles. And your reaction is probably the same as mine was: Huh? Well, history and nature have been formidable allies in the preservation of the island. When the U.S. Navy left Culebra in the early 1970s, the local government did a rare thing: It swooped in and zoned the land *before* big commercial enterprises had a chance to discover Culebra's treasures. How did this impact the island? To make a long and complicated story short, the 1-acre, 5-acre, and 25-acre plots of land assigned and distributed by the government for development (over 60 percent of the island was designated for residential-only construction) prevented resort developers from planting sprawling hotels right on Culebra's most marketable asset: its spectacular beaches.

The interior terrain was zoned into larger parcels, so a private homeowner had to purchase a 25- or 50-acre plot of land on which to build a house. The hotels wanted nothing to do with this land, since it was far from the beaches and had rugged or nonexistent roads and no infrastructure whatsoever. Impractical for both private and commercial developers, these chunks of land stayed, and remain, relatively unspoiled. The one big resort hotel that tried to make it work—Costa Bonita—ran into all the expected problems of staffing and maintenance, and now lies empty; locals call it the "eyesore of Culebra."

The turtles did their part as well. Leatherback, hawksbill, loggerhead, and green turtles call Culebra home, and leatherbacks and hawksbills come to the island's beaches to nest. When the navy left Culebra, much of the territory fell into the hands of the U.S. Fish and Wildlife Service. In large-scale urbanization, the commission logically saw an imminent threat to nesting turtles and other wildlife, and rushed to preempt any such development. Their swift action secured this ancient nesting ground for several species of turtle. To this day, all the waters around Culebra, which are an essential habitat for green turtles, are protected.

Of course, turtles and tourists aren't the only ones to enjoy Culebra's rugged hospitality. While the rest of the world stayed away, other visitors made—and still make—good use of the island. The mangroves, coral reefs, and cays are home to thriving communities of marine life. And bird-watchers and divers love Culebra for its visual cornucopia.

Culebra isn't for everyone; any local will spend all day trying to convince you of this basic fact (with little success). Tourists who come here for a five-star resort experience are bound to be sorely disappointed; the ones who hear about Culebra's fabulous beaches and expect state-of-the-art facilities are in for a nasty shock; and the ones who come with an open mind must understand one thing, for their own sake—they're not in San Juan anymore.

Once you've become familiar with Puerto Rico's island getaways, you'll reach an interesting conclusion: Culebra is different from Vieques. At first blush, the casual observer may think the two are basically the same—off the beaten path, a bit quaint and old-fashioned, but with great beaches and a thriving tourist industry. Dig a little deeper and you'll find important differences. Vieques does a much better job of catering to the well-heeled crowd who demand resort-class accommodations and service. Culebra cannot, and will not, match the luxury boutique hotels of its cousin. In more subtle ways, the two are psychologically apart. There is even something of a sibling rivalry between them. Culebra doesn't have the social divide between the locals and foreign residents that you see in Vieques. It also doesn't have the same petty-crime issues.

Why? Because size matters. Culebra is so small that everyone knows each other. People tend to get along, because there's nowhere to go if you don't; and there's a general, communal camaraderie. Stealing from your neighbor is practically the same thing as stealing from *everybody's* neighbor. Also, there is no unemployment on Culebra. Again, this is directly attributable to the size of the island. As unemployment and crime are common bedfellows, it follows that Culebra is one of the safest places you'll ever visit. It's also one of the friendliest places around. Culebrenses are laid back, affable, and welcoming. English is understood, if not spoken, everywhere. A couple of days is all you'll need to start recognizing faces and making friends.

DEWEY STAY OR DEWEY GO?

Culebra has one town, Dewey, with two roads leading out of it. Nobody calls it Dewey; it's just *pueblo,* or "town." And the town looks a bit dilapidated. The iron bridge over Ensenada Honda looks like it might fall apart one of these days (if you pass underneath it and look up, you'll see what I mean). Even some of the popular eateries and hotels appear in need of a face-lift. But this is where the action, such as it is, and the commercial heart of Culebra lie. Dewey houses the island's City Hall, tourism office, gas stations, police and fire station, hospital, bank, school, post office, and churches. The ferry dock is in Dewey, and the airport is minutes away. Water taxis, dive shops, and sailing charters operate out of the town. And, as you might imagine, there are quite a few restaurants, shops, and hotels in town. As Dewey shuts down at 11 every night, you can guess how many nightclubs there are.

It's interesting to note that lodging options vary greatly if you don't stay in town. Most of the hotels in Dewey are guesthouses that cater to budget travelers. Nothing fancy, these range from bare and bleak to simple and comfortable. And while the few hotels near town, like the **Club Seabourne**, are quite nice, the real luxury accommodations in Culebra are the private cottages, villas, and apartments

Keep Your Shirt On

It's a bit surprising in such a tranquil, easygoing place as Dewey, but there is one rule of thumb visitors must strictly adhere to : Men are required to have a shirt on, and you will be stopped if you're loafing about bare-chested. Women also need to cover their bathing suits. Call it a sense of island style.

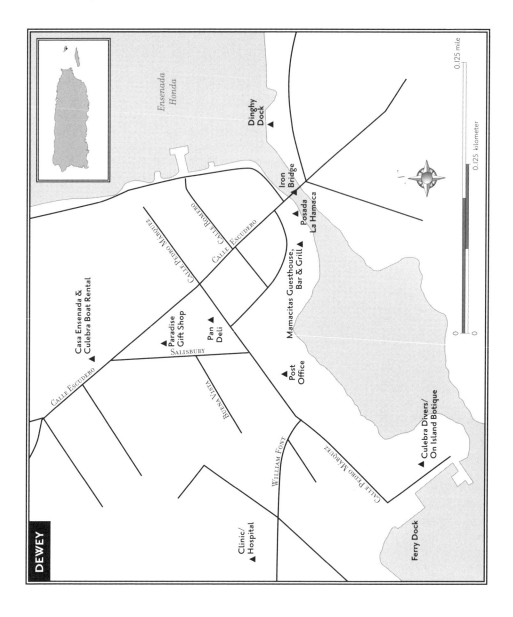

available for rent. Some of these are gorgeous, secluded homes that allow you to live lavishly for a week or two.

Regardless of where you sleep, if you remain in Dewey while you're here, you're pretty much missing the whole point of coming to Culebra. Treat the town as your pit stop (if you're staying here) or as your fueling station, but get out of town to enjoy the island's resources. Some of the better hotels, and all of the best home rentals, are located elsewhere. You'll also find great restaurants in other parts of the island. There's not much to see and do outside Dewey—then again, there's not a whole lot to see and do *in* the town either. But that's why you're here. And once you leave Dewey behind, you'll start to truly appreciate what

Culebra is all about. You're not here to shop, except for the occasional souvenir or two. You're not here to gamble. And you're not here to spend your vacation in Dewey.

So, now that we've established that Dewey is *not* the place to spend the majority of your time, the obvious question is: what to do? There are three plausible answers: Get to the birds, get to the beach, and get off the island. Culebra is one of the oldest wildlife refuges in the world. Designated as such since 1909, the island has been a preserve for over 13 species of migratory seabirds, including terns, red-billed tropic birds, pelicans, and boobies. It's for the dedicated birder rather than the casual observer.

As for beaches, while Culebra may not have the astounding number and variety found on Vieques, it holds its own fairly well. And it does have one bona fide superstar that blows away anything you'll find in the rest of Puerto Rico.

Flamenco Beach

I know I should be listing these in alphabetical order, but I'm taking a bit of license here, because Flamenco Beach belongs in its own stratosphere. This is the kind of place that makes your jaw sag. Framed by hills, Flamenco Beach is a long and deep horseshoe of sand against which the most dazzling variegated blue waters lap. It's a Blue Flag beach that stretches for miles, an idyllic place that has more services and facilities than any other beach in Culebra. It's also the most accessible; *públicos* journey between Dewey and the beach throughout the day. The beach has a large, sectioned campground; kiosks selling food, drinks, camping gear, and clothing; information booths, lifeguard towers; and volleyball nets. But all that is secondary to its incredible beauty.

Mired in the natural paradise is a poignant memorial to the island's past military occupation: Head north along the beach and you'll come to one of two rusted tanks, partially

Flamenco Beach

painted over, half-submerged in the water. The second tank is reached by the walking path running parallel to the beach, next to the campgrounds.

Brava Beach

By the time I got to Brava, I was bleeding from several scratches, dirty, and sweaty. I was also the only one on this beautiful, isolated stretch of sand, with only a recalcitrant crab for company. The only way to get to this beach is to drive to the end of a residential street, park, ignore the frenzied barking of the neighborhood dogs, walk past the NO ENTRY sign, and follow the trail for a good half mile. For the most part, it's an easy-to-moderate hike, but you can easily miss the narrow entrance to the beach—I did—and then you'll find yourself fighting through a gauntlet of tree limbs, mangrove roots, and cobwebs. With its booming surf and spotless beauty, it's a lovely place to visit, surf, and bodyboard, but the rough waters aren't great for swimming.

Carlos Rosario

Carlos Rosario, on the northwest side of Culebra, is easily accessed via a short hike from Flamenco Beach (you can also get to Carlos Rosario from Tamarindo Beach). It's a small beach that has the distinct advantage of giving you the best snorkeling on the island. Dive in and swim out to the channel marker, turn right, and you'll find yourself floating above a spectacular coral reef teeming with marine life. It's as close to a *National Geographic* special as you'll get.

Dakity Beach and Soldier's Point

On the south side of the island, this pebbly beach is good for beachcombers and snorkeling, but it's not worth going out of your way to visit if you're in Culebra for only a short time. A good kayak destination from town.

Melones Beach

Framed against Cayo Luis Peña, the sunsets are beautiful at this popular local beach close to Dewey. There's good snorkeling in nearby reefs, but there are better places to sunbathe.

Resaca Beach

If you think the trek to Brava Beach is tough, forget about getting to Resaca. Of the big, beautiful beaches, this is the most difficult one to reach, and unless you relish a challenging hike, you'd be better off getting here by boat. It's also a mirror image of next-door Brava Beach. *Resaca,* incidentally, means "undertow," so I wouldn't recommend swimming too far out to sea.

Tamarindo Beach

On the way to Flamenco, you'll see signs for Tamarindo Estates and Tamarindo Beach. This is a smaller beach that is at times soft and sandy, and at other times a pebbly mix of sand and coral. You can bathe and bask within easy view of Cayo Luis Peña.

Zoni Beach

If Flamenco is too crowded and you don't feel like hiking, Zoni might be your best bet for white sands and calm waters. A quiet beach on the eastern side of the island, Zoni has beautiful, up-close views of the Cayo Norte and Culebrita islets.

Hail a (Water) Cab

So you think taking a taxi in New York City (or San Juan, for that matter) is expensive? Wait till you shell out the bucks for a water taxi. This is the main mode of transportation to Culebra's cayos, but it's worth the price. Here are a few numbers you can call:

Cayo Norte Water Taxi
787-742-0050

Culebra Water Taxi
787-360-9807

Isleño Water Taxi
787-314-6163

A water taxi at the ferry dock in Dewey

In addition to the popular beaches, you can find tiny, isolated stretches of sand around the island, especially near some of the private homes available for rent. It's not hard to reach the water in Culebra, but the beaches and reefs aren't found only on the main island. Some of the best destinations in Culebra lie just offshore.

Culebrita and Cayo Luis Peña

Culebrita and Cayo Luis Peña are two of Culebra's largest offshore keys. (A third islet, Cayo Norte, is privately owned, and everyone is waiting to see what becomes of it.) Both destinations are worth the trip, for different reasons, and both will make you feel just a bit like Gilligan: Culebrita has only one artificial structure, and that's one more than the other islet. And for both, the boat journey is part of the fun. In February, you might see humpback whales in these waters. Dolphins and turtles are among the more familiar, year-round sights.

Culebrita

If you have time for only one trip off the island, make it Culebrita. The name is an affectionate term meaning "little Culebra," and it makes sense. Just a mile off Culebra, this chunk of land boasts six beaches and is home to just one building, the famous Culebra Lighthouse. Culebrita is easy to cover by foot, with walking trails connecting the islet's best beaches and its only landmark.

West Beach on Culebrita

View from the eastern end of Playa Tortuga

The water taxis drop you off and pick you up after several hours, so it's good to bring provisions (among these, make sure to bring water and snorkeling gear—two essential items). Once the boat is out of site, you'll forget all about civilization as you trek along under the open sky with nothing but nature around you. About a mile in length, Culebrita is a wonderful place to explore and swim. Of the islet's beaches, **West Beach** is my favorite: a long, thin stretch of sand with a multihued tapestry of blue waters. The Culebrita Reef, called Los Corchos by the locals, is on the south side of the island.

The most popular beach lies on the north side of the island, and it's called **Playa Tortuga** (Turtle Beach). As you can probably tell by the name, the turtles like it here. So do humans. This is a large and picturesque crescent whose turquoise waters are protected on either side by long, encircling arms of rock. You can sunbathe, swim, and snorkel to your heart's content, but you shouldn't miss out on the easternmost point of the beach. Walk along the sand, then negotiate the rougher, coral banks, and you'll get to a unique little corner: a place with shallow tidal pools and flats that are ideal for children and wading (when the surf is not too rough). A small hill here offers commanding views of the island, the lighthouse, and St. Thomas.

A trail connects Playa Tortuga to **Trash Beach,** so called because a lot of debris due to carelessness or indifference washes up here. I haven't seen evidence of that; instead, I was treated to a smaller twin of Tortuga, with the added advantages of no people around and lovely views of St. Thomas in the distance. Unfortunately, the surf here is rough and not recommended for swimming.

You might be tempted to visit the much ballyhooed lighthouse. Built in the 1880s, it's one of the oldest in the region, and it gets a lot of hype. But I found it to be a singularly overrated attraction on the island, and, unless you're a serious lighthouse enthusiast, I wouldn't recommend the detour. The hike, along an overgrown trail that's tough to find (but does get easier as you climb), winds its way up a hill. There are lovely views along the way, but the lighthouse itself is closed to the public. A wire fence stretches around it (although there is an opening), and the structure is considered unsafe. Let's put it this way: Out of a group of six people, I was the only one to veer off in search of the lighthouse, and by the time I returned to find everyone else excitedly talking about the turtles and rays they had spotted in the water, I realized they were a lot happier for their decision.

It's Good to Be Lazy

I'm in the boat with Walter, of **Culebra Divers** (see "Tours" on page 268), and two other passengers. We skim through the water, the eastern coast of Luis Peña growing as we near our dive site. The shores are a mix of coral, rock, and sand, and we pass just one idling boat before we come to a stop. Walter helps us into our gear—no wetsuits, but tanks, weight belts, masks, and flippers—and I leap rather clumsily into the deliciously temperate water. We head for shallow ground and then go through the basics of diving, Walter guiding us in the precision art of how to breathe, monitor pressure, and acclimate to the environment and the equipment. He keeps imploring us to stay relaxed, take it easy, not thrash about or try to do too much.

When it comes to diving, he says, it's good to be lazy. When we're comfortable, we set out, exploring the reef and scanning our surroundings for marine life. I'd seen plenty of schools of fish when I went snorkeling, so I was looking for something different. We don't see sharks or turtles, but it transpires that Walter has chosen a good spot. Our first encounter is a baby lobster, which we each cup in our hands before moving on. Next, Walter spots a sea cucumber on the ocean floor. He picks it up, tickles it, and passes it to us so we can feel its carpet-soft body. A little farther on, Walter and I see something at the same time, and we both point excitedly: Scurrying along in plain sight is a beautiful moray eel. We hover inches above it, watching it slither its way to the safety of a large coral. Even Walter is excited by the rare appearance of the reclusive creature in the open. We round out our one-tank dive with a few menacing-looking barracuda before saying good-bye to Luis Peña's underwater kingdom.

Walter Rieder of Culebra Divers

Cayo Luis Peña

CAYO LUIS PEÑA
Luis Peña offers a different type of playground. The beaches aren't as grand as the ones on Culebra and Culebrita, and there are no easy hiking trails. Along with Culebrita, Luis Peña is the only part of the **Culebra National Wildlife Refuge** that is open to the public, and visitors love to come here for rugged nature walks and scenic views. Most people who travel to Cayo Luis Peña, however, bring their diving and snorkeling gear: This is a popular destination for those who want to explore Culebra's underwater world. The coral reef on the southwestern side of the island is a good place to start.

LODGING

Bahía Marina Resort
787-742-0535
www.bahiamarina.net
Punta Soldado Road, Km 2.4, Culebra
00775

At press time, there was a lot of construction going on around the Bahía Marina hotel, part of a huge expansion. This won't hinder guests, who get to enjoy the feel of living in a furnished studio apartment (complete with futon in the living room and kitchenette) with an ocean view at this condo-hotel. Bahía Marina has a nice bar, restaurant, and pool, and an overall rustic look with wooden decks and walkways between the rooms. There are disabled-access rooms as well. $$–$$$.

Casa Ensenada
1-866-210-0709; 787-742-3559
www.casaensenada.com
142 Escudero Street, Culebra 00775

Located right on the *ensenada* (harbor), Casa Ensenada gives you a lot for the price.

For one, the back of the hotel is a pier where guests have access to a free kayak and boat rentals through **Culebra Boat Rentals** (see "Attractions, Parks & Recreation"). Lockers for storing your luggage after you check out let you enjoy your last day on the island to the fullest. The small guesthouse has spacious bedrooms with a private entrance, air-conditioning, satellite TV, kitchen, and private bathroom. On the water, there's a communal patio with a barbecue grill and picnic tables. Plus, if you're staying a week or longer, the seventh day is free. $–$$.

La Casita

787-742-0803
www.culebradivers.com
Bo. Resaca 326, Culebra 00775

This lovely little cottage, owned and managed by Walter and Monica of Culebra Divers (see "Tours"), is a picturesque and quiet retreat, perfect for a vacationing couple. Perched at the top of a hill, the cottage has a four-poster bed, a fully equipped kitchen, air-conditioning, a porch with barbecue grill, and a wading pool out front with a great view of the bay. While most private rentals require a week, La Casita has only a three-night minimum. It's outside Dewey, and you'll need your own transportation to get here. $$.

Club Seabourne

1-800-981-4435; 787-742-3169
www.clubseabourne.com
State Road 252, Playa Sardines Ward, Culebra 00775

A short drive from Dewey, Club Seabourne is the nicest-looking hotel on the island. Guest rooms are located in eight plantation-style chalets and are beautifully decorated in a Colonial tropical style. The room's balconies have lovely views of the gardens and the bay. Guests get a complimentary Continental breakfast and all the amenities

of a luxury boutique hotel. Special touches include a free one-hour kayak rental and bike rental. Leave your cabanas and walk along the manicured grounds to the main building, which houses a very good open-air bar and restaurant, small pool, and comfortable communal lounge. Club Seabourne also has all-
inclusive and honeymoon packages. $$$.

Culebra Island Realty

787-742-0052
www.culebraislandrealty.com

Culebra Island Realty lists beautifully appointed, privately owned homes. After touring many of these homes and seeing the quality of the lodgings, cleanliness of the homes, and privacy they provide, I found this to be a top-class agency with prime properties. If you're spending a week or more on the island, owner Jim Galasso is your man. Below are just a few of his listings (all rentals are on a weekly basis). $$–$$$$:

Casa Coquí and Casita Coquí
With its stone walls and open-air showers, you could call this a modern-style Swiss Family Robinson home. Casa Coquí is a unique property of three separate buildings interconnected with decks and walkways. The Casita, with its sloped wooden roof, tiled floor, and writing desk in a corner, is full of rustic charm. Both properties are among my favorite choices for something a little different.

Casa del Mar and Casita del Mar
Ideal for families and larger groups, the Casa and Casita del Mar are two adjacent homes that can be rented separately or together. They are both very close to the water, with wooden walkways leading down to the water. Both are furnished in a clean, contemporary style, and the electronic shutters open to a magnificent view. Casa del Mar is the larger of the two, and has a

View from Harbour View Villas & Suites Courtesy of Harbour View Villas & Suites/Juanita Bananas

pool table and entertainment area. The large patio is perfect for lounging and enjoying the visual panorama; and the walkways, manicured gardens, landscape, and private kayaks put you in mind of living in a well-groomed park.

Casa Nueva
One of the few listings in Dewey, Casa Nueva has an architect's touch. It's a new property with three bedrooms, modern kitchen, and wooden french doors opening out to a covered balcony. If you want to stay in town while you're in Culebra, you should check out this place.

Casa Zoni
The dark and light wood decor, high ceilings, rustic porch, and lovely kitchen make Zoni a quaint rental home. The house has three nicely furnished bedrooms, each with a bathroom. You can relax in the hammock overlooking Zoni Beach, or walk 500 yards to reach the beach.

Nido de Amor
Nido de Amor (Lover's Nest) is big on charm and privacy. This one-bedroom cottage of a large estate is separated from the main house by a forest, so guests are ensured privacy. It's a waterfront property with lovely views, and there's a trail leading to an unnamed strip of beach that is practically your own if you stay at Nido de Amor. You even get a two-person kayak for your use.

Flamenco Beach Campgrounds
787-742-0700
At Flamenco Beach, Culebra 00775

Some people never check into a hotel when they get to Culebra. Rather, they go straight to Flamenco beach and pitch their tents. The only campgrounds in Culebra, these are some of the best facilities you'll get. They're run by the municipality and are sectioned into separate but adjoining campsites. I'm told that each campground has developed its own personality: Sites A and B cater more to families; C is louder and younger; D and E attract couples. No matter where you belong, you'll have access to outdoor showers from 4–7 PM and bathrooms at all times, and you're mere steps from spectacular Flamenco Beach. At $20 per day, it's small wonder that the grounds can get busy. Some people camp at Flamenco for months at a time. $.

Harbour View Villas
787-742-3855
www.culebrahotel.com
Barrio Melones, P.O. Box 216, Culebra 00775

The vibe at Harbour View is relaxed and mellow—even by Culebra standards. This is the kind of place where they chuckle if you lock your door, because, up on a private hill overlooking the bay, there's really no need. Harbour View is well named, and the best way to enjoy that view is to rent one of the rustic wood villas, with their high-beamed ceilings, french doors, and wooden balconies providing a feast for the eyes. You can either get a one- or two-bedroom villa, complete with kitchen and bath, or an individual room with private bath. In addition to the view of the water, you're surrounded by lush flora. Arguably the best restaurant on the island, **Juanita Bananas**, is in the main house. $–$$.

Hotel Kokomo
787-742-3112; 787-742-0003
www.culebra-kokomo.com
Six Pedro Márquez Street, Dewey, Culebra 00775

After staying in a room that was nothing more than a bed, side table, and four walls (with the bathroom down the hall), I find it hard to recommend Kokomo. But this is also the cheapest lodging in town short of a tent, and the "you get what you pay for" adage has been meticulously followed. If you can afford more, make sure you get more. $.

Mamacita's Guesthouse
787-742-0322; 787-742-0090
www.mamacitaspr.com
64 Castelar Street, Dewey, Culebra 00775

The 10 rooms of Mamacita's Guesthouse are typical of a Dewey hotel: nothing great, but well kept and clean. Two of the rooms come with a kitchen, and all have air-conditioning (which is not always the case in Culebra). You can also get a room with a small fridge, microwave, satellite TV, and DVD player. Guests with boats can dock them here. One of the better, and livelier, restaurants is in Mamacita's, along with the adjacent Caribbean Bar, right at your feet. $–$$.

Posada La Hamaca
787-742-3516
www.posada.com
68 Castelar Street, Dewey, Culebra 00775

Among all the budget options in Dewey, Posada La Hamaca is one of the better deals. There's nothing too fancy about the rooms, but they're clean, all have air-conditioning and private baths, and one of them has satellite TV. Guests are provided with coolers, beach towels, and ice for their trips to the beach. This place blends in perfectly with the sleepy, relaxed spirit of the island. $–$$.

Villa Boheme
787-742-3508
www.villaboheme.com
368 Fulladosa Street, Culebra 00775

A cute and colorful guesthouse right on the water, Villa Boheme is a pleasant lodging option. There are 11 rooms, some with their own kitchen and others sharing a communal kitchen. Some rooms also have a balcony overlooking the bay. If you have a boat, you can dock it here for a small fee. The hotel has a long outdoor patio with outside showers so you can clean up before your flight, even if you've already checked out. $–$$.

Villa Melones

787-765-5711; 787-742-0343
www.culebra-island.com

Perched on a hill overlooking Melones
point, this gorgeous villa is a great example
of luxury rentals in Culebra. Owner Susan
Hubbell is an affable host who will pick you
up at the airport and take you to your new
home. And you might feel like buying it
from her after you see it. The house has a
beautiful, high-ceilinged and wood-beam
living room with attached kitchen and three
well-appointed bedrooms. There's a small
pool on the premises, and a road leading
directly down to Melones Beach; but the
fabulous deck with a hammock and a panoramic view of the sea, Cayo Luis Peña, and
Melones point really drew my eye. A two-
night minimum stay is required. $$$.

DINING

Barbara-Rosa's Restaurant

787-397-1923
Along Route 250 west of Dewey, Culebra

No waiter service, no wine service, no
problem. Just walk up to the kitchen, order
one of the delicious fresh seafood dishes,
and grab a seat (you can bring your own
wine or beer). The crab soup, fish-and-
chips, lump-meat blue crab cakes, and
shark nuggets (a favorite), are all excellent,
and Barbara is a friendly and pleasant host.
Open Thursday through Monday 11:30
AM–9:30 PM. $–$$.

Café Isola

787-742-0203
At the ferry dock, Dewey, Culebra

The people who introduced draft beer to
the island are also known for their Spanish
tapas, burgers, pitas, and salads. It's a small
restaurant with good food at reasonable
prices. The biggest trick might be actually

getting to dine here. The restaurant has an
"open when we feel like it" philosophy. $$.

El Caobo

787-742-0505
Muñoz Marin Street, Dewey, Culebra

El Caobo, or "Tina's," is one of the best
places in Culebra to get solid Puerto Rican
food. They are known for their seafood, and
dinner is a good time to try cobia, a fish
found in these waters, or any of the other
fresh catches of the day. Other favorites
include Tina's grilled pork and chicken with
rice and beans. Open Monday through
Saturday 4–10 PM. $$.

Dakity Restaurant

787-742-0535
www.bahiamarina.net
At the Bahía Marina Resort, Punta Soldado
Road, Km 2.4, Culebra 00775

Of the three restaurants at Bahía Marina,
this is the place to go for fine Puerto Rican
dining. Seafood is the star, with grilled
mahimahi, *chillo entero* (whole red snapper), and Caribbean lobster headlining the
menu. The *churrasco* steak is also a popular
item. The dining room setting follows
through the rustic decor of the hotel and
offers wonderful views. Open 6–9 PM for
dinner. $$–$$$.

Dinghy Dock Bar-B-Q Restaurant

787-742-0024; 787-742-0233
www.dinghydock.com
372 Fulladosa Street, Culebra

That's "dinghy," not "dingy" (although it's
not the fanciest of places). The boats will
tie up along the bar here, and its passengers will disembark for a quick drink
(happy hour daily from 3 to 6 PM) or for a
meal. The Dinghy Dock serves up a hearty
breakfast (try the rum-coco french toast),
a decent lunch (8-ounce burgers, wraps,
burritos, and criollo specials), and a

Entrance to the kitchen at Juanita Bananas Courtesy of Harbor View Villas & Suites/Juanita Bananas

better-than-average dinner. The fresh seafood is simply but tastefully prepared, the steaks are certified Angus beef, and the barbecue is the restaurant's specialty. You also get an unlimited (but very basic) salad bar and even a nightly show ... of sorts: The spotlights on the water illuminate the large tarpon swimming lazily just under the surface. $–$$.

La Guarida del Zorro

787-340-7058
On road to Resaca Beach, Barrio Resaca, Culebra

"The Fox's Lair" is one of the newer restaurants outside Dewey that has been drawing islanders and tourists looking for something different. Besides the very cool name, there's a nice, casual ambience (no waiter service). The space is divided between the bar area with pool table and the dining

room. Chef Susie Hebert calls her menu "tropical latitude" food—that's criollo cooking with international accents (try the Szechuan-style *churrasco* as an example). Another nice thing: No dish is above $15. Open Wednesday through Sunday 5–10 PM for dinner. $–$$.

Heather's Pizzeria & Bar

787-742-3175
14 Pedro Márquez Street, Culebra

The slogan here is "more than pizza," and while this is true, I'd still recommend sticking to the specialty. The very good, thin-crust pizza comes with ingredients that range from the typical to the original (like eggplant, chorizo, feta cheese, and artichoke hearts). Try one of Heather's combo pizzas, or order by the slice. There are also pasta specials and sub-style sandwiches. Open daily 6–9 PM. $–$$.

Juanita Bananas

787-742-3171; 787-402-5852
www.juanitabananas.com
At Harbour View Villas, Culebra

If there is one reason to wait till high season starts before coming to Culebra, Juanita Bananas is it. Widely considered the best restaurant on the island, Juanita Bananas is only open from December 15 to July 30, and visitors have to jockey with the locals for space. You just don't get this kind of food elsewhere on the island. For starters, Juanita's has the freshest ingredients. In addition to fruit trees and fresh seafood, there's a full hydroponic garden with homegrown herbs and vegetables. Sushi Monday features creative rolls like the "Juanita Bananas" (tuna, papaya, slaw, and chives) and "Culebra Special" (cobia with scallions). Their signature entrées include guava barbecued ribs with "crispy little spiders" (calamari) and panko-crusted grouper in a coconut-lemongrass sauce. Or, you can sample from the menu of *bananeos*, which are tapas-style dishes heavy on fresh seafood and local flavors. And you can finish off with their chocolate truffles. In a relaxed and artistically casual setting, Juanita Bananas is a breath of fresh gourmet air. Make a reservation and plan on dining here at least once. Open Friday through Monday 5–10 PM for dinner. $$–$$$.

Mamacita's

787-742-0322; 787-742-0090
www.mamacitaspr.com
64 Castelar Street, Dewey, Culebra

The menu, written on a chalkboard at the entrance, changes every night at Mamacita's, but the quality doesn't. For consistently good food in a friendly and lively atmosphere, you can't beat this popular hometown spot. The dishes are a celebration of the tropics, prepared with more flair and flavor than you might expect from a casual, dockside joint. You can't go wrong with their fresh fish dishes with a side of yucca mash. Whatever you get, make sure you leave space for the fabulous peanut butter pie drizzled with chocolate. At lunch, humans aren't the only ones to enjoy Mamacita's; as you munch on burgers (try

the excellent grouper burger), fajitas, and salads, you'll be joined by the large, lazy iguanas who love to sunbathe on the deck. Open daily 10:30 AM–4 PM for lunch and 6–9:30 PM for dinner.

White Sands Restaurant

787-742-3169
www.clubseabourne.com
At Club Seabourne, State Road 252, Playa Sardines Ward, Culebra

Much like the hotel, Club Seabourne's White Sands is fancier than many other places on the island. The restaurant has seating on the porch of the main house and overlooks the landscaped gardens, and the ambiance is one of laid-back elegance. You can also dine indoors and even in the walk-in wine cave, if you like. And the food, like the Caribbean bouillabaisse, menu of ceviches, and award-winning plantain-crusted scallops with shredded duck *ropa vieja,* is an inventive mix of criollo and international cuisine. The same creativity is put into desserts like the chocolate ravioli with fig sauce. Open Wednesday through Sunday 6–10 PM for dinner. $$–$$$.

ATTRACTIONS, PARKS & RECREATION

Culebra Anglers

404-317-2896
www.culebraanglers.com

Aboard Captain Bonnie Anderson's two boats—the 30-foot *Andy* and the 14-foot *Gary-Marc*—you can fish for just about anything these waters have to offer, from snapper to marlin. The *Andy* has a fighting chair for big-game fish, and the *Gary-Marc* is available for both fly-fishing and light spinning-tackle guided trips. Rods, reels, and lures are provided. $$$$.

Culebra Boat Rentals

1-866-210-0709; 787-742-3559
www.culebraboatrental.com
142 Escudero Street, Culebra

Experienced sailors can rent a CBR motorboat or a sunfish sailboat if they want to chart their own course around the island. The 16- and 18-foot motorboats come with cell phones, life jackets, and a cooler. $$$$.

Tours

Aquatic Adventurers
787-209-3494
www.culebradive.com

A PADI Master Instructor and U.S. Coast Guard–certified captain, Captain Taz has been taking people snorkeling and diving for years. His 26-foot boat, *Razmataz,* makes two trips daily. The reefs off Cayo Luis Peña are a popular destination, and trips include a light lunch and soft drinks. $$–$$$.

Culebra Divers
787-742-0803
www.culebradivers.com
Four Pedro Márquez Street, Culebra

Whether you're an experienced diver, a novice, or just want to go snorkeling, Culebra Divers can accommodate you. There are daily boat trips (for one-tank and two-tank dives), and Walter—a U.S. Coast Guard–licensed captain, an AHSI CPR Instructor, and a NAUI Scuba Dive Instructor—will do his best to find an ideal dive spot. Sites range from drop-offs to caves to shipwrecks and are determined by the weather conditions and your experience. You can even get your certification here. If I go diving in Culebra, these are the people I call. Trips include gear and instruction for beginners. $$$.

Chris Goldmark
787-742-0412
www.culebraflyfishing.com

Just about everybody on the island recommends Chris Goldmark for fishing tours. With over 15 years of experience in these waters, Chris specializes in fly-fishing and light-tackle fishing for beginners and experts alike. His services are available from October to May. $$$–$$$$.

Tanamá Glass Bottom Boat
787-501-0011

Perfect for those who want to see Culebra's coral reefs and marine life without getting wet, Captain Pat and Captain Jack's glass-bottom boat lets you explore the Culebrita's cays, Luis Peña, and the reefs of Carlos Rosario. $$.

Wildeye Snorkeling
787-950-2111

This six-passenger boat makes two reef stops (or one reef and one island stop, if you prefer) on its half-day snorkeling excursions. The trips include equipment and lunch, and the boat has a generous amount of shade (a small but important benefit). One feature that makes these tours unique is the education that Captain John will give you about the significance of the reefs and the impact of the ecosystem. There's also a sunset cruise around Culebra. $$$.

Culture

If you've come here for the museums, you might want to catch the next ferry back. Culebra hasn't developed facilities that promote or celebrate its culture, and its two major landmarks aren't open to the public. The lighthouse on Culebrita is one of the oldest in the Caribbean, but due to safety issues, visitors are prohibited from entering. At press time (2007), the island's only museum, located in an old brick munitions house built in 1905, wasn't scheduled to open for another year or so.

Nightlife

El Batey Bar
787-742-3828
Route 250, Km 0.7, Culebra

On a weekend night, El Batey might be the hottest ticket in town. And one visit to the bar will tell you all you need to know about nightlife in Culebra. Set on the outskirts of Dewey, El Batey is a typical roadside bar and restaurant. There's a pool table and little else in the way of decor, but this can be a noisy and fun place after a long, hard day on the beach. Home to some of the best burgers on the island, it's also outside Dewey, so it can—and does—stay open until 2 AM on weekends. $.

El Eden
787-742-0509
P.O. Box 836, Dewey, Culebra

In high season, you get a little more time to relax on the porch, hang out at the funky tiki bar, and enjoy a cocktail or a glass of wine. El Eden is out of the way from center of Dewey, but it's an easy walk and the place has an offbeat charm. Open until 9 PM during high season. $–$$.

Heather's Pizzeria & Bar
787-742-3175
14 Pedro Márquez Street, Dewey, Culebra

For a few drinks after a day of sand and water, check out one of the few typical bar atmospheres in Dewey. Bathed in perpetually dim lighting, Heather's attracts a mix of locals and tourists, and you can order a slice of pizza to accompany your drink of choice. Open daily until 9 PM. $.

Mamacita's Caribbean Bar

787-742-0322; 787-742-0090
www.mamacitaspr.com
64 Castelar Street, Dewey, Culebra

After the sun goes down, a lot of people head to Mamacita's. During the week, the bar stays lively, sometimes showing a game on the big screen. There's a DJ on Friday and a live band on Saturday, playing salsa, meringue, and reggae music. Like the rest of Dewey, it all closes down at 11 PM. $.

Shipwreck Bar & Grill

787-742-0535
www.bahiamarina.net
At the Bahía Marina Resort, Punta Soldado Road, Km 2.4, Culebra

It's day- and nightlife at Shipwreck's, with happy hours starting at noon on weekends and 4 PM on weekdays. There's live music on Saturday night, but Culebra-style, the action stops at 10 PM.

SHOPPING

Culebra Beach House & Bike Shop

787-742-2209
372 Fulladosa Street, Dewey, Culebra

As the name implies, this cute shop specializes in things beach-related. You can rent beach chairs, umbrellas, coolers, and snorkel and bodyboard gear (also available for sale). The store also rents bikes and sells camping gear, a small selection of bags and beaded bracelets, and unique home accessories for island life, like white mosquito nets to hang above your bed. Open daily 9 AM–6 PM. $–$$.

Culebra Divers

787-742-0803
www.culebradivers.com
Four Pedro Márquez Street, Dewey, Culebra

The source for all your diving needs (including rentals), Culebra Divers also carries T-shirts, jewelry, and accessories. Open daily 9 AM–1 PM and 2–5 PM. $–$$$.

Culebra Gift Shop & La Cava

787-742-0566
138 Escudero Street, Dewey, Culebra

Billing itself as a "Caribbean General Store" is just about right. From souvenirs to beach clothing and accessories, the store has mostly the kind of standard fare one finds in the tropics. Of course, there are Puerto Rican originals here and there, but it's more an all-purpose store for anybody heading out to the beach. You can rent kayaks, bodyboards, fishing rods, floats, and underwater cameras. There's also a food section with meat, fish, and ice cream. Open daily 9 AM–6 PM. $–$$.

Fango
787-435-6654
Castelar Street, Dewey, Culebra

There's something about this tiny, atypical store that catches the eye. Partly, it's the bongos lining one wall (these aren't for sale—they belong to the band that plays next door at Mamacita's). Partly, it's the collection of cool, unique print T-shirts, framed art, and Afro-Caribbean drawings, music, and artifacts—everything made in Culebra. And a lot of it has to do with the engaging owner, Jorge Acevedo, a man who in some ways epitomizes what being a Culebrense is all about. It's worth dropping by. Open "most days" 10 AM–1 PM and 3:30–7 PM. $$–$$$.

Flamenco Tent City
787-226-0232
www.hometown.aol.com/flamencotent
At Flamenco Beach, Culebra

This kiosk, one of several at the entrance to Flamenco Beach, is not quite a "city," but it does stock just about anything you need for the beach and for your camping needs. It's amazing to think that clothing, hats, beach chairs, snorkel gear, sleeping bags, ice, oil, bug spray, underwater cameras, and other items can all be found here, but there you have it. If you've landed up at Flamenco Beach with nothing but your bathing suit, make this your first stop. $–$$.

Island Woman
This brightly painted little shack, just across from the bridge, is one of the most photographed spots on the island. Why? Because people can't get enough of the OPEN SOME DAYS, CLOSED OTHERS sign when the shop is closed. When it is open, it sells a mix of sauces, jewelry boxes, bracelets, and other knickknacks. Open . . well, some days, not others. $.

On Island
787-742-0439; 787-742-0704
At the ferry dock, Dewey, Culebra

Part of the main strip along the ferry dock (with a second store above the Dinghy Dock Bar-B-Q Restaurant), On Island sells block-print T-shirts, flax linen clothing, handcrafted jewelry, and beachwear and beach accessories. Open most days 10 AM–5 PM. $–$$$.

Paradise Gift Shop
787-742-3569
Six Salisbury Street, Dewey, Culebra

There's a funky collection of art, island clothing, sombreros, jewelry, and miscellaneous knickknacks and souvenirs here. Among the more unique items are sea-themed toys, cool octopus- and crab-shaped lamps, and a collection of T-shirts, coasters, and hats printed with a nautical map of Culebra. Open daily, except Wednesday, 9 AM–6 PM. $–$$$.

Food Purveyors, Liquor & Cigars

Antojitos Chiquí's
This roadside stall on Dewey's main street draws lines for its wide array of *piraguas* (shaved ices), ice creams, and milkshakes. Open daily 11 AM–9 PM. $.

El Eden
787-742-0509
P.O. Box 836, Dewey, Culebra 00775

Walk across the bridge and toward the pier, and then turn left onto a large and near-empty lot. At the end, you'll find El Eden, a pleasant surprise in Dewey. This multipurpose store is equal parts deli, bakery, café, liquor store, and tiki bar. The fresh-baked breads and pastries are quite good, and the made-to-order sandwiches are perfect for beach lunches. You can get fancier foods as well, like grilled eggplant lasagna, shiitake mushroom soup, and home-made meatballs. The liquor section is well stocked with a selection of wines and champagnes from Chile, California, Italy, Spain, and Australia, as well as more local produce like rum and *coquito.* Worth the walk if you're staying in town, and definitely worth the drive. Open Monday through Saturday 9 AM–6 PM (9 AM–9 PM during high season), Sunday 9 AM–2 PM. $–$$.

Panadería Fontanez
787-742-0374
In a small lot near the airport, along Route 250, Culebra

This convenience store and bakery with seating area is open seven days a week, which is a rarity on the island. In addition to hot, fresh-baked bread and many types of sandwiches, Fontanez sells basic groceries and liquor. Open Monday through Friday 5:30 AM–7 PM, Saturday and Sunday 5:30 AM–9 PM. $.

Pandeli
787-742-0296
17 Pedro Márquez Street, Dewey, Culebra

You'll probably make at least one stop at Pandeli, either for basic groceries, liquor, pastries, fresh-baked bread, the selection of deli sandwiches, or great breakfasts. It's open early, so you can fuel up on eggs, bacon, french toast, pancakes, and *mallorcas* before you hit the beach. Open Monday through Saturday 5:30 AM–5 PM, Sunday 6:30 AM–5 PM. $.

Good to Know About . . .

Colmado Milka
787-742-2253
374 Escudero Street, Dewey, Culebra

A grocery store with a fresh meat center in addition to all your basic needs. You can access Milka by foot or by boat. Open Monday through Saturday 7 AM–7 PM, Sunday 7 AM–1 PM.

Excétera

787-742-0844
126 Escudero Street, Dewey, Culebra

The main "business center" in Dewey, Excétera provides Internet access, mailing supplies, fax and copy machines, phone stations, and magazines. There's also a 24-hour ATM. Open Monday through Friday 9 AM–5 PM, Saturday 9 AM–1 PM. $.

Exquisite Laundry Service

787-742-0722

On a small island where you don't always have access to laundry machines, it's good to know there's a place that offers same-day, drop-off and pickup services.

Superette Mayra

787-742-3888
118 Escudero Street, Dewey, Culebra

A small, well-stocked grocery store in the heart of Dewey. Open Monday through Saturday 9 AM–1:30 PM and 3:30–6:30 PM.

Useful Numbers

Bank (Banco Popular)
787-742-3572

Coast Guard
787-729-6800

Culebra National Wildlife Refuge
787-742-0115

Fire Department
787-742-3530

Gas Stations
Gulf
787-742-3506
Garaje Ricky
787-742-3194

Hospital
787-742-3511

Police
787-742-3501

Post Office
787-742-3862

Puerto Rico Tourism Company
787-742-1033

WEEKLY & ANNUAL EVENTS

Culebra International Regatta

March
787-785-2026; 787-635-2979
www.caribbeanracing.com
In and around Dewey

The second leg of the prestigious Caribbean Ocean Racing Court is the Culebra International Regatta. It returned to the island in 2006 after three years off. Free.

Turtle Nesting Season

Seasonal, typically April to June
787-742-0115 (Culebra National Wildlife Refuge)
www.fws.gov/caribbean

Sun-loving humans aren't the only ones who love Culebra's beaches. Nesting leatherback and hawksbill turtles also come to Culebra's sands. The leatherbacks love Brava, Resaca, and Zoni beaches, while nesting hawksbills are found all over the island. Reproductive cycles depend on the species: Mating season for hawksbills is practically year-round but especially from August to October; and for the massive leatherbacks—the largest turtles in the world (they can grow over 6 feet in length and up to 1,800 pounds)—from March to July. Culebrenses are fiercely protective of their hard-shell friends, and nesting beaches are closed from sunset to sunrise during the season. The Department of Natural Resources sometimes runs a volunteer program that gives you up-close access to hatching leatherbacks. Visitors should also check with the Culebra National Wildlife Refuge (see the phone number at the beginning of the entry) for general information on turtles and how best to enjoy their presence without impacting the environment. (For example, one problem caused by eager humans is the footprints left in the sand below the tide line, in which hatchlings get trapped and die).

Carnaval Deportivo
July
787-742-3521, ext. 441
Dewey

This annual festival celebrates a variety of land and water sports, with contests, prizes, food kiosks, and music. Free.

10

PUERTO RICO ON A . . .

The amazing thing about Puerto Rico is that you can enjoy a remarkably different vacation each time you go there. In this chapter, I've put together a few ideas for people with specific tastes or needs, targeting diverse groups of people to better illustrate the versatility of the island as a tourist destination. I hope to show you what Puerto Rico offers to visitors who don't have a lot of money to throw around; to the cruise ship crowd who get only a day to scour the island; to the thrill-seeking, bungee-jumping adrenaline junkies; and to the sappy romantic in all of us.

PUERTO RICO ON A . . . SHOESTRING BUDGET: HOW TO HAVE FUN WITHOUT BREAKING THE BANK

No one will tell you that Puerto Rico is a cheap place to visit. The Caribbean, in general, is a playground for the wealthy, and you'll need to spend some money to enjoy Puerto Rico's better hotels, fine restaurants, and other amenities. After all, this is home to a sizable number and variety of luxury resorts. But that doesn't mean you can't enjoy the island without taking out a second mortgage.

'Tis the (Off) Season

If you want to enjoy spectacular deals on lodging, go during the off-season, from May to November. The winter months are peak travel times to Puerto Rico, and the entire island is in tourist mode. Do your research online and by phone, and you'll be surprised at the deals you'll find.

Entertain Yourself

The island offers numerous free or very cheap sources of entertainment. The most obvious of these, of course, are its beaches. Beaches in Puerto Rico are free, with the exception of a nominal parking fee at *balnearios,* and there are over 230 miles of them

Kite flying in front of El Morro in Old San Juan

Cheap Thrills

Here are a few things you can do in Puerto Rico that won't cost much, if anything:

Attend a festival—The pantheon of Catholic saints and the festive nature of the Puerto Rican people make a good recipe for street festivals, and these take place year-round throughout the island. In San Juan, the more famous ones are San Juan Bautista Day in June and Fiestas de San Sebastián in January, but there are numerous smaller, local parades celebrating each town's patron saint. You can get a calendar of *festivales patronales* (patron saint festivals) from the **Puerto Rico Tourism Company** office (787-721-2400) in Old San Juan, and you can get a Público to take you there for very little money. It's not just about the saints, either. Puerto Ricans *love* festivals, and everything from antique toys to hammock weaving gets its own special day. In addition, the LeiLoLai program instituted by the tourism office offers year-round music and dance concerts that cost as little as $3.

Commune with Nature—This is something of a no-brainer, but Puerto Rico's greatest asset—its natural resources—is free. It costs you nothing beyond transportation to trek through El Yunque or explore the island's many beaches.

Do-It-Yourself—Many tour companies run tours around San Juan and other major tourist cities, but you can see and do a lot by yourself if you show a little initiative. For example, tours to the Bacardi distillery from Old San Juan, while convenient and comfortable, will cost you a lot more than the 50¢ ferry ride from the pier in Old San Juan to Cataño, and the few dollars for the taxi to take you to the factory. Once you're here, the tours are free and you even get a free drink for your efforts.

to tempt you. They range from isolated stretches of sand to glitzy, ritzy spreads in front of five-star hotels.

Puerto Rico's cultural and historical sights are also extremely affordable. The entrance fees to all the major forts, museums, and important sites are either free or less than $5, and you can easily spend a few days doing little more than visiting the island's wonderful monuments. In addition, Puerto Ricans are extremely proud of their musical heritage, and enjoy sharing it with the world. As such, you can partake of music and dance, and culture, either for free or for a nominal fee. Travelers should check with the **Puerto Rican Institute of Culture** (787-724-0700) to see what is planned during their stay.

Hostels and Paradores

There is no shortage of cheap seaside hotels, motels, and bed-and-breakfasts that rent rooms for less than $100 a night, even in the most tourist-heavy areas. All of these lodgings are listed in this guidebook (see the Lodging Index), but here's a short directory of my favorites, by location:

Old San Juan
La Caleta Apartment Rentals
Da House at the Nuyorican Café

Condado
At Wind Chimes Inn (off-season rates are
    a bargain)
Casa del Caribe

Ocean Park and Isla Verde
Coqui Inn
Numero Uno Guest House
Tres Palmas Inn

La Caleta Rentals apartment in Old San Juan

Culebra Island
Casa Ensenada
Posada La Hamaca

Vieques
Casa La Lanchita
Sea Gate Guest House

If you're exploring the rest of Puerto Rico, you can book yourself at one of the many Paradores (countryside inns), that dot the island. Check out **www.gotoparadores.com** for a listing of hotels under this special program, which is aimed at providing affordable but good-quality lodging.

Cheap Eats

Dining in Puerto Rico can be fun, fattening, and budget-friendly. If your budget demands fast food, forget about Burger King and try one of these chains:

Pollo Tropical

A chain that serves tasty grilled chicken and other meats with rice and beans. Check out the one in Isla Verde.

The Taco Maker

Many consider this a more authentic upgrade of Taco Bell. In Old San Juan right near Plaza de Armas, it's one of the cheapest options you'll find.

El Mesón

Great sub-style sandwiches, with a brunch conveniently located in Plaza de Armas in Old San Juan.

You'll always find hearty and cheap sandwiches at *panaderías,* which are popular and located all over the island. And don't forget about the kiosks. You don't have to go to Luquillo to get your fill of these eateries. From Old San Juan to Vieques, there are plenty of opportunities to sample fried everything, *pasteles,* and other snacks for a few dollars. Finally, if you hit the open road, stop at a roadside restaurant. What's lacking in decor is made up in price and taste.

PUERTO RICO ON A . . . SCHEDULE: THINGS TO DO IF TIME IS SHORT

This is an easy one. If you're a first-time visitor disembarking at San Juan with one or two days to spend on the island, and no clear agenda, focus on the old city (unless, of course, you're hell-bent on finding an isolated beach and setting up camp for the duration of your stay). Your best bet is a walking tour of Old San Juan. From the tourism office at La Casita, travelers can

> **iPod Ready**
>
> Log into the iTunes store and type in "Old San Juan Walking Tour." This will take you to an excellent, free Podcast of a walking tour of the old city, narrated by Orlando Mergal.

pick up a well-marked map with dotted-line itineraries specifically for shopping, scenery, monuments, and historic walks. There are also recommended shortcuts if time is of the essence. This is a great way to breathe in the city, stopping wherever you see something that interests you, and covering a good cross-section of activities, including parks, restaurants, and historical monuments.

To maximize your experience, consider taking a guided tour. "Legends of San Juan," offered by **Legends of Puerto Rico, Inc.**, is one of the best. The tour lasts two hours, covers 14 sites in detail, and leaves you at Cristo Street, where you can do some timely souvenir shopping. If you're staying overnight, you might prefer "Night Tales in San Juan," offered by the same company, which gives you a unique and romantic account of the island's history.

If you've seen and done Old San Juan, here are a few one-day agendas to consider:

Surf & Turf

Rent a car for the day, start early, and combine El Yunque and Luquillo in one journey that lets you enjoy beach and mountain. You can spend the morning in the rain forest, hiking for a few hours and taking a dip under La Mina Falls, and then drive down (maybe stopping at the kiosks for lunch) to Luquillo beach in the afternoon. Given that the round-trip will take between two and three hours, you'll want a full day to do this, but it can be a great way to get away from the city and enjoy the best of Puerto Rico's natural environment. Both El Yunque and Luquillo are off Route 3 as you head west from San Juan.

Stop & Shop

You'll need a car for this one too. Shopaholics can ignore history, beaches, and mountains and spend a full day (or more) in Puerto Rico doing what they love most. While San Juan is a mecca for souvenirs, jewelry, and fashion, there are three major centers for shoppers outside the main tourist areas:

Plaza Las Américas
787-767-5202
525 F. D. Roosevelt Avenue, Hato Rey, San Juan
www.plazalasamericas.com

Plaza Las Américas mall in Hato Rey

Massive enough to keep you busy for a day . . . or three. Open Monday through Saturday 9 AM–9 PM, Sunday 11 AM–5 PM.

Belz Factory Outlet World
787-256-7040
www.belz.com/shopping/canovanas.aspx
18400 Route 3, Barrio Pueblo, Canóvanas

Over 400,000 square feet of retail space to tempt you, including Polo Ralph Lauren, Tommy Hilfiger, Nike, Guess, and Reebok outlet stores. Open Monday through Saturday 9 AM–9 PM, Sunday 11 AM–5 PM.

Prime Outlets
787-846-5300
One Prime Outlets Boulevard, Barceloneta

A bit farther from San Juan, Prime is still chock-full of name-brand outlet stores like Calvin Klein, Polo Ralph Lauren, and Zales. Open Monday through Saturday 9 AM–9 PM, Sunday 11 AM–5 PM.

Science & Nature

Many tour companies offer a combined excursion to the Camuy caves and the Arecibo Observatory, and both are amazing in their own way. Camuy's stalactites, stalagmites, sinkholes, and dramatic—almost alien—landscape offer a completely different experience from the technological marvel of the world's largest single-dish radio telescope. It's a tour package that shows you the impressive achievements of science and nature.

PUERTO RICO ON A . . . DARE: ADVENTURE PACKAGES FOR THE BOLD AND THE BRAVE

For those looking for something a little more heart pumping than the beach, Puerto Rico offers a few adventurous diversions. As you might imagine, most of these activities center in or under the water, but the mountains and the caves play their parts as well.

Get Wet

For all the aboveground attractions that the island boasts, the wonders below the surface have long been a huge draw for people from around the world. The volcanic activity that shaped the island is also responsible for creating a breathtaking underwater kingdom filled with coral reefs, sunken wrecks, sheer drops, and deep tunnels. Beyond that, Puerto Rico's astounding variety of marine life is one another reason for its reputation as a fabulous diving and snorkeling destination. There are dive spots all over Puerto Rico; beginners are better off in the waters off the eastern shores of the islands—especially off Vieques and Culebra—which have calmer seas. The best reef and cave-diving is off Fajardo, located on the northeast tip of the main island. Here are a few cool places to don your flippers and explore:

School of Blue Tangs, Courtesy of Erin Go Bragh Sailing & Snorkeling Charters

A Few Dive Operators

Caribbean School of Aquatics (San Juan)
787-728-6606
www.saildiveparty.com

Caribe Aquatic Adventures (San Juan)
787-281-8858
www.diveguide.com/p2046.htm

Ocean Sports (Isla Verde)
787-268-2329
www.osdivers.com

Coquí Dive Puerto Rico (Fajardo)
787-636-3483
www.coquidivepuertorico.com

Nan-Sea Charters (Vieques)
787-741-2390
www.nanseacharters.com

Culebra Divers (Culebra)
787-742-0803
www.culebradivers.com

A stingray in the waters off Fajardo
Courtesy of Erin Go Bragh Sailing & Snorkeling Charters

The 22-Mile Wall

The dive equivalent of Disneyland, the famed Wall is about 2 miles off La Parguera, at the southwestern corner of the island. At the Wall, drop-offs yawn up at you from depths of more than 1,500 feet, with visibility from 60 to 150 feet. The most popular spot is Fallen Rock, so named because of an underwater promontory that broke off thousands of years ago, carving a deep trench where, today, all kinds of marine life gather. From octopi to sharks to moray eels, you can find it all around the black coral orchards here.

Desecheo

Desecheo Island is inaccessible, but its waters are fair game. The island is less than an hour away by boat from the main island's west coast, and home to spectacular coral reefs and diverse marine life. Check out Yellow Reef, underwater caves, and brightly colored tube coral.

Mona

This island, considered a mini Galapagos, is home to many species of iguana, seabirds, and turtles. Underwater, over 270 species of fish congregate around Mona. Dolphins, sharks, and—during the winter months—even humpback whales with their young can be spotted here. The caves, reefs, and walls surrounding Mona will also keep you satisfied.

Aboard the ERIN GO BRAGH

There's nothing wrong with the larger and more modern catamarans, but one trip aboard the *Erin Go Bragh* was enough to convince me that this is the way to sail the Caribbean. It was a clear day and our destination was set: Cayo Lobos, part of the archipelago of islets between Culebra and Fajardo. The *Erin Go Bragh III* (vessels I and II were sold as bigger boats were acquired) eased out of the marina under motor power, but it wasn't long before her sails were unfurled and we pushed west. A 50-foot yacht, the *EGB III* is fully equipped with cabins belowdecks for longer trips, a kitchen, and two bathrooms. Captain Bill decided to let out the spinnaker—a huge sail with a large shamrock proudly on display as it caught the wind—and we cruised along, chatting about the science of biobays, exchanging one-liners from Monty Python movies, and enjoying a perfect day at sea. Captain Bill and Ingrid, a husband-and-wife team, have been doing this for a long time. They were the first to offer overnight and multiple-day trips from Fajardo. And their chartered trips are as much a passion and pastime as they are a profession.

As we snacked on tortilla chips with Captain Bill's "famous" mango salsa and an artichoke-and-olive salad, we passed the keys of Palominos (private playground of the Wyndham El Conquistador Resort) and the almost unnaturally picturesque Palominitos. This latter islet has been the site of numerous photo and video shoots; its unique landscape (a clump of trees at one end and a smooth, clean patch of beach at the other) is the effect of Hurricane George's random path through the tiny island.

We pushed on and soon dropped anchor just off Lobos, slipped on our masks and flippers, and enjoyed snorkeling among the reefs and schools of brightly colored fish. After a grilled-on-board lunch of barbecued chicken and ribs, we returned to the idyllic Palominitos for another round of snorkeling and sunbathing, then sailed back to the marina. Our journey was a full day, and it was over too soon.

Ingrid at the spinnaker, aboard Erin Go Bragh

The Wit Power

Off Culebra, the *Wit Power* is a sunken tugboat lying just 40 feet below the surface. Divers can have a field day swimming in, around, and through gaps in the largely intact, coral-encrusted wreck. Turtles, angelfish, groupers, and other marine life live in the waters around the wreck.

Vieques

A good place for "easy" dives, Vieques has several abundant reefs to choose from. Check out Patti's, Angel, and Blue Tang reefs.

Get Strapped In

Think you can snag a 200-pound marlin? Well, at least it's easy to hop on half- or full-day charters out of San Juan, Fajardo, Culebra, and other ports throughout the islands. Puerto Rico has among the best fishing grounds in the Caribbean for blue marlin; it also has excellent wahoo, tuna, dorado, and mahimahi fishing.

The following are some of the charters you can reserve from San Juan:

Benitez Fishing Charters
787-723-2292

Castillo Tours & Watersports
787-791-6195

Grand Illusion Charters
787-380-4645

In Culebra, you can try:

Culebra Anglers
404-317-2896
www.culebraanglers.com

In addition to the big game fish, you can also enjoy light-tackle fishing and fly-fishing excursions for tarpon, snook, barracuda, and mangrove snapper.

Get Windblown

Okay, so maybe you don't need to be intrepid to get in a boat and cruise around the island, but it's still an adventure, and there is something to be said for letting the wind power you through the water. You can get into just about any kind of vessel in Puerto Rico, from Jet Skis to 50-foot catamarans. There are numerous kayaking tours to different parts of the island, and yacht cruises ranging from short-term jaunts around the bay to overnight trips. Fajardo, the boating capital of Puerto Rico, is the place to be for sailors or for those looking to charter a boat. As most visitors to Vieques or Culebra pass through Fajardo, it is easy to plan a day out on the ocean from there. And, of course, the two islands offer many options to enjoy a day of sailing and snorkeling. Operators include the following:

Adventures by the Sea (San Juan)
787-374-1410

San Juan Waterfun (Isla Verde)
787-643-4510
www.waterfun-pr.com

Erin Go Bragh Sailing & Snorkeling Charters (Fajardo)
787-860-4401
www.egbc.net

Salty Dog (Fajardo)
787-717-6378
www.saltydreams.com

Traveler (Fajardo)
787-863-2821
www.travelerpr.com

Marauder Sailing Charters (Vieques)
787-435-4858

If you're a little more daring, you might want to learn how to surf, windsurf, or kite surf. For that, I'd recommend one place above all others:

Velauno (Punta Las Marías)
1-866-PR-VELA-1; 787-728-8716
www.velauno.com

Get Roped In

If you prefer to stay on land while you get your adrenaline rush, El Yunque and Camuy will serve you ably. Ever been canyoning? Know what canyoning means? Well, imagine rappelling, crossing Tyroleans (a fancy word for a rope stretched between two high points with a chasm below you), using Via Ferrata climbing routes (a relatively easy type of mountain climbing route), and jumping out into the open sky and down into a river. Now imagine doing all of that in a rain forest.

Or maybe you prefer being under the ground rather than above it. Maybe caving's your thing. If that's the case, strap on a lamped helmet, life jacket, and harness and prepare to rappel straight down the mouth of one of the deep chasms of the Camuy cave system. As you explore this subterranean landscape, you'll end up mud sliding, body rafting, and free jumping through the darkness. If you want to feel this rush, call one of these people:

Acampa
787-706-0695
www.acampapr.com

The Gallery Inn in Old San Juan

Aventuras Tierra Adentro
787-766-0470
www.aventuraspr.com

PUERTO RICO ON A . . . HONEYMOON:
THE MOST ROMANTIC SPOTS

Destination weddings are a booming business in the Caribbean. Puerto Rico is no exception, and it's easy to see why: Getting married on this island gives you a choice of almost fantasylike settings. You can tie the knot on a mountaintop under a crystal blue sky or on a pristine beach with the gurgling surf accompanying the bridal waltz. You can have your reception in a natural cave or in the botanical gardens. And, of course, you don't have to go anywhere else for your honeymoon.

Julio Cintrón and Emilio Olabarrieta, owners of **Arquetipo** event planners (see page 286), have organized weddings for Puerto Rico's elite as well as international celebrities. Based on their clients' preferences, they have chosen locations as diverse as a rustic Colonial hacienda in the foothills of El Yunque, a yacht afloat in San Juan Bay, and the atrium of the Museo de Arte de Puerto Rico. Their specialty is carrying through a consistent theme, from location to cuisine to decor—what Emilio calls "sophisticated Caribbean"—that maintains a tasteful, understated elegance.

If my sister's wedding is any indication—she worked with **Akua** (see below) and its event manager, Ariadne Comulada, and held a spectacular and flawless reception at the Hotel El Convento—then I can see why Puerto Rico is such a popular wedding destination. The service, setting, and entire experience are sure to provide you with an unforgettable event. But romance isn't limited to weddings.

All of the natural and artificially constructed luxuries of the island are at the disposal of couples chasing romance. And Puerto Rico has a full array of businesses dedicated to helping your special event come true. Many hotels in San Juan, Vieques, and Culebra offer wedding and honeymoon packages, some more elaborate than others. You can spoil your loved one at a fabulous, intimate hotel; seduce him or her with a gourmet dinner; and take full advantage of Puerto Rico's many idyllic backdrops and landscapes. The rest is up to you.

For those planning a wedding, honeymoon, or just one heck of a first date, below are some useful contacts. I haven't listed price ranges because, let's face it, you'll spend a nice chunk of cash to impress your other half. Also, these are by no means your only options for romance-related lodging, dining, and services. By and large, this is an admittedly biased list of my favorites.

Event Planners & Services

Akua
Owner: Javier Martinez
787-727-0137; 787-727-5903
800 Calle del Parque, Santurce, San Juan 00909

Arquetipo
Owners: Julio Cintrón and Emilio Olabarrieta
787-268-5228
1762 Ponce de León Avenue, Santurce, San Juan 00909

One of Puerto Rico's premier wedding and event planners.

Guillén
787-781-6252
www.guillenphotography.com
1115 Piñero Avenue, Río Piedras 00920

Digital and conventional photos and video services.

Hotels with Honeymoon/Romance Packages

At Wind Chimes Inn
1-800-WINDCHIMES; 787-727-4153
www.atwindchimesinn.com
1750 McLeary Avenue, Condado, San Juan 00911

While most of the options listed here are on the higher end of this book's price ranges, At Wind Chimes Inn is a bargain bet for honeymooners or couples looking for an intimate alternative to a big-budget hotel. The honeymoon package includes a deluxe king-sized room, sangria and wine or champagne, a gourmet breakfast, fresh flowers, and the friendly personalities of the staff.

Club Seabourne
787-742-3169
www.clubseabourne.com
State Road 252, Playa Sardines Ward, Culebra 00775

The three-day honeymoon package includes transportation to and from the hotel as well as around Culebra (Jeep rental, bikes, and kayaks), breakfast and dinner, poolside massages, and deluxe villa accommodations.

The Gallery Inn
787-722-1808
www.thegalleryinn.com
204–206 Norzagaray Street, Old San Juan 00901

For a truly artistic wedding, or just a romantic getaway, complete with piano recitals, wine tasting, and a parrot entourage, the Gallery Inn will appeal to your more eclectic tastes.

Hotel El Convento
787-723-9020
www.elconvento.com
100 Cristo Street, Old San Juan 00901

The package starts with the two-room bridal suite, which is in a secluded section of the hotel, close to the small, terraced pool. Features include complimentary afternoon wine and hors d'oeuvres, a signature bag, a plate of chocolates, fresh flowers in the room and, of course, champagne on ice.

Inn on the Blue Horizon
787-741-3318
www.innonthebluehorizon.com
Route 996, Km 4.2, P.O. Box 1556, Vieques 00765

Blending nature and luxury is an art at the Inn on the Blue Horizon, and this hotel has an air of romance around it. Their weddings are petal-strewn, tea-light-bathed, flower-filled affairs nestled against the backdrop of the sea. Additional touches like silver-framed photos of each guest serving as place settings, and the attentions of the resident chef, make it an idyllic setting for a bride and groom.

The Ritz-Carlton, San Juan Hotel, Spa & Casino
1-888-451-9868; 787-253-1700
www.ritzcarlton.com/hotels/san_juan
6961 Avenue of the Governors, Isla Verde, Carolina 00979

The wedding package includes a ceremony site, bridal bouquet, groom's boutonniere, champagne, limo transfer to and from the airport, and one hour of a wedding photographer's time. On top of that, you have a smorgasbord of luxury options, from a violinist or guitar player to a four-course dinner on the beach.

Romantic Restaurants and Gourmet Meals

311

787-725-7959
www.311restaurantpr.com
311 Fortaleza Street, Old San Juan

Among the fun and flirty restaurants on Fortaleza Street, you can escape here for an
evening of long looks across the table in a quiet, elegant setting. Go with the wine-and-
food-pairing menu.

Ajili Mojili

787-821-9195
1006 Ashford Avenue, Condado, San Juan

If your partner pouts about missing out on the best of Puerto Rican food, head straight for
Ajili Mojili for excellent service, divine food, and a beautiful, formal dining experience.

Café Media Luna

787-741-2594
351 Antonio G. Mellado Street, Isabel II, Vieques

On Vieques, it's hard to duplicate the ambience and flavors of Media Luna. The tables by
the balcony are very romantic, and the creative food will likely induce a little fork-play.

The private dining area at Delirio in Miramar

Carambola

787-741-3318
www.innonthebluehorizon.com
At the Inn on the Blue Horizon, Route 996, Km 4.2, Vieques

Creative food, a lovely setting, and the sea breeze blowing through your hair. Whether you sit outside on the patio or in the more formal indoor dining room, you'll appreciate what Carambola gives you.

Delirio

787-722-0444
762 Ponce de León Avenue, Miramar, San Juan

You're sure to impress your date if you bring her here for dinner; and you're likely to blow him or her away if you arrange for a private dinner at which the chef cooks just for you.

Panza

787-289-8900
329 Recinto Sur Street, Old San Juan

Warm lighting, spare-no-expense decor, sumptuous food, an intimate setting, and excellent service. What more do you need?

White Sands Restaurant

787-742-3169
www.clubseabourne.com
At Club Seabourne, State Road 252, Playa Sardines Ward, Culebra

In rustic Culebra, White Sands does its best to create an environment of soothing luxury and under-the-stars intimacy.

Shopping

The Basket Company

787-782-1084
20 Blay Street, corner of Bechara Industrial Park, Puerto Nuevo

Creative and cute designs for your wedding.

Cappalli

787-289-6565
206 O'Donnell Street, Old San Juan

San Juan's queen of lace has a selection of bridal gowns in addition to her other lines.

E'Leonor

787-725-3201
1310 Ashford Avenue, Condado

Looking for your Vera Wang gown (and maybe something a little sexier for the next night)? This is where you want to be.

Harry Robles

787-727-3885

1752 Loíza Street, San Juan

Custom-made wedding gowns don't come easy, and don't come cheap, so book an appointment well in advance if you want a Harry Robles original.

Suggested Reading

Puerto Rico, Borinquen Querida, Roger A. LaBrucherie, Imágenes Press, 2001

Puerto Rico—The People and the Culture, Erinn Banting, Crabtree Publishing Company, 2003

Puerto Rico—Trials of the Oldest Colony in the World, José Trias Monge, Yale University Press, 1999

Speaking Boricua, Jared Romy, Publicaciones Puertorriqueñas, 2005

Vieques, A Photographically Illustrated Guide to the Island, Its History and its Culture, Gerald A. Singer, Everbest Press, 2004

Yes Beach, Early Artis, Gone Cat Publishing, 2006

General Index

Lodging by Price

Dining by Price